Language and Neoliberalism

Language and Neoliberalism examines the ways in which neoliberalism, or economic liberalism, finds expression in language. In this groundbreaking original study, Holborow shows at once the misleading character of ideological meaning and the underlying social reality from which that meaning emerges.

In universities, it is now the norm to use terms like *entrepreneurial* and *business partnerships*. How have these terms become a core component of education and gained such force? *Markets* have become, metaphorically, a power in their own right. They now *tell* governments how to act and *warn* them against too much public spending. Post-crash, the capitalist market continues to be crisis-prone, and in that context the neoliberal ideology remains contested.

Free of jargon and assuming no specialist knowledge, this book will strike a chord internationally by showing how neoliberal ideology has, literally, gone global in language. Drawing on Vološinov and Bakhtin, Williams and Gramsci, and introducing concepts from Marxist political economy, *Language and Neoliberalism* is essential reading for all interested in the intersection of linguistics/applied linguistics and politics.

Marnie Holborow is a lecturer in the School of Applied Language and Intercultural Studies in Dublin City University, Ireland. She is a co-author of *Neoliberalism and Applied Linguistics* and has written widely on the presence of neoliberal ideology in language.

LANGUAGE, SOCIETY AND POLITICAL ECONOMY

Series editor: David Block, Institució Catalana de Recerca i Estudis Avançats, Universitat de Lleida

This series aims to publish broadly accessible monographs which directly address how theoretical frameworks in political economy can directly inform the critical analysis and discussion of language in society issues. Contributions to the series include extensive theoretical background, dealing with an aspect or area of political economy, before moving to an application of this theoretical discussion to a particular language in society issue. The series takes up the challenge of interdisciplinarity, linking scholarship in the social sciences in general (and political economy in particular) with the kinds of issues which language in society researchers have traditionally focused on. The series also aims to publish books by authors whose ideas fall outside the mainstream of language in society scholarship and by authors in parts of the world which have traditionally been underrepresented in relevant international journals and book series.

Forthcoming titles:

The Narratives of Capitalism: Everyday Economics and the Production of Public Discourses
Christian W. Chun

Global English and Political Economy: An Immanent Critique
John O'Regan

Language and Neoliberalism

Marnie Holborow

LONDON AND NEW YORK

First published 2015
by Routledge
2 Park Square, Milton Park, Abingdon, Oxon OX14 4RN

and by Routledge
711 Third Avenue, New York, NY 10017

Routledge is an imprint of the Taylor & Francis Group, an informa business

© 2015 Marnie Holborow

The right of Marnie Holborow to be identified as the author of this work has
been asserted by her in accordance with sections 77 and 78 of the Copyright,
Designs and Patents Act 1988.

All rights reserved. No part of this book may be reprinted or reproduced or
utilized in any form or by any electronic, mechanical, or other means, now
known or hereafter invented, including photocopying and recording, or in any
information storage or retrieval system, without permission in writing from
the publishers.

Trademark notice: Product or corporate names may be trademarks or
registered trademarks, and are used only for identification and explanation
without intent to infringe.

British Library Cataloguing-in-Publication Data
A catalogue record for this book is available from the British Library

Library of Congress Cataloging in Publication Data
Holborow, Marnie.
Language and neoliberalism / by Marnie Holborow.
pages cm. -- (Language, society and political economy)
1. Language and languages--Study and teaching--Political aspects.
2. Applied Linguistics. 3. Neoliberalism--Social aspects. I. Title.
P53.6128.H65 2015
320.51'3014--dc23
2014037988

ISBN: 978-0-415-74455-3 (hbk)
ISBN: 978-0-415-74456-0 (pbk)
ISBN: 978-1-3157-1816-3 (ebk)

Typeset in Sabon
by Taylor & Francis Books

Contents

	Acknowledgements	vi
1	Introduction: language and neoliberalism – issues and framework	1
2	Neoliberalism and language as a commodity	13
3	Markets, metaphors and neoliberal ideology	34
4	Language and the market metaphor	52
5	The neoliberal reinvention of *entrepreneur*	71
6	Austerity and the entrepreneurial university	96
7	Conclusion: implications for understanding ideology in language	127
	References	132
	Index	149

Acknowledgements

Any book is a collaborative effort but this one seems more than usually so, as it has been very much shaped by discussions and exchanges that I have had with others. First, I would like to thank the editor of the series Language, Society and Political Economy, David Block, for inviting me to start off the series, and who has offered sound advice all through the project. Some time ago, David saw the need, with some shrewd foresight, for a radical and/or Marxist critique of neoliberalism within the field of applied linguistics, and I am delighted and honoured that he involved me in his plan. I would also like to thank John Gray who, true to form, came up with detailed and constructive comments. John also provided me with an opportunity to get great feedback when he kindly invited me to a seminar on language and neoliberalism, held at the Institute of Education in London in June 2014. There are several people that I would like to thank for their detailed comments on drafts of the book. Joseph Sung-Yul Park gave me a detailed response to my take on linguistic markets in general and on Bourdieu in particular. John O'Regan magnanimously tolerated my criticisms of Foucault and offered many helpful comments. I would specially like to thank Kenneth McGill for reading nearly all the manuscript and for his incisive remarks which made me rethink things considerably. The final book owes much to the comments and input from all of these people, but, of course, I am responsible for the opinions expressed and for any shortcomings it may have.

My colleagues in Dublin City University have been very understanding of me while I was writing the book. Special thanks go to John O'Sullivan, whose responses to my work constituted, in their own right, the beginnings of a book. My thanks go to everyone in the School of Applied Language and Intercultural Studies (SALIS) for their generous collegiality given despite these individualistic, neoliberal times. I would like to thank Mary Phelan, Michael Cronin, Barra O'Seahdha, Maria Loftus and Pat O'Byrne for being there to bounce ideas off, Veronica Crosbie for being a regular source of interesting books, Niamh Kelly for useful practical suggestions and Jenny Bruen for being so obliging as the research officer in the school. I would also like to thank Siobhan Dunne, Shauna McDermott, Samantha Seery, Marie Byrne and others, in Dublin City University library who went to great lengths to track down books and articles for me. I am indebted to John Kearns for his proofreading and for his knowledge about all things linguistic; without his input, getting the book ready in time would simply not have been possible. The book received financial support from the Faculty of Humanities and Social Sciences Book Publication Scheme at Dublin City University, for which I am very grateful, as I am to Dorothy Kenny for the support she gave me during the writing of the book.

I would like to thank everyone at Routledge, and particularly Louisa Semlyen, for her enthusiasm for the series from the beginning, and Sophie Jacques and Rosie Baron for their practical advice. I would especially like to thank Laura Sandford for her patience with my emails and her kind help during the production process, and Jaya Dalal for her meticulous copyediting, which has greatly improved the final text. Many thanks, too, to Andrew Watts for seeing the production process through so smoothly.

I would also like to thank Willy Cumming, John Molyneux and Kieran Allen, who have read drafts, corrected mistakes and offered sound advice. Finally, special thanks go to my daughter, Kate, for her constant encouragement.

Publisher's acknowledgements

We are grateful to the *Financial Times* for granting permission to reproduce an extract from the article entitled 'We Must Listen to What Bond Markets Tell Us' by Martin Wolf, which appeared in the *Financial Times* on 6th September 2011. We are also grateful to Patrick Freyne of the *Irish Times* for permission to reproduce an extract from his article entitled 'How You Can Help Fix Ireland' which appeared in that newspaper on 15th March 2014.

1 Introduction

Language and neoliberalism – issues and framework

Optimizing the customer footprint across geographies was how one very large financial services multinational described, in a press release, how it was axing over a thousand people across its branches. Such language hardly surprises us as we have become only too aware of company buzzwords, PR language, management speak, corporate phrases all around us. *Value added transparency* and *customer-centric* may be what fills strategic plans and brochures in private companies and increasingly the public sector, but this corporate-speak now figures strongly across society as a whole. *Mission* has replaced policy, *entrepreneurial* has become the most prized social trait, *valued customers* are what we are and *competitive* and *market efficient* what we could be. The widespread use of financial language, as in *leveraging*, and of management speak as in *deliverables*, has permeated many areas of our lives (Kellaway 2007; Seacombe 2011; Beckwith 2006). The existence of *Brand Me* portals to help students prepare themselves for the employment market is an indication of the depth of penetration of the market into the way we speak.

Why has such pervasive use of corporate jargon arisen? The 'marketization of language' (Cameron 2001; Hasan 2003; Kelly-Holmes and Mautner 2010; Fairclough 2010) may have been evident across much of the English-speaking world for a generation, but does its presence now – paradoxically more pervasive since the market crash of 2008 – indicate that it has irrevocably become part of our social world? Is it symptomatic of a deeper ideological shift which reflects the apparent unassailable position of neoliberalism? The sweeping presence of what one writer calls 'creeping linguistic neoliberalism' (Mirowski 2013: 117) certainly raises forcefully the relationship between language and ideology. This is the subject of this book.

'Vocabularies of the economy', Doreen Massey claims, have altered our everyday encounters. A T-shirt worn by an attendant in an art gallery bearing the words 'customer liaison' converts a spontaneous discussion about a picture into a commercial transaction. Being described as 'customers' on trains, buses and in hospitals means that 'a specific activity is erased by a general relationship of buying and selling that is given precedence over it' (Massey 2013: 3). 'The vocabulary of *customer, consumer choice*, of *markets* moulds both our conception or ourselves and our understanding of and relationship to the world'

2 *Language and neoliberalism – issues and framework*

(2013: 5). She describes the use of this language, in a Gramscian framework, as 'crucial to the formation of the ideological scaffolding of the hegemonic common sense' and to 'the establishment of neoliberal hegemony' (2013: 4).

Her claim is that this new dominant ideology, 'inculcated through prevailing names and descriptions, steers us towards being "enrolled in a self-identification" process', just as strong as any 'material entanglement in debt, pensions and mortgages' (2013: 5). These vocabularies, which reclassify our roles, identities and relationships, 'embody and enforce the ideology of neoliberalism' (2013: 6). She identifies various bundles of economic words, such as *wealth*, *output*, and *growth*, which reinforce in their terms the dominant conception of the well-being of both individuals and societies. The widespread use of *investment, expenditure* and *speculation,* and also *earned* and *unearned income,* contribute to the financialization and marketization of our society. These 'vocabularies of the economy' and the attendant neoliberal ideology they imply is the stronger for their being accepted by all mainstream political currents, including social democracy, which 'accept the dominant architecture of the system in place' (2013: 6). 'The assumption that markets are natural is so deeply rooted in the structure of thought that even the fact that it is an assumption seems to have been lost to view'; 'this is "real hegemony"' indeed, she claims (2013: 16). Her call is for the current 'common sense' of language to be challenged root and branch (2013: 17).

Massey's observations touch on the central theme of this book: how language and ideology intersect and how neoliberalism has deeply influenced the language of today. This introductory chapter will first present some theoretical issues concerning the interplay between language and ideology, and then outline how the term 'neoliberalism' will be used in the chapters that follow.

Ideology, 'common sense' and language

The inclusion of Gramsci's terms in Massey's discussion of language and ideology is apt. Gramsci developed a distinctive interpretation of the dynamic and tensions of ideology and how these were reproduced in language. Gramsci's discussion of language and ideology provides a useful starting point to examine the articulation of neoliberal ideology in language. His writings have been recently reinterpreted, highlighting his sensitivity to the social and political importance of language (Ives 2004; Thomas 2009) and re-translations of his work (Gramsci 2011) have opened new avenues of understanding of his sometimes densely expressed ideas.[1] The brief section which follows makes no pretensions to capture fully his understanding of ideology and hegemony; rather it aims to identify the strands of Gramsci's thought which serve as an entry point into a discussion of the presence of ideology in language and which, interwoven with other Marxist interpretations of language, underpin the approach taken in this book.

First, Gramsci identified metaphor as being crucial to the articulation of ideology in language. For Gramsci 'language is always metaphorical' (Gramsci 1971: 450) and ideology often lies metaphorically embedded in language. Identifying the ideological role of metaphor involves a 'critical and historicist conception'

Language and neoliberalism – issues and framework   3

of language (1971: 451) which locates the metaphorical–ideological significance of a word in its accumulated social history. One example he gives is the word *disgrace*, whose metaphorical origins are woven so deeply into its structure that the religious connotation has faded from view (1971: 452). Gramsci described how a 'new metaphorical meaning spreads with the spread of the new culture which gives a precise meaning to words acquired from other languages' (2011: 187). Words can mutate over different societies and historical periods, absorbing 'in metaphorical form' (1971: 451) meanings from the past but they can also be infused with new ideological meanings by new ruling orders. He gave as an example the metaphorical language of religion, which is given different ideological inflections by different social classes. The 'popular turns of phrase' (1971: 328) are cultivated within 'the whole mass of the faithful' who adopt a conception which is not their own, but is 'borrowed from another group' yet which they affirm 'verbally' because this is 'the conception which it follows in normal times' (1971: 326–28). The historical residues within language, as Peter Ives notes, are 'fundamental in operations of power prestige and hegemony' (Ives 2004: 88). Gramsci also implies in parts of his writings that he sees language as metaphorical in the broader sense that it can be used as a metaphor for social and political relations.[2] However understood, metaphor, by drawing together unlike things and declaring that they have something in common, provides a linguistic mechanism for the articulation of ideology in language. As I show in Chapters 3 and 4, the personification of the market and the market as metaphor, in different forms and guises, carries deep ideological significance and serves as reinforcement of the neoliberal message.

Gramsci's historico-ideological understanding of metaphor flows naturally from his dialectical appreciation of language and social change, a view more fully outlined (contemporaneously) by Vološinov, who speaks of the 'social life' of the verbal sign (Vološinov 1973: 21). This theme is also repeated in historical approaches, which have seen the metaphorical dimension to the meaning of words as a complex expression of changing political consciousness. Words both inherit meanings from the past but also incorporate new meanings reflecting the political priorities of social classes in the present. Christopher Hill's study of the changing significance of the word 'revolution' in the seventeenth century is a case in point (Hill 1990).[3] The appropriation of words from the past for the neoliberal lexicon – such as *entrepreneur*, as we see in Chapters 5 and 6 – and used in different contexts with different meanings, adds the authority of tradition to new ideological turns.

Second, both ideology and language are linked for Gramsci to the question of social consciousness. Language represents our potential to form a general view of the world which means, as Gramsci puts it, 'everyone is a philosopher, though in his own way unconsciously, since even in the slightest manifestation of any intellectual activity whatever, in "language", there is contained a specific conception of the world' (Gramsci 1971: 323; 2011: 352).[4] (Gramsci often writes language in inverted commas, indicating his awareness of the conventional and the new meaning of words, and how ideology can take shape through marking

4 Language and neoliberalism – issues and framework

the different semantic layers of a word).[5] Insofar as both language and ideology involve the ability to generalize beyond the particular and the present, to make abstractions about the world in which we live, they overlap and are interconnected. Gramsci writes 'language is essentially a collective term which does not presuppose any single thing existing in time and space' (1971: 349). Without having read *The German Ideology*, he arrives at a remarkably similar view to that held by Marx of language and ideology. Marx saw language as the mode of being of thoughts, as a form of 'practical consciousness' (1974: 51).[6] Similarly, language for Gramsci is a concrete social activity in which everyone is engaged and, in so far as it forms how we see the world and interpret it, it is also effectively ideological. This coming together of language and ideology for the individual, Gramsci stresses, takes place in response and reaction to socially dominant ideological conceptions of the world 'mechanically imposed by the external environment' (1971: 323) by the dominant social class, which attempts to shape social consciousness within the confines of existing social relations.

Third, Gramsci's well-known concept of common sense also has a linguistic dimension. Gramsci alludes repeatedly to the role of language in the legitimization of common sense. Common sense, for Gramsci, consists of a spontaneous set of beliefs which together express a conception of the world which takes the social order as 'the way things are'.[7] It is apparently the 'spontaneous feelings' that people have, 'the traditional popular conception of the world – what is unimaginatively called "instinct" although it too is in fact a primitive and elementary historical acquisition' (1971: 199). Common sense gains currency through language. Gramsci describes it as 'a conception of the world "in whatever language"' (1971: 323), and 'superficially explicit or verbal', 'inherited form the past and uncritically absorbed' (1971: 333).

Because we use language as it already circulates in society, because we socially inherit linguistic use, our 'unthinking' engagement in language can often appear to accept uncritically its ideological meanings. For example, when we are told that our local health centre has a *customer care policy*, it may appeal in an immediate sense in that it tells us we are being looked after but, at a deeper layer of meaning, it draws us into a world in which all services are seen in market terms. Or when we are told that we are living in an *information* or a *knowledge society* these phrases may seem, on the face of it, to reflect accurately the changes brought about by the digital revolution. Yet they also subtly detach human capacities from the humans that possess them, and make society appear to be driven by 'things', not people. The apparent immediate acceptance of such meanings represents, for Gramsci, a way of thinking that is 'fragmentary, incoherent and inconsequential' (1971: 419) in that it places us in a passive position *vis-à-vis* the social world. Common sense as propagated by ruling orders is often, as he puts it, 'neophobe or conservative' (1971: 423), representing a view of the world which reinforces the existing social order. Gramsci's common sense, as Kate Crehan (2011) notes, encompasses its 'givenness' in that it confronts us as an external reality. But this does not mean that it does not contain contradictions and the potential for change.

Common sense is linked to Gramsci's concept of hegemony and the economic order and this connection is particularly important in matters of ideology and language. Hegemony is often loosely understood as consensual power or, following Raymond Williams, the 'structures of feeling' (Simpson and Mayr 2010; Woolard 1998: 238). However, it is important to understand that Gramsci sees hegemony primarily as a socially imposed and historically specific method of rule. Though hegemony is manifest at many different levels of society – economic, institutional, cultural and linguistic – it derives its force from those who, in Gramsci's well-chosen words, have material forces as their 'content' and ideologies as their 'form' (1971: 377). Gramsci's writings were very much grounded in Marx, and following Antonio Labriola (upon whose translations of Marx Gramsci relied) he considered that the ultimate shaping forces in human history were a society's basic economic structures and social class system (Gramsci 1971: 459; Labriola 2005; see also Crehan 2011). In some places in the *Prison Notebooks*, Gramsci makes the source of hegemony in capitalist society very clear: 'the "spontaneous" consent given by the great masses of the population to the general direction imposed on social life by the dominant fundamental group ... is historically caused by the prestige and consequent confidence that the dominant group enjoys because of its position and function in the world of production' (1971: 12).[8] Meanings in language are also subject, albeit more diffusely and not straightforwardly, to the same social pressures from the ruling class, involving the manufacture of consent. The apparently agentless workings of the market (which I explore in Chapter 4) or the representation of society as a collection of individual *entrepreneurs* or *human capitals* (described in Chapter 5) are verbal attempts to linguistically 'manufacture' neoliberal consent, and its articulation through powerful public channels, as I show, disperses this 'common sense' far and wide. Through oft-repeated phrases, used in set contexts, specific ideologies are asserted on behalf of specific social interests. Exhorting everyone and society as a whole *to live within their means* may seem like a logical statement for survival, but when uttered by a politician addressing the population at large it represents a conscious erasure of differences of wealth, a dimension which actually affects the feasibility of the proposition. *Austerity* may sound like a sensible response to an economic crisis but, as I will show in Chapter 6, it subtly covers over the reasons why it is supposedly needed and the fact that it hits the poorest hardest. The ideological theme takes shape from the class interests of its speakers, and gives it what Vološinov calls a 'uni-accentual' character.

Fourth, ideological hegemony is not a settled question, neither from the point of view of those who promote it nor for those at its receiving end. Gramsci's discussion of hegemony was understood as an overall strategy which included consent but also included force, and was deployed throughout society in a homogeneous politico-economic bloc. Peter Thomas emphasizes that hegemony in Gramsci is 'a theory of *class power*' (2009: 224, emphasis in the original) – a social strategy which runs in two directions, most weightily from above in terms of existing capitalist ruling class power but also, and a characteristic often omitted from cultural commentaries, from below in the struggle of the masses of ordinary

6 Language and neoliberalism – issues and framework

people to envisage and establish a different social order. Hegemony, as Mayr notes, is only ever achieved partially and temporarily as 'an unstable equilibrium' and one that requires constant remaking (Mayr 2008: 14). This changing dynamic of ideological hegemony is not captured in static notions, such as 'inculcation' (Massey 2013), or 'internalisation' (Mesthrie et al. 2009: 316). The power of Gramsci's common sense was that it was neither fixed nor guaranteed, but constantly tempered by people's actual experience of the social world. Common sense 'inherited from the past and uncritically absorbed' can under certain conditions move 'beyond common sense' and become 'a critical conception' or 'good sense' (Gramsci 1971: 423, see also 333–34; 2011: 369). In other words, our daily experience of the social world seems both to confirm and to run counter to many of the truisms of established common sense. This can jolt us abruptly into new ways of thinking and speaking about the world – what Gramsci called 'good sense'. The articulation of this new awareness, informed by practical social experience, can only prevail and supplant traditional forms of common sense, Gramsci was at pains to point out, if it is given collective organization and political expression.

The same tensions and contradictions are present in the articulation of ideology in language. A dominant ideology may say one thing about people's lives which their immediate life experience contradicts and leads them to say something different. Despite the apparent weight and overwhelming diffusion of neoliberal ideology, social consciousness is never smooth and singular; it is fractured and contradictory. A verbal and ideological rupture is most evident in the emergence of new collectively articulated language in mass social movements. Against a backdrop of the official neoliberal language of *trickle-down economics*, or *the need for austerity*, deepening social deprivation and greater social inequality can give rise to alternative representations. One such representation was the verbal labelling of *'the one per cent'* for the top wealthy few who were profiting from the crisis, a designation which rapidly caught on across the world. It struck a blow against neoliberal common sense and became what one might call 'good sense'. As Noam Chomsky put it at the time of the US Occupy Movement, 'there were things that were sort of known, but in the margins, hidden, which are now right up front – such as the imagery of the 99% and 1%' (Chomsky 2012). Christian Chun (2014), in his interesting study of language of the LA Occupy Movement, has also shown how protest signs can serve as tools for rethinking dominant discourse and, reinforced collectively, can become critical language in action. An example he gives is one of the signs made up by the occupiers, which read *Corporate Welfare – all the rewards of capitalism with none of the risks*. This 'marked an important disruption to the common sense discourse of welfare in the US that had prevailed in the past 30 years' (Chun 2014: 183). The clash between prevailing common sense and actual social experience is also lived out in a fragmented form in everyday language. In post-crash Ireland, words such as *zombie, toxic* or *the bankers* as terms of abuse passed into common usage and disrupted the common sense of business as usual (Holborow 2012a). The dualism of common sense and good sense is played out, as Gramsci noted, in the 'concrete historical act' of human activity (1971: 372–73) and is vital to understanding both the weight of 'common sense' language and its potential to unravel.

If the challenge to the common sense of neoliberalism arises from the raw experience of its effects, as Gramsci noted, this may manifest itself only 'occasionally and in flashes' (1971: 327). For it to survive it needs to find coherent expression, practically and theoretically. Gramsci, himself writing amid the effects of a long period of deep crisis in the 1930s, dramatically evidenced by his own imprisonment, saw that the struggle against the existing order had to take place on all fronts, ideological as well as practical and organizational. He claimed that it was often in times of crisis that the ideological terrain became intensely important since the ruling orders sought 'to conserve and defend the existing structure' and would make every effort to cure them and within certain limits to overcome them' (Gramsci 1971: 178). The widespread presence of neoliberal ideology in language is one sign, this book contends, of a concerted project for ideological hegemony on behalf of powerful social interests and therefore uncovering the ideological meanings in its use must also be part of the challenge to it.

Neoliberalism: its nature and political dimension

When dealing with interpretations of neoliberalism, two cautionary remarks need to be made. Neoliberalism is referred to in very different ways and used to cover a diverse range of developments of different scales and origins. It is a new form of capitalism (Duménil and Lévy 2004), a series of successive waves of 'rule regimes' (Brenner et al. 2010), a restoration of capitalist class power (Harvey 2005), a collection of political projects, a cultural or ethical set of shared beliefs (Hilgers 2010), even individual behaviours and norms (Ong 2007). Not surprisingly, therefore, it has been described as a 'rascal concept' (Brenner et al. 2010: 184). An early collection of studies of neoliberal experiences noted that 'precise definitions of neoliberalism were difficult' because although the basic feature of neoliberalism is 'the systematic use of state power to impose (financial) market imperatives in a domestic process that is replicated internationally', it 'straddles a wide range of social political and economic phenomena' (Saad-Fihlo and Johnston 2005: 1–3). It is therefore necessary to clarify my approach to neoliberalism in this study.

Second, because neoliberalism was identified as a political project of capitalist elites (Harvey 2005) and because it became the target of the anti-capitalist movements of the early 2000s it was from the outset a political term, used widely by anti-capitalist activists as well as academics (Klein 2007; Harvey 2005; Callinicos 2003). One of the first to recognize neoliberalism as being 'an immense political project', and to foresee its significance, Pierre Bourdieu (1998) described it as 'the strong discourse', 'because it has on its side all of the forces of a world of relations of forces', an understanding which, for Bourdieu and many others, led logically to the fusion of academic analysis and political activism. The political dimension attached to critiques of neoliberalism has ebbed and flowed. The

8 *Language and neoliberalism – issues and framework*

social effects of the economic crisis and recession which unfolded after the market crash of 2008, and in response to the poverty and social dislocation that neoliberal economic policies caused, led to an upsurge of radical anti-capitalism, demonstrated most dramatically in the uprisings of Arab Spring but followed closely by the Occupy Movement in the US and in Europe, notably Spain, alongside mass opposition to the neoliberal terms of debt repayment in Greece. At the time of writing in 2014, these movements have for the most part receded, but it is clear that political tensions and contradictions around neo-liberal rule remain and these have fed into a new wave of interest in the nature of neoliberalism.

This is certainly the case for accounts of neoliberalism in applied and socio-linguistics and linguistic anthropology. It has only been since the economic crash of 2007–8 that neoliberalism has become a recognized point of reference in these disciplines and there are many examples. The discourses of neoliberalism have been explored in language teaching in the English language industry and in the marketization of language teacher education (Chun 2009; Gray 2012; Kubota 2011) Discourse analysis of performance-based versions of citizenship, as articulated in residents' accounts of the 'desirable' urban citizen, has been set in the context of neoliberal urban transformation (Weninger 2009). Linking neoliberalism to applied linguistics as an overall theme has led to investigations into the presence of neoliberal keywords in public discourse, 'economizing' identity and neoliberal representations of celebrity in text books (Block et al. 2012). Neoliberal ideology has been analysed through the metaphors in circulation in the US media after the Wall Street bail-out (Horner 2011). Neoliberalism has also provided a backcloth to studies dealing with the commodification of language (Duchêne and Heller 2012) and the marketization of English language skills in relation to the neoliberal 'promise' of employment (Park and Wee 2012). The 'neoliberal imaginary' has been cited as a cause of employees thinking of themselves as bundles of (language) skills to be sold on the labour market (Urciuoli 2008; Boutet 2001; Flores 2013). As these examples indicate, reference to neoliberalism involves introducing questions of political economy into linguistic anthropology and sociolinguistics, specifically around the nature of 'language work' in contemporary capitalism and a revisiting of social class (Block 2014).

In this book, I shall be dealing with neoliberalism primarily as an ideology for reasons that I set out below. This is not to minimize the importance of neoliberalism as an economic policy regime implemented by governments or as various strategies which aim to raise profitability levels for capital, nor, indeed, to ignore the very real and tangible effects that neoliberalism has on many people and societies across the world. It flows rather from the recognition that ideology is a core reference point for analysis of neoliberalism in language and an analytical tool for highlighting more generally the inconsistencies and contradictions of neoliberalism, whether in its notions of human capital (as I examine in Chapter 2), its reification of the market (Chapter 3) or its entrepreneurship claims for society and the university (Chapters 5 and 6).

Neoliberalism as ideology

First, neoliberalism operates at the level of 'appearances' and in accordance with its own version of an ideal world, characteristics generally taken to be those of an ideology. What neoliberalism says and what it does constantly diverge. The main tenet of neoliberalism is that the best outcomes will be achieved if the demand for and supply of goods and services are allowed to play out 'without interference by government and other forces' (Crouch 2011: 17). But, as Harvey points out, what the neoliberal state was in theory was not what it practised (2005: 64–70). The same governments which were declaring their commitment to these neoliberal policies, even before the crash of 2008–9 were 'interfering' very directly to construct a 'free' market to defend the interests of capital. Although governments were publicly rejecting state intervention in the economy, their actions proved that capitalism needed the state just as much in the neoliberal era as it had done in Keynesian times. Chris Harman gives details of direct government intervention to stop market pressures closing down car plants, hedge funds and banks and of increased state expenditure in the advanced capitalist countries over the period 1990–2001. This was financed not through free market principles but through 'Keynesian' methods of borrowing secured precisely because, in the case of the US, they were strong states (Harman 2007: 97). Accounts which describe neoliberalism as a 'coup' on behalf of a new financial elite against the old production-based order (Duménil and Lévy 2004), tend to ignore these continuities in relation to the state. Indeed, as Mirowski argues, neoliberalism is built on 'double truths' (Mirowski 2013: 68), on proclaiming publicly one thing while doing something very different. This dissonance reached unparalleled proportions during the economic crash of 2008–9. The trillions of dollars poured into failing banks demonstrated how far states were prepared to go to protect the interests of the 'free market'. Self-contradiction – or 'regulation in denial' (Peck 2010: xiii) – graphically reveals the broader character of neoliberalism which, for all its 'actually existing' status claimed by both its proponents and its critics, is the expression of a wished-for world, one that offers the promise of market equilibrium 'an endless utopia' of market freedoms (Bourdieu 1998), a vision not necessarily realized in the real world. Identifying this mismatch reveals its deep ideological and political bias and also its own potential vulnerabilities. The characterization of neoliberalism as an ideology, in other words, provides a crucial avenue for critique of both the doctrine and the political project, which, as we shall see, has relevance for its various ideological representations in language.

Second, neoliberal ideology is a ruling ideology. In a succinct summary of the Marxist interpretation of ideology, Jorge Larrain claimed 'ideology for Marx, as a distorted consciousness, has a particular negative connotation whose two specific and connected features are, firstly, that it conceals social contradictions and, secondly, that it does it in the interests of the dominant class' (Larrain 1979: 48). Interpretations of ruling ideologies in class terms are often dismissed in various disciplines (especially those addressing language and discourse) as reductionist, out of date and irrelevant to the contemporary world of micro-patterns of social

10 *Language and neoliberalism – issues and framework*

consciousness (Torfing 1999; Woolard 1998; Van Dijk 2008). Those who have written extensively on neoliberalism clearly identify the powerful channels – academic, corporate and political – through which the political project of neoliberalism has been steered (Mirowski 2013; Mirowski and Plehwe 2009). Mirowski, however, specifically refrains from using the word 'ideology', preferring to characterize the political project dimension as driven by a 'Neoliberal Thought Collective' and as 'a modern social epistemology in a distributed setting'.[9] Yet it would seem that the class dimension of neoliberalism, both as a doctrine and as a political project, can hardly be ignored, and that ruling ideology fits neoliberalism particularly well. It is uniform on a scale unthinkable in the nineteenth century when Marx alluded to ruling ideologies (Marx and Engels 1974). Channels of communication, with strong ties to corporate interests, have probably never been so streamlined nor, as I show in my analysis of the reproduction of neoliberal keywords across different arenas of official discourse, so amenable to uniform reproduction of a dominant ideology. Finally the wealth of the current ruling elite of capitalism has reached proportions of concentration not seen, Thomas Piketty argues, since the nineteenth century (Piketty 2014). Given that these elites are generally unanimous on the merits of market capitalism, this enables neoliberal ideology to have a formidably powerful platform. While local variations of neoliberalism vary in emphasis and neoliberal ideology is by no means monolithic, its ties to a concerted political project on behalf of governments and corporations, in what Harvey has called 'the restoration of class power', was precisely what enabled it to become 'the hegemonic mode of discourse', now 'incorporated into the common-sense way many of us interpret, live in, and understand the world' (2005: 3). Being the ruling ideology, as my earlier description of Gramsci's 'common sense' makes clear, in no way implies it is monolithic or that it constitutes anything as materially constraining as 'an ideological state apparatus' (Althusser 2008), but it does draw attention to the fact that neoliberal ideology is hegemonic, and that it is so probably on a scale unprecedented even for ideologies that were claimed to be dominant in the past.

The theme of ruling ideology has become more relevant post-crash. Contrary to some expectations (Birch and Mykhnenko 2010), neoliberalism appeared to re-emerge reinvigorated; the doctrine seemed to experience not only a 'non-death' (Crouch 2011) but a newfound resurgence. Deep near-global economic recession accompanied by a dramatic redistribution of wealth in favour of the rich required neoliberalism to justify its about-turns and its social effects. The point of departure for this book is ideological legitimization in relation to neoliberalism, of which Ireland, which provides much of the material which will be discussed, is a particularly strong example. Amid the imposition of austerity policies which resulted in the most serious erosion of living standards for the vast majority for decades, containment of social unrest was the overriding priority for Irish governments. The ideological strategies employed, including the linguistic–ideological representations of *entrepreneurship* alongside *austerity* in official discourse, as we discuss in detail in the context of higher education in Chapter 6, were focussed and streamlined and strongly constituted, I argue, the promulgation of a ruling ideology.

Third, neoliberalism as ideology raises the question as to why I have chosen not to describe ideology in language as *discourse*, as has tended to be typical of this type of study. Ideology has featured less in social and cultural studies than it did twenty-five years ago, a phenomenon that has been attributed to the 'simultaneous decline in salience of social class as a theme and a category' (Fairclough 2010: 26). Although ideology is loosely recognized, many critical discourse accounts often tend to rely on the Foucauldian discursive nexus, which involves 'orders of discourse', 'discursive regimes of truth', and other 'discursive practices' (Foucault 2002; Fairclough 2010: 58). Foucault rejected ideology because he considered it too identified with the social and material world, and with notions of truth and Marxism (2002: 119), and this thrust has largely characterized the 'discursive turn' since.

Of course discourse means many different things from many different standpoints. At an everyday level it can mean simply sub-text or narrative, and incorporates the very ideological aspects of language that are of interest to me here. Equally, discourse analysis has extended the boundaries of language to include other disciplines, and introduced social and critical theories as a means of deconstructing meaning, which is as I have argued in the first section of this chapter, very much the concern of this study. But discourse *à la* Foucault, which defines 'subjects' and positions them in so far as it lays down who it is possible to be and what it is possible to do, would seem to cede too many norm-giving powers to discourse and downplay the role of social forces. Equally, the non-inclusion of the material world – in this case, the social relations of the capitalist market – merely leaves it alone rather than challenging it. Ideology explicitly retains the link with the material and social world which an extensive understanding of discourse obscures. For this reason I have chosen to retain ideology as a vital tool of analysis, both for the presence of a ruling ideology in official language and for neoliberalism itself, as I hope the following chapters will make clear.

Notes

1 One reason for the fragmentary and sometimes abstruse form of Gramsci's writings is the fact that he wrote them under the harsh conditions of prison. In 1928 he received a twenty-year jail sentence under Mussolini's fascist regime for his political activities.

2 Some commentators have taken this further to argue that different types of grammar are metaphors for hegemony (see Ives 2004: 85). Marx also used the same metaphor that social relations were the 'language of life' (1974: 47).

3 Tony Crowley and Marc Steinburg, from different angles, provide historically based views of language which highlight their ideological content (Crowley 1996; Steinberg 1999).

4 Gramsci uses the Italian *linguaggio*, with the meaning of language in general, which is different to the Italian *lingua*, which he uses when speaking of a national language. English does not have this distinction.

5 See Showstack-Sassoon (2010).

6 *The German Ideology* was first published while Gramsci was still in prison but it is possible that he was aware of its content via others (Harman 2007: 116). See

12 *Language and neoliberalism – issues and framework*

Holborow (1999) for an account of Marx's view on consciousness and language. See also Beaken (2011).

7 The Italian term *senso comune* refers simply to the beliefs and opinions supposedly shared by the mass of the population and has less of the positive connotations of common sense in English (i.e. good, sound practical sense; see Crehan 2011).

8 Gramsci's words echo those of Marx in *The German Ideology* where he claims that those with means and wealth also exert disproportionate influence on ways of thinking. 'The class which is the ruling *material* force of society is at the same time its ruling *intellectual* force' (Marx and Engels 1974: 64).

9 This claim is made in his response to a discussion of his book hosted by *Antipode* in 2013 (see http://radicalantipode.files.wordpress.com/2013/11/mirowski-reviews_authors-response.pdf, accessed 10th December 2014).

2 Neoliberalism and language as a commodity

In the late 1980s, linguist and anthropologist Susan Gal, in an article entitled 'Language and Political Economy', observed that what were missing in critical approaches in language studies were the linguistic and symbolic aspects of world-wide processes. Investigations were needed to examine the relationship between language structure and language use to political economy (Gal 1989). Her comments about the gap between linguistics and political economy are a reminder of the radical critique prevalent within linguistics at the time, but they also hint at why it is a subject worth revisiting now. Linking language to political economy required, according to Gal, a critique which took on the structuralist principle of separating the linguistic sign from the material world. This conceptual divide had allowed an intellectual division of labour to develop between the 'idealists' who specialized in cultural and linguistic phenomena and the 'materialists' who investigated economy and ecology (1989: 346). Yet the political economy debates about 'base and superstructure, structural determination versus human agency, and local versus global forces', she maintained, could be fruitfully shared with those interested in cultural, symbolic and ideological matters. Indeed, the analytical tools of political economy were essential, Gal noted, for locating linguistic practices in larger systems of inequality and, more generally, for 'conceptualising the role of cultural practices' in a socio-economic framework (1989: 348). Authorized or hegemonic linguistic practices, she claimed, are not simply forms; they also carry cultural definitions of social life that serve the interests of dominant classes. She understood denotation as one of the core links between language and the material world, and issues of ideology 'fundamentally implicated in relations of domination' (1989: 348). Control of the representations of reality was not only a source of power but also 'a likely locus of conflict and struggle' and 'even the so-called dominant discourse was rarely monolithic but rather a field of competition for power among elites' (1989: 348, 361). For the analysis of the social role of language, Gal's explicit terms of reference, like those of Dell Hymes (1996), were that capitalism was a system of social classes, of conflict and of struggle, and that consideration of the political economy was vital to understanding language as social practice.

The kernel of her observation – language as social practice within a political economy – resonates directly over the decades to our world, a social world in

14 *Neoliberalism and language as a commodity*

which the material effects of social class, of inequality, of capitalist instability, despite post-structural counsels to the contrary, are inseparably bound up with culture and language. Presciently, she spoke of the need to avoid the pitfalls of those analyses of power in language or discourse which, in her words, 'leave notions of ideology, class and social control under-theorised' and which sometimes 'seem to assume that there is an unproblematic reality that it is the linguist's responsibility to reveal', thus failing to account for the political implications of language as social action (Gal 1989: 358–59). With this in mind, it would seem essential, in this account of neoliberalism and language, to include political economy and its relationship – both material and ideological – to language.

One aspect of the relationship of political economy to language is the way in which language itself has become treated as a commodity in contemporary capitalism. This chapter will begin by examining how commodification in capitalism is seen as a natural state of affairs in neoliberal thinking while, in Marxist analyses, it is regarded as a process whose roots and nature lie in the specific social relations of capitalism. The chapter will then discuss whether language as used in work can be considered a commodity. It will argue that a Marxist interpretation of generalized commodity exchange in capitalism provides a theoretical basis for the understanding of ideology, and can serve as a framework for investigating its presence in language, as later chapters will show.

Commodification and political economy

Commodification has expanded into every corner of social life. It was no accident that Karl Marx, more than a century and a half ago, chose to begin his magisterial analysis of nineteenth-century capitalism with a discussion of the commodity. What struck Marx about the commodity form in capitalism was its all-pervasive character; '[t]he wealth of societies in which the capitalist mode of production prevails appears as an immense collection of commodities; the individual commodity appears as its elementary form' was how he opened *Capital* (Marx 1974). His compelling discovery was that commodity relations in capitalism apply not only to things but also to people, and that this outcome deeply affects our experience of the social world and our ideas about it. What appeared to be a simple commodity was in fact the product of someone's work and the embodiment of specific social relations. This concealment at the heart of capitalist commodity exchange resulted in the human dimension disappearing under 'the fantastic form of a relation between things' (Marx 1974: 165). Creative human effort, when put to use in the work process, becomes reduced to mere objects with a price tag, appearing, even to those involved in their creation, as stripped of all particularity. This insight seems all the more relevant to us today when commodities confront us at every turn, when we spend ever greater amounts of time shopping for them, wanting them or choosing between them and every social activity increasingly has a market price. At many different levels, as Harvey notes, we depend on commodities for our survival (Harvey 2010a: 15), and commodification appears in a very real sense to overshadow contemporary social life.

We ourselves are subjected to commodity logic as the value of our work, in the form of wages or salaries, is determined not by the amount of effort, skill or expertise we can offer, but by the 'labour market' – the place where a price is stamped on our work, decided according to what employers or society deem acceptable to pay. People are obliged to sell their potential to work in the labour market because this is the only way to earn a living and to pay for things that they need; however, once they enter the work system, their creative potential becomes something over which they have little or no control. Work becomes an input into a production or service-giving process with our outputs paid less than the value of the effort put into them and rendered equivalent to dispensable commodities (Burawoy 1982: 198; Harvey 2010a; Harman 2009: 26; Marx 1974: 361). The vast changes in the organization and technologies of work have in many ways added to the commodification of work since they are used to break work down into evermore quantifiable segments. Commodification has expanded to encompass many aspects of human endeavour, even the most abstract. The process of education has been repackaged to attract student-consumers; healthcare has been redefined in terms of patient throughput or profitability; familiarity with information technology, skills in different fields and knowledge in general has been rebranded as human capital; new ideas arising from human creativity and imagination have now become materialized as intellectual property. Furthermore, the process of commodification is felt more intensely today as human work, put up for sale on an expanding global market, is undervalued and undersold, and frequently, as widespread unemployment persists, unable to command a price at all. The greater the complexity and range of the technology and skills employed, the fewer employees overall are required, which further intensifies competition in the job market. The result, as noted by sociologists of work, is that ever more highly skilled and knowledgeable people earn ever less for ever more complex and intricate work (Brown and Lauder 2006; Brown and Lauder 2012). Labour in general – what Marx called labour power, as seen from the overall perspective of the working class as a whole – is getting less and less in relation to what it contributes to the productive process.

Neoliberal thinking shares with Marxist analysis the recognition that the commodity is central to the political economy of capitalism, but starts from a different standpoint and draws very different conclusions. For neoliberals, the commodity form is a straightforward input or output of capitalist production, and is stripped of all social relations. In human capital theory, which is a main plank of neoliberal thinking, commodification applies – as if self-evidently – to human knowledge and skills. What humans can do and learn to do must be scientifically measured in order to evaluate their 'returns' potential, for the individual and for the economy as a whole. Gary Becker, an early proponent of the theory from the Chicago school of economics, sought to incorporate the labour component into economic theory and hit upon 'human capital' as part of the 'utility function' within an economy. Human capital, for Becker and other early neoliberal thinkers, now came to be the determining factor in modern 'information' economies, indeed announcing the 'age of human capital' (Becker 2002: 3; see also Becker 1992).

16 *Neoliberalism and language as a commodity*

This marks a considerable ideological shift in that human capital has increasingly replaced conventional concerns with macro-societal factors to become openly and without reserve, in neoliberal thinking, the pivotal factor of economic performance (Mirowski 2013: 114–15). Equating humans with capital ignores the fact, as Piketty (2014: 46) notes, that outside slave-owning societies, 'human capital cannot be owned or traded on a market (permanently at any rate)'. This objection highlights how far down the crude economic reductionist road neoliberals have come. 'Human capital', when it was first coined by Becker in the 1950s, was considered to be too debasing for general use in popular texts (see Holborow 2012a: 46). David Harvey considers human capital theory to be 'one of the weirdest, widely accepted economic ideas that could ever be imagined' (Harvey 2014: 185).

In effect, neoliberal ideology places individualized human capital at the centre of a competitive market world. It presents commodification in a highly individualized fashion, with commodities – for people to consume and as parcels of themselves – as the means by which people interact with the world. Human knowledge is repackaged as a tangible asset, a commodity belonging to an individual, which competes on the market against the knowledge and skills sets of others. If the person can develop, usually at their own cost, their own skills and capabilities, their own 'human capital' is expanded and they can gain the edge over others on the labour market and secure a 'premium' or a higher salary. In this scheme of things, higher education, now reinvented as a finely tuned skills processor to serve the economy, becomes a key performer in the realization of competing human capitals. Education, now an enabler of human capital development, becomes the crucial driver of the economy, a power-house of economic potentiality from which anything non-functional, not measurable in monetary terms or not immediately economically useful, is expelled. Educational products compete on the market for student consumption and then the knowledge that students acquire is sold on as human capital on the wider employment market. The logic of commodities engulfs the whole field of education, and snuffs out any earlier established notions that learning may have any intrinsic or social value (Ball 2012; Collini 2012; Holborow 2013; Walsh 2012; Ward 2012).

Language commodified?

Scholars of applied and socio-linguistics have also turned their attention to language as a commodity in contemporary capitalism and to whether linguistic skills function as added value in the labour market (Block 2014; Heller 2010a, 2010b; Tan and Rubdy 2008; Park and Wee 2012; Flores 2013). Language is described as 'a saleable commodity with regard to business and marketing' and represents 'an investment in cultural capital which can then be exchanged within the global labour market' (Rassool 2007, quoted in Tan and Rubdy 2008: 3). Joseph Park and Lionel Wee, drawing on Bourdieu's theory of a linguistic market, describe how 'language varieties, linguistic utterances, accents, and their embodiments are all like commodities on a market – the linguistic market' (Park and Wee 2012: 27).[1]

Language skills, now less valued as badges of identity, have become 'caught up in processes of commodification' and 'are emerging as resources and a source of profit for businesses' (Boutet 2012: 207). This development is seen as a parallel development of the 'worldwide economy of information and communications' which 'has made it possible to rationalize the process of articulation and introduce a category of workers who are "language workers"' (2012: 224). Language thus becomes 'a bounded commodity traded in borderless commerce, realised in education and training' (Joseph Lo Bianco, in Tan and Rubdy 2008: xii) and marks, in the case of English, the transformation from language of empire to language of economy. More broadly, English as a commodity, as John Gray notes, cannot be separated from neoliberal policies which 'seek to incorporate as many aspects of human experience and activity as possible into the sphere of the economy and subject them to market forces' (Gray 2012: 138).

Monica Heller maintains that linguistic resources have always been able to be 'mobilised in markets as interchangeable with forms of material capital' (Heller 2010b: 102). But she argues that language in late capitalism acquires a specific and emergent 'exchange value' which has replaced the liberal values of linguistic prestige afforded by breeding, taste, intellectualism, rational thought, or 'good' schooling. Securing a job in some sectors depends less on having physical or other attributes than on having suitable communication skills (Cameron 2000). This shift is seen as part of a wider development in contemporary capitalism in which social position has become determined by access to symbolic resources. Heller holds that language can now be considered to occupy a more central role in the economy since it has become the vital complement to the accomplishment of work and itself a product of labour (Heller 2010b: 102–4). She claims that commodification of languages has occurred in two ways: by language constituting symbolic 'added value' to industrially produced resources in the niche markets of tourism, advertising, language teaching, translation and call centres and by converting language into a technical skill amenable to managerial measurement. Drawing on Bourdieu (1991), Coupland (2003), Fairclough (2006) and Castells' notion of communication power (2009), Heller argues that the 'struggles over social difference and social inequality on the terrain of language move away from political frames ... towards economic ones, changing the nature of discourses that legitimise power and the nature of criteria used in social selection' (Heller 2010b: 102). She notes, however, that the commodification of language-as-skill and language-as-identity in the new economy, gives rise to 'a troubled space of contradiction' (Heller 2010b: 103) and that language needs to be analysed within a political economy framework which pays more attention 'to the circulation of symbolic and material resources' in order for speakers to claim ownership of linguistic resources, the right to control their production, their circulation and the value attributed to them' (2010b: 110). In order to judge whether language can be considered in these commodity terms, it is necessary to delve a little deeper into the nature of commodities.

Commodities and their 'mysterious' nature

Few would dispute the effects produced by commodification: 'objectification, interchangeablity, measurability and money equivalence' (Ball 2012: 25). However, to explain why commodification has expanded across so much of social life, even to the most intimate and personal aspects of our lives (Russell Hochschild 2003; 2012), and why commodities seem to have such compelling power and influence, we need to unravel what it is that makes commodity exchange in capitalism socially distinctive. Marx's description of commodities, as pointed out above, highlighted a dualism. Commodities seem to be 'simple things, obvious and trivial', but, on analysis, are revealed as being very 'strange things, abounding in metaphysical complexities and theological niceties' (Marx 1974: 71). However, Marx also pointed out that commodification in capitalism is neither complete nor self-sustaining.

The mysterious nature of commodities, according to Marx, arises from their capacity to appear as something simple, an elemental form of the capitalist market, when in fact under the surface they constitute something different. Commodities cover an immensely diverse range of 'goods', all with very different material qualities – from yoghurt to jeans, iPads to houses, cars to carbon emissions, kilowatts to kitchens. They are quantified differently, and have different degrees of usefulness – what Marx called use-value – but when each is given a recognized exchange value their differences dematerialize under their transformation into 'the material bearers of exchange value' (Marx 1974: 126; Harvey 2010a: 15–19). What allows commodities to have an agreed value – expressed in money – is their commensurability with other commodities, whose reference point is the very material fact that they have been produced by human labour. Commodities carry the human labour embodied in their production.

However, the labour involved in any one product or service is very different to another, and so in order to arrive at equivalence, a more generalized notion of labour is required. This is what Marx called 'abstract labour power', by which he meant not the specific nature of labour in any one productive area, but a general value given to labour taking into account skills and levels of technology in use and what society considers enough for a person to survive on (Marx 1974: 274). Thus labour power is also an exchangeable commodity with any individual possessor of it able to sell it for a price on the market. Wages and salaries are 'only special names for the price of labour-power', 'for the price of this peculiar commodity, which has no other repository than human flesh and blood' (Marx 1999). Abstract labour power, while sharing something of the abstraction of human capital, is a generality which operates, not between competing individuals, but between conflicting social classes. Capital treats all labour as equivalent and labour power rests on a level of abstraction that strikes out, in the interest of profit maximization, the differences among types of work and the many actual life-experiences of those who carry out the work. This, as noted by David Block, is 'the source of the disconnect between the social relationship of production processes and end products' (Block 2014:

136) and goes some way to explaining why 'labour as commodity' has deeply alienating overtones.

Language, on its own, may seem to be a commodity, especially when developments in information technology have provided it with new effects and communication paths, and even endowed it, according to some, with a 'high exchange value' or 'high trading value' (Lam and Wang 2008). English seems especially well positioned for the commodity label, for it seems to be growing as a global resource with an exchange value (Tan and Rubdy 2008: 3–5; see also Heller 2010b: 104–5) and is widely promoted as such. The era of the knowledge economy would seem to have hastened the commodification of language, and marked a departure from earlier 'production-based' economies, as Nikolas Coupland (2003: 467) indicates. Language, to all intents and purposes, in these accounts, has 'materialised' and become commodified as part of the changes in a 'post-industrial' society.

These seemingly common-sense impressions, however, echo the dominant neoliberal theme which assumes that commodities are the basic unit of society, but stripped of any social relations dimension. Joseph Lo Bianco identifies this overlap when he says that 'linguistic commodification reflects the ruling rationality of markets' in our times (in Tan and Rubdy 2008: xii–xiii; see also Gray 2012). Nikolas Coupland, on a similar theme, highlights more broadly the danger of blurring sociolinguistic theoretical premises with prevailing globalization narratives. Linguistic analysis should be cautious, he warns, of becoming a 'service discipline which fills out empirical detail in an effort to validate pre-existing generalisations' (Coupland 2003: 465). Heller also notes that we need 'to shift our focus away from taking dominant ideas about categories as somehow objectively real, or as units of analysis that can be presupposed rather than problematized' (2010a: 361). But to take this critique further, we need to turn to social theory and political economy for the theoretical tools to describe the commodification of language in ways which allow us to move beyond the parameters of neoliberal orthodoxy.

Nelson Flores invokes something of this dimension when he describes language commodification as part of 'neoliberal epistemology that moulds world's languages into market niches for transnational corporations' and how the promotion of plurilingualism represents the pursuit of ever greater profitability across global cultures rather than any commitment to cultural diversity. Flores sees resistance to this neoliberal commodification as springing from 'new subject positions' which create more fully rounded, culturally specific interpretations of language and which use 'the tool of plurilingualism' against what he defines, somewhat loosely, as 'the grain of neoliberal governance' (Flores 2013: 500). Heller, referring to language as a technical skill as part of the work process and the work product, also argues, that politically what matters is who defines the 'values of linguistic commodities or more broadly who regulates the market' (Heller 2010b: 103). However, not making explicit whether or not language as a commodity is being used metaphorically avoids the central question about whether language can actually be treated as 'a product of labour' (Block 2014: 137) or as a dimension of labour power (Gray 2010).

Language, labour and work

To help clarify these issues, the commodification of language needs to be understood as part of work in capitalism as a whole. When people sell their labour on the job market, all of their skills, including their linguistic skills, are made available for capitalist production. Social relations in capitalism are such that the products of human labour are owned not by those who possess the skills but by those who are in a position to exploit them. In this respect, language commodified, as a presumed factor in the labour process, represents an extension of already recognized elements of a production system driven by profit (Wood 1998: 39). Put another way, the language skills of an individual employee appear compellingly as a commodity to those who will make profits out of their exploitation – employers.

Language is a crucial skill and ability that can, if carefully exploited, secure greater profits, in production, in customer care, in after-sales and across the service sector. Managing the linguistic behaviour of employees, as Deborah Cameron notes in her study of the monitoring and surveillance in call centres, is what capitalist organizations seek to do and 'the exploitation of linguistic resources ... cannot be separated from the exploitation of human resources more broadly' (Cameron 2005: 10). Employers have an interest in measuring very precisely exact outputs of labour power, and class relations drive the objectification of knowledge and language skills. This dimension is crucial to understanding the tensions and ambiguities of the commodification of language. Or, as Kenneth McGill (2013: 88) puts it, 'the commodification of call centre work is achieved via the commodification of general abilities, effort and attention of the person doing the work, rather than in terms of the commodification of any specific linguistic or communicational competence' and this being the case, 'it remains worthwhile to focus on the more broad nature of the alienation involved rather than solely on its entanglement with language use'. This perspective has the merit of situating language skills within the more general commodification of labour power and the social relations which sustain it. Without the overall dimension of social relations between capital and labour, language as a commodity risks echoing neoliberal determinations of language as 'human capital'.

Neoliberalism presents all human skills as simple commodities with a price tag. Skills used at work are separated from social relations and are presented simply as individuals putting them to use for the rewards – or wage 'premiums' – that they can bring. But as Marx pointed out, individual employees, once they start working, have no control over how their skills are put to use. The large, factory-like halls, almost anywhere in the world, full of knowledgeable IT workers are evidence that, for the vast majority, the work of skilled employees unfolds not for the benefit of the individual, or even with the potential for them to use their skills to the full, but for the benefit of the company and in conditions over which the employees have very little control. Capital has its own motives for slicing up human abilities into quantifiable commoditized entities: to streamline production with a view to leaner production methods and increasing profits.

The distinction between labour and labour power, referred to above, is important when it comes to assessing whether language in the labour process can be considered a commodity. An individual who sells her labour on the market receives a salary which has been arrived at through the going rate for that sort of job. This going rate – or the price of labour power – takes into account the average amount of labour time performed by a worker of average skill and productivity working with the technology currently in use to produce this product – what Marx called 'socially necessary labour' time (Marx 1974: 129; see also Harman 2009: 25).[2] It is an average cost given to a person as a unit of labour. But when labour power is put to work, when employee Maria puts into practice her skill set, she produces more value than what Maria receives in salary. This applies whether Maria is producing something or whether her work is indirectly adding value via sales, advertising, communications, etc. In this sense, language and IT and communication skills are no different to dexterity and literacy in the past in that they are both vital parts of the work process. Indeed language as part of human capabilities in the work potential, even if its applications have become vastly more sophisticated, has always been part of labour power within the productive process and within service industries. To put it another way, human skills in capitalist relations of production, in the concrete, contribute towards producing surplus value, or extra value (in the system as a whole) over and above what the employee has been paid in wages.[3] This point is important because casual reference is made to post-industrial work as if the use of different skills and networked work patterns, or 'communication power' (Castells 2009; Hardt and Negri 2000), have altered social relations. But extraction of surplus value still takes place even if it is through the exploitation of communication skills, multilingualism or IT skills within an overall system of production. And workers, for all their higher levels of skills, for all the neoliberal talk of individual choice, are compelled to sell their knowledge and skills to make a living and so are compelled to enter the world of work under these conditions.

In other words, language in the labour process cannot be separated from the social relations of work in capitalism, something which is obscured in glib claims for the transformative nature of the 'knowledge economy' (Doogan 2009; Brown et al. 2011). Language as a commodity works well for capitalism; language as commodity, from the point of view of the employee, is constantly undersold.

Language and new technologies

Because new technologies give greater access to information and allow language to overcome geographical limitations, it is tempting to believe that new information technologies have transformed the nature of language and catapulted human speech into the position of a 'materialized' object. From the point of view of language in the labour process, present developments may be understood as the continuation of the division of labour into ever more discrete tasks and skills,

22 Neoliberalism and language as a commodity

rather than as representing a qualitative change from the 'industrial past'. Where Taylorist production methods of the twentieth century sought to capture, codify and adapt crafts and skills to increase production on the assembly line, today, open-plan, regimented offices effect an intensive re-engineering of digital and linguistic skills in order to repossess them as working knowledge. Language skills in particular are amenable to being packaged, 'transmitted and manipulated by others, regardless of location' (Brown et al. 2008: 11). Assessment of the value of language in the labour process is less a novel development specific to the 'knowledge economy' than a characteristic of the capitalist process of production which recasts all human skills and labour to suit its own purposes.

In the 1970s, Henry Braverman drew attention to the fact that, in Western economies, the extension of white collar work served to increase output, efficiency and distribution of goods. But he also described how the new office regime continued (contrary to the myth that every white collar worker was 'middle class') the same, strict, factory separation between the conception and execution of work (Braverman 1974). Today the same feature may be observed in work regimes supported by information technology and intense surveillance systems which make companies like Wal-Mart and Amazon, a 'surreal world of digital control in which the human element is in eclipse as just another factor of production' (Head 2014: 29). Every human skill has long been quantified for its contribution to the work process, and priced, taking into account the prevailing levels of technology, according to its contribution to the overall productive process. Today the skill components of production have extended far wider than in Braverman's day, yet the price which is paid for them and the manner of their deployment, like in the past, remains outside the control of the skilled worker or employee. In the 'information economy', work discipline may appear less intrusive than that experienced on mechanical assembly lines, but information workers continue to be tightly beholden to machines, with these more likely to be PCs, laptops, and ear and mouth pieces than giant moving sections of iron. Technology today, although it may seem to give its users greater autonomy, is used to make work more efficient and productive within the existing social relations of production.

Accordingly, language workers may be required to be linguistically adept and flexible, but at the same time, as Heller remarks, the language routines prescribed are mind-numbingly uniform (Heller 2010a: 357). Accounts of the repetitive work in call centres bear this out. One employee in an Irish centre, for example, describing himself as a 'call-centre drone', reported: '"Thank you for calling, my name is Noel, can I have your home telephone number please?" I have spoken this exact sequence of words at least two thousand times' (Burke 2008; see also Bunting 2004). For all the glowing neoliberal accounts of higher education now opening the way to interesting and rewarding jobs, the reality for many graduates is that they, like Noel, will be in drudge jobs requiring the use of only a tiny part of their skills, knowledge and potential. The 'knowledge economy' may conjure up an image of flexible work processes without physically demanding and repetitive routines, but contemporary mass offices represent the new daily grind of work, frequently involving relative de-skilling and often as exhausting and alienating as assembly lines of the past (Brown and Lauder 2012: 5; Holborow 2012b). The undervaluing of the skills that these workers possess, with the low pay that they receive, as Kenneth McGill points out, hardly puts language workers in a position to command a wage premium, or the 'skills rent' of professional employees in the past (McGill 2013: 90). Of course, some graduates will be able to use their language and other skills to secure high-tech and well-paid jobs and some will reasonably aspire to management positions.[4] However this fortunate layer of graduates is a narrowing one. If some graduates have been able to use their skills as valuable commodities and appear to draw ahead of others, it is because there has been a sharp decline in incomes of those who did not go to college (Brown et al. 2011: 17). And overall, even highly skilled graduates are not guaranteed higher salaries, as Brown et al. argue, because demand for all types of highly skilled employees has not significantly increased overall. In fact, their research points to the fact that the market price for labour, however skilled, can fall, even in periods of boom, and that the trend overall is that increasing numbers of graduates have resulted in a widening gap among college graduates within the same occupations. As they put it succinctly, 'there is a growing void between brain power and market power' (Brown et al. 2011: 124) and the human capital promise that learning is earning is forever crashing on the rocks of oversupply. What they call the 'global auction' for all skills has shifted into reverse gear and larger swathes of graduates from many countries are losing out. If language skills represent a commodity from the labour market standpoint, they do not appear to offer any significant advantage to those who possess them.

Finally, even within the rigid confines of call centre work, while in terms of labour power work is a commodity, in its concrete form its full commodification is not guaranteed. The language skills of an individual employee can never wholly transmogrify into a commodity because they emanate from a rounded, unpredictable and social human being. The same is true for any specific aspect of human creativity which is fed into the productive process. This real life distinction, which leads to all sorts of difficulties in the world of production, creates contradictions that do not conveniently evaporate in our commodity-centred world. The commodification of human skills ignores the real, living use value dimension of labour and reduces work to a mere input into the production profit-making process. Much though any exploiter of labour might wish otherwise, craftsmanship, technical knowledge, or language skills can never be reduced to quantifiable units with fully dependable outcomes, as each carries the unpredictable element of human agency. When Henry Ford famously bemoaned: 'Why is it every time I ask for a pair of hands, they come with a brain attached?' he was drawing attention, with surprising candour, to this fact.

Pressures from capitalist production may give a certain justification to the labelling of call centre workers as 'language workers', but such passive objectivism is seldom adopted by the workers themselves. While these workers may indeed be what Josiane Boutet calls 'the emblematic figures of late capitalism', she also notes that language workers 'feel they are on the same side as the "white collar workers" in modern companies' (Boutet 2012: 224), an indication that, despite the constraints, the employees continue to see their language as their own. When discussing the designation and re-designation of skills, it is important to recognize its social and ideological intent and how this drives the reclassification process. Asaf Agha, in his description of 'commoditised speech', describes this labelling as promoted by the corporations, who for their own social interests, see workers only as labour inputs, and who want to see everyone else adopt their discourse. 'It can be used by job seekers to re-describe themselves as a bundle of skills'; by doing so the job seekers are employing 'the ventriloquated speech of the corporation in which they hope to be embedded as wage labour' (Agha 2011: 44). There is no reason to believe, however, that employees succumb so passively to this process of self-labelling: the worker may well describe herself as 'a bundle of skills' for the pragmatic purposes of getting the job, but not generally identify herself as this at all.

Certainly in call centre work, as studies have shown, employees do not fully submit to the commodification of their language: their conversations do not always rigidly conform to time constraints; they do not always stick to the prescribed conversation routines; they certainly do not stop having attitudes to their work which, like our Irish employee above, may run counter to the 'always smiling' employee handbook. An employer can never be sure that they are getting pliable language speakers who will always produce the desired 'customer talk' (Holborow 2007: 65–70). Cameron recounts how call centre workers felt humiliated by the abuse they get from angry callers and resented being instructed not to retaliate (Cameron 2005: 16). She also points to a case of flight attendants working for Hong Kong Cathay Pacific Airlines who, in dispute with their company, withheld their 'smile on demand' as part of their industrial action (2005: 17), showing that workers can use the prescribed verbal and non-verbal communication for their own ends. Language as commodity cannot be guaranteed, as Heller puts it, because language is 'not about autonomous forms but rather about social practices [which] necessarily escape the strict confines of marketisation' (Heller 2010a: 358). Workers are not a submissive bundle of skills in the hands of those who run service industries. The most elaborate of human qualities, whether on an assembly line or in a hall of workstations, 'will always resist being reduced to one more commodity input' (Albritton 2012: 67). In this political sense, language can never be fully commodified.

Cameron highlights how managing language serves the ideological purpose of further stratification and exclusion and control in the labour market (2005: 21). The desire to compress language into the tight confines of commodification is part of a wider political project to naturalize commodification in the interests of maintaining existing social relations. This aspect of the categorization of language as a commodity would seem important to emphasize if we are to understand the political motivation for neoliberal ideology to reduce language knowledge and skills to a market commodity and if we are to offer alternative, more socially rounded and agency-oriented views of language.

Neoliberalism and surface relations

Bonnie Urciuoli notes that communication skills 'take on a reality through the ways that they are fetishised' and that 'communication skills in particular are fetishised as sure fire techniques that can bring in the bucks'. They are packaged discursively with intentional 'denotational vagueness', which is central to their central strategic use, 'linked as they are to their users' alignment with corporate values' which is to reinforce the idea of the neoliberal self (Urciuoli 2008: 213–15; see also Urciuoli and LaDousa 2013). It is worth examining in a little more detail what is meant by fetishization or the reification of skills, as it is directly linked to the articulation of neoliberal ideology.

Capitalist commodification which envelops all aspects of social and human life and erases human agency constituted what Marx called 'commodity fetishism'. Commodity fetishism is the process through which the definite social relation between people takes on the appearance of being a relation between things. This appearance of commodities is made possible because of 'the peculiar social character of labour which produces them' (Marx 1974: 165). This thing-like appearance of commodity exchange is not false; it exists but conceals the social relations involved. Commodities become stripped of all the concrete characteristics of the human effort that went into producing them. The exchange of commodities represents a double act of abstraction: that which makes the commodity an equivalent to a sum of money and that which, irrespective of its inherent value, makes it possess the same value as another commodity for which it is being exchanged. This complex hub of commodity exchange, which subjects every aspect of social life to its dictates, makes people relate to each other not directly as human beings but through the mediation of things (money and commodities), and leads to a situation where commodities dominate humans rather than the other way round. Taking commodities as 'things' separated from their human origin annuls their social dimension, and this appearance confounds reality (Albritton 2012; Geras 1990; McNally 2001; Žižek 2012a).

The way society appears to us is affected by this commodified appearance of things. The integral unity between work and its rewards is broken and wealth seems something removed from the humans who produce it. Society appears to us as an upside-down world in which capital appears, not as the result of people's input, but as a source of wealth generation in itself. To put it in Marx's rather gothic-sounding terms, 'Monsieur le Capital' 'does its ghost walking as a social character and at the same time directly as a thing' (Marx 1991: 809). Once different forms of value are reified, the social relations which explain their existence are obscured and the interrelations between them – market prices, interest rates, booms and slumps in production, the cost of credit, consumer confidence, market crashes – appear as 'overwhelming natural laws that irresistibly enforce their will over people and confront them as blind necessity' (Marx 1991: 10). The practical effect of all such fetishism, as noted by Bertell Ollman, 'is the blanket ignorance it imposes on anyone trying to understand the economic system' and surface relations become everything (Ollman 1971: 201).

26   Neoliberalism and language as a commodity

Neoliberal ideology is based on surface relations. If good wages are the just returns for the costs of your education and up-skilling, then being underpaid is nobody's fault but your own. When capital is merely a sum of money which an individual is fortunate enough to have at their disposal, then its increased value becomes a simple reward for risk-taking or hard work. When profit-making is simply the result of meeting demand in the market, then profits are the well-earned rewards for the work of an entrepreneur. Presented as a host of atomized decisions about benefits and costs, society as a collective evaporates behind a throng of individuals whose social interventions consist mainly of competing against one another. For Chicago school of economics neoliberal Gary Becker, for example, all economic activity boils down to individuals competing freely in a world of other individuals. 'Human capital analysis starts with the assumption that individuals decide on their education, training, medical care, and other additions to knowledge and health by weighing the benefits and costs. Benefits include cultural and other non-monetary gains along with improvement in earnings and occupations, while costs usually depend mainly on the foregone value of the time spent on these investments' (Becker 2010). Becker's assumption is that the market operates independently of us and if an individual chooses to engage with this market, they will receive rewards proportionate to what they have invested. Disparities of income are explained also on the free-market assumption that everyone has access to education and training; 'since earnings are gross of the return on human capital, some persons may earn more than others simply because they invest more in themselves' as Becker puts it (1962: 9). He adds that 'because "abler" persons tend to invest more than others, the distribution of earnings could be very unequal' (1962: 49).

Becker's view, as this last statement shows, is ideological in that it promotes the market as the ultimate arbiter for fair exchange and wealth distribution. The market thus described erases pre-existing social inequality and defines poverty as failure to be sufficiently market aware. The merit of Marx's analysis of the commodity form in capitalism is that it allows a systematic unpicking of the myth of the market as a site of socially neutral exchange.[5] The identification of human labour as the common value component to a commodity and the recognition that commodity exchange in capitalism is based on labour being bought for less than it produces, strips the market of its supposed anodyne character and situates it within specific social relations. Human capital theory also recognizes the labour component but sees it not in relation to capital's ability to extract profits, but in discrete units taken as the accumulation of individuals' decisions and actions. It was Foucault's singular insight in his discussion of the Chicago school of economics, to point out that neoliberal economics 'is no longer the analysis of the historical logic of processes; it is the analysis of the internal rationality, the strategic programming of individual's activity' (Foucault 2008: 223).[6] Neoliberalism takes the capitalist economy as a functional given, with social inequality depicted as differences between individuals' investment and the use of their human capital. Marx's method, as Jorge Larrain highlights, is to expose the nature of commodity fetishism as mystifying in two senses: 'the mystification which consists of reducing the social objectivity of phenomenal forms to a natural objectivity and the mystification which reduces social objectivity to social subjectivity' (Larrain 1979: 59). The sham of the level playing field of commodity exchange is revealed through tracing of the value of commodities to the exploitative transaction between unequal social players.

But the method of stripping off appearances to reveal underlying social relations also points to how ideology can arise in the practical reproduction of social relations and their appearances. The seeds of ideology develop around partial perceptions of reality, which has relevance for our understanding of neoliberalism. Neoliberal ideology, as will be highlighted in Chapter 5, is often presented as a power whose logic and force has bamboozled all of us as individuals into compliance. However, ideology is never a simple question of domination, brain-washing or inculcation. It is able to connect to popular consciousness because it is constructed on what seems to be true. The originality of Marx was to show the connection between the social appearance and experience of commodity exchange in capitalism and distorted views of society and how these could become the basis of ideologies and mobilized on behalf of the capitalist class. What Marx called 'vulgar' economics, makes a 'violent abstraction' of the nature of commodities, operates at ever greater degrees of remoteness from the world of production, and thereby acts as a preventative guard to seeing beyond the activities and ideas which reproduce existing society. 'Everywhere vulgar economics ... relies here as elsewhere on the mere semblance as opposed to the law which regulates and determines the phenomena' (Marx 1974: 421–22). Commodities and their means of exchange – money – thus come to stand for everything else and acquire a 'seemingly transcendental power' (Marx 1973: 146). This apparent self-standing power of money as an independent source of wealth, Marx tells us when explaining the exploitative nature of capital, is 'of course, a godsend' because it is 'a form in which the source of profit is no longer recognisable' and which results in the capitalist production process seeming to acquire an autonomous existence, with commodities and money driving the system. Commodities – or money or capital – as wealth-creating in their own right come to seem as 'natural as a pear tree bearing pears' (Marx 1981: 516–17). Commodity logic thus naturalizes existing social relations. Neo-liberal ideology could be said to operate in the way that Marx describes and could therefore be aptly described as the 'vulgar economics' of our day, with the same ideological effects.

Commodity fetishism, ideology and critique

The temptation in a world in which neoliberal thinking has become so dominant is to believe that what exists today can only be grasped on its own terms, through its own language and ideas, with no reference to the social and economic relations from which it has emerged. Yet any ideology is neither supremely secure nor wholly 'imbued' by its recipients. The ideology of neoliberalism, like other ideologies, is constructed on specific social phenomena that appear to be true.

28   *Neoliberalism and language as a commodity*

It derives from aspects of our experience of the capitalist market and particularly from the exchange abstraction of the commodity-form, an abstraction which seems, at one level, to make sense to us. Marx drew the analogy of religion, whose origins lay in real human conditions and relations and carried the same distortions that were in society. The process was one of the 'reifiying of an abstract category, treating it as a thing in itself and attributing to it powers that properly belong to human beings' (Arthur 1974: 19). So it is with commodity logic. The impression of being dominated by things arises from capitalist economic relations in which things and people are actually treated as commodities. It may be accepted at one level and resented at another, or it may be passively experienced as simply as the way the world is, or it may be felt as self-alienation, as Marx termed it in his early writings (Marx 1964: 120–34). Marx incorporated alienation into his theory of commodity fetishism, which forms the basis both of a critique of capitalist political economy, but also of a theoretical understanding of the origin of ideology.

Commodity fetishism allows an understanding of ideology, not as a fixed mentality, but as 'tacit social consciousness' (Wayne 2005: 193) or the potential for generalization about how society works which arises from the particular social relations of capitalism. Human relations, perceived as the mere exchange of things, lead to a distorted perception of social reality in which the social character of labour is hidden. As Terry Eagleton explains, society becomes fragmented by commodity logic, which makes it more difficult to grasp it as a totality (Eagleton 2007: 85). Ideology thus understood is not, as is often assumed, a question of simple 'false consciousness' (a term not used by Marx) – a blind submission to 'wrong' ideas. Nor is it mainly a wilful conspiracy to confound on the part of the capitalist class, although it can frequently be that, as government broadcasting almost anywhere in the world regularly attests. Rather, ideology arises also as the result of a 'duplicity built into the very economic structures of capitalism, such that it cannot help presenting itself to consciousness in ways askew to what it actually is. Mystification, so to speak, is an "objective" fact, embedded in the very character of the system' (Eagleton 2007: 86), although contradiction may express better the fissured reality of commodification. In other words, the capitalist economy itself, as Alex Callinicos notes, produces 'its own misperception' (1983: 131). Ideology thus understood is written in the political economy and consciousness and reality united in the same phenomenon (Larrain 1979: 46). Misperception can be fragmentary rather than roundly and permanently 'false', can exist as common sense alongside other conflicting views and can be altered and re-conceptualized by social relations and social conflict.[7]

Marx's subtle interweaving of the material and consciousness in his discussion of the commodity has exerted a strong influence, for good reason, in the social sciences and in cultural studies. According to Slavoj Žižek, its dialectical method offers 'a distilled version of a mechanism offering us a key to the theoretical understanding of phenomena which at first sight have nothing whatsoever to do with the field of political economy' (Žižek 2012b: 306). Yet scholars of applied linguistics and socio-linguistics have up until now tended to ignore the

Neoliberalism and language as a commodity 29

role of commodity fetishism in the making of ideology. For example, in her examination of ideology in the introduction to a collection of essays on language ideologies, Kathryn Woolard does not refer to commodity fetishism, even when discussing Marxist views of ideology. Ideology is defined as 'lived relations by which subjects are connected ... to the dominant relations of productions and distribution of power' in society (Woolard 1998: 6), but with no reference to social class or capitalism. Susan Phillips, in the same volume, refers to material aspects of ideology not in terms of the material economic relations in society but through a form of 'materializing' ideology, following Raymond Williams's formulation about culture, so that 'the material and the ideological become as one' with neither being more determining (Phillips 1998: 215). Michael Silverstein, in his contribution to this collection, sees ideology as 'the construal of inherently dialectical indexical processes', arising from indexical semiotic processes. Evaluation of the relationship of ideology to the social world, for Silverstein, appears to automatically include a falsity–truth dichotomy, which he dismisses as the 'intellectual salvos of dele-gitimisation'. Claims that the 'mystifications and distortions of an ideology' have a hold over 'otherwise silent or non-discerning victims' represent 'a move of committed advocacy', he argues, a 'stance of otherness', either 'from an epistemo-logical viewpoint or a "frankly political" one' (Silverstein 1998: 126). Silverstein judges such analyses as 'self-styled scientific' emanating from 'some versions of (generally left-wing) political economy' and notes that even the pronunciation of ideology is indicative of a partisan commitment to one set of social theories or another.[8] Along similar lines, Woolard establishes a distance between her interpretation of ideology and what she characterizes as 'an outmoded base-superstructure model in which material life relations are seen as primary and real and the ideological as derivative, predictable or illusory' (1998: 20). The econo-mically reductive base/superstructure model referred to by Woolard is, I think, something of a caricature, and one which Marx, in all likelihood, would have rejected as well. Nevertheless, economic reductionism is regularly imputed to the Marxist base/superstructure model and this, encouraged by Althusserian and other interpretations, can result in ideology being defined, in counter-response, as completely *detached* from political economy. Woolard veers so sharply from what she perceives as economically reductive interpretations of ideology that she risks inverting the material/ideational framework, stating that ideology is 'of interest more for its efficacy to transform the material reality'(Woolard 1998: 11). Given this now familiar eagerness to 'materialize ideology', it would seem useful to indicate briefly, in conclusion to this chapter, why this study takes political economy and commodification as central to the analysis of ideology.

To assert that in some circumstances, material production does exert a primary determining force on certain phenomena need not be either economically reductive or over-mechanical. To observe, as does Terry Eagleton, that 'within a multitude of social determinants some are finally more determinant than others' (1989: 168) is merely to note that society cannot be treated as some undiffer-entiated whole in which every social element is as determining as the next. Contrary to common belief, Marx recognized that ideology plays a decisive role

30 *Neoliberalism and language as a commodity*

in social change and indeed spent a great deal of time writing about 'super-structural' issues and their role in revolutionary situations.[9] The recognition that 'definite forms of social consciousness correspond to the economic structure' or that 'the mode of production of material life conditions the social political and intellectual life process in general' (Marx 1969: 502) is not the same as saying that economic relations call all the shots. The interweaving of consciousness with the material world is no straightforward process. Capitalist commodity exchange may be a determining factor in the way we see the world but, as I have argued here, the process is always uneven and incomplete and consciousness can never be wholly reduced to commodification. Political economy, in this view, is merely the starting point for analysis for ideology, and the basic context which exerts an influence on the shape and nature of social life and (today much more extensively than in Marx's time) in increasingly uniform ways.

Second, when referring to ideologies in and of language the distinction between discursive representations of the world and the real social world needs to be made explicit; otherwise we are robbed of a vital critical tool. The predication that there is a 'difference between how society presents itself in the discourses that seek to legitimize it and its real structures constituted by exploitation and class antagonism' (Callinicos 2006: 246) is what continues to make Marxism relevant as a critical method. The relationship of language and ideology to political economy constitutes a multi-layered concept of reality in which purposeful human agency takes place within social relations of production, but is not reducible to them.

More recently within applied linguistics, there have been some steps made towards adopting a critical approach based on an inclusion of the dimension of political economy. In our analysis of the commodification of language, I have drawn on some of this work (for example, McGill 2013). In addition, others have pointed out that linguistic critique can benefit from the inclusion of political economy analysis, with its focus on capitalist social relations. John O'Regan (2014), for example, has argued for a theoretically grounded *immanent critique* of the claims and ideological suppositions of English as a lingua franca (ELF), as proposed by Seidlhofer, Jenkins and others. Immanent critique is associated with the Frankfurt school and, as explained by O'Regan, uses historical context to interrogate the inner logic of a theory to demonstrate how its assumptions may reflect conflicts to be found within prevailing social conditions (O'Regan 2014: 2). This method involves introducing concepts 'from the outside' – from political economy – to interrogate those taken as given by the object of study and 'confront it with what it is' (O'Regan 2014: 3). O'Regan's study draws eclectically on both Marxist and Foucauldian theoretical perspectives in order to confront the ELF movement with the contradictions contained in its own texts and thereby uncover its actual, albeit not declared ideological positions. He notes that the discourse of ELF is marked by slippages between difference and *deficiency*, *standard* and *non-standard*, which together, O'Regan argues, 'invent' ELF as a variety, making it appear as a thing-in-itself, which is a form of hypostatization. To cover the case of suppositions being artificially

Neoliberalism and language as a commodity 31

concretized, he also draws on commodity fetishism as a parallel stating that 'this type of fetishism finds its metaphorical equivalent in ELF' (2014: 8). While ELF is neither a real commodity nor a product of labour, the hypostatization of ELF is nevertheless an 'irreal mystification', similar to what Vološinov and others have called 'abstract objectivism'. If reification in O'Regan's model appears to operate on the ideational plane – with partiality and totality understood theoretically rather than from the social relations of capitalism – nonetheless, a clear and convincing connection between commodity fetishism and ideology is given and surely points the way towards a fruitful form of analysis and critique in the field.

Third, raising the relationship between language and political economy does not have to involve making language into an economic 'thing' or 'materializing' it in some way. Neoliberal theories of human capital, as recounted here, 'commodify' human abilities, both to lure individuals to 'invest' in them, and in order to quantify them to make them more productive in the capitalist economy. Partly as a challenge to this, 'language as commodity' has been taken up by sociolinguists as an attempt to both introduce language into a wider socio-economic landscape and to redress the functionalist, neutralizing accounts of language which have often prevailed in global English tropes. However, I have argued here that language as commodity may too readily objectify language and underestimate how language as used at work can never quite mutate into a commodity. The notion of 'language workers', it has been shown here, does not fit the perceptions that people have of themselves, nor is the language they use guaranteed to be the pliable, profit maximizing tool that employers seek. In discussion of this anomaly, I have drawn on political economy analysis to describe the nature of commodity exchange in capitalism, how capitalist commodification attempts to expunge class conflict and how these insights point to some of the limitations of the notion of language as a commodity. Materializing language, I have noted, also echoes some of the themes of neoliberal ideology. More generally, perhaps the desire to 'materialize' language runs the risk of what Terry Eagleton noted, with reference to 'materializing culture' – that it is less an explanatory account of real social processes than an attempt at a re-description, in seemingly materialist terms, of phenomena which have been ideologically misperceived as 'immaterial'(Eagleton 1989: 169). Certainly, accounts of language which attempt to show that language is now a commodity rather than a cultural product, and to see this more generally as a paradigm shift towards an 'immaterial' economy, may fall too quickly into this trap and paradoxically come to repeat dominant neoliberal narratives about the 'knowledge' economy (Brown and Lauder 2012; Holborow 2012b).

Conclusion

This chapter has shown how neoliberal ideology places commodities at the centre of its social world, representing them as straightforward input or output of capitalist production and economies. From the neoliberal standpoint, language

32 *Neoliberalism and language as a commodity*

too is treated like a commodity, either one that employers make use of in the service industries or one which those who possess it can use to their own material advantage. I have argued that neoliberal views of language as a commodity fail to take account of the social relations which deprive 'language workers' of control over their skills and which lead to them being underpaid and unable to use to the full the skills that they have. The often tedious, highly supervised work regime of language workers exposes the myth that the knowledge economy has ushered in more autonomy for these workers, or that information production is run along freer, 'post-industrial' lines. To characterize language simply as a commodity is a reflection of the influence of neoliberal ideology in that it denies the reality of language in work situations and the potential of speakers to refuse to fit into the commodity slots allocated to them.

This chapter has also discussed the nature of capitalist commodity exchange, revisiting the question of ideology in the Marxist theoretical framework of commodity fetishism. Often ideology is dismissed as unconvincing because of its supposed 'false consciousness' dimension. I have tried to show that the way society appears to us is affected by the commodity appearance of things which explains how neoliberal ideology, by reproducing the surface relations of things, can superficially seem to be true. This understanding of ideology will be taken up in our investigation of metaphors of the market in the next chapter.

Notes

1 See Chapter 3 for a more detailed discussion of language and markets.
2 'Socially necessary labour time' as described by Marx in his account of how the value of a commodity is reached 'is the labour time required to produce any use-value under the conditions of production normal for a given society and with the average degree of skill and intensity of labour prevalent in that society'. Marx goes on to add that this varies enormously from society to society 'determined by amongst other things by the workers' average degree of skill, the level of development of science and its technological application, the social organisation of the process of production, the extent and effectiveness of the means of production and the conditions found in the natural environment' (Marx 1974: 129–30). Socially necessary labour is often taken to be synonymous with abstract labour (Bottomore et al. 1983: 448).
3 Surplus value was Marx's term for excess value produced by the exploitation of workers. It forms the basis for the profit of the individual capitalist plus what he pays out to others in the form of rent, interest payments and taxation (plus what he or she spends on non-productive activities such as after-sales, advertising distribution, etc.). See Harman (2009: 31–35) for a discussion of this, and also in the glossary of Marxist terms in the same book (2009: 400).
4 The degree of alienation depends on the type of work and where the employee is situated in the work hierarchy. Joseph Park (2013) convincingly shows how language as commodity is used as a mechanism of control even in promotion procedures for middle management in multinational corporations in Korea. Discrimination in the form of non-promotion is exercised against those not comfortable using English, despite the company's declared diversity policy (Park 2013: 564).
5 The question of the market and how it is presented in neoliberal language will be analysed in much more detail in the next chapter.

Neoliberalism and language as a commodity   33

6 Although Foucault saw this not as an ideology but as an 'actually existing regime'. See Chapter 5 for a full discussion of his understanding of neoliberal economics.
7 See Callinicos (1983: 131–35) for a discussion of this issue and his rejection of a theory of fetishism which is deterministic, in favour of a more nuanced view which starts with the conceptualization of social phenomena in their specific, complex and differential relations of determination.
8 Strangely, Silverstein chooses to highlight the two phonological forms: [ay]deology and [i]deology which he sees as identity badges of, on the one hand, the Cultural Anthropologists and the other of 'Sociological Anthropologese or even Sociologese/ Political Economicists [sic] among others'. Silverstein has little sympathy for the latter camp (Silverstein 1998: 126–27).
9 Actually Marx did not write exclusively about economic production. Many of his works, besides *The German Ideology*, were philosophical; *The Eighteenth Brumaire*, written by Marx during the upheavals in France between 1848 and 1852, is exclusively dedicated to political questions with hardly one reference to the economy or to production.

3 Markets, metaphors and neoliberal ideology

Central to the ideology of neoliberalism is the notion that the market captures a basic truth about human nature and social organization. It redefines the relationship between the individual and society with social behaviour being guided, not by collective institutions and interaction, but by supply and demand, by entrepreneurs and consumer choice, by individual companies and individual people. Social activity and exchange becomes judged on their degree of conformity to market culture. Neoliberal ideology can thus be justly described as 'shorthand for market rule' (Birch and Mykhnenko 2010: 2).

The idea that everything works through the market is so accepted that it has become part of the social and mental scaffolding of our daily lives. Markets work best when left alone; nothing should be done to undermine or interfere with free competition in the market; societies must be structured to facilitate market imperatives; individuals need only taper their talents to the dictates of the market to realize their potential. As noted by David Harvey a decade ago (2005: 2–3), official policies of most states everywhere automatically simply accepted without question that human well-being could best be advanced by booming markets and that governments should provide the institutional framework to achieve this. After the economic crisis of 2008, it was predicted, with some justification, that the bursting of the market bubble would force neoliberalism into retreat (Duménil and Lévy 2011). But neoliberalism bounced back with increased vigour, albeit with greater contradictions. Neoliberalism's favoured protagonists, the financial markets became again the fount of all economic wisdom. Quickly forgotten was their recent collapse under the strain of their ballooning speculative activities. Financialization was already playing a much larger role in the economy before the crisis; financial markets now stepped squarely into the role of the main drivers of public policy. One sign of this was the appointment, in an unprecedented step, of a government entirely made up of people from finance. On 16 November 2011, Mario Monti (formerly EU Competition Commissioner and adviser to Goldman Sachs, Coca-Cola and the ratings agency Moody's) was invited by the Italian president to become prime minister of Italy as head of a technocratic government composed entirely of unelected professionals.

This context of crisis has meant that states changed their official tune: they now threw off their carefully woven cloak of invisibility and emerged more openly as managers of the market. Most notably, via the financial institutions of the Eurozone, they injected colossal sums of money into private banks to pay off their debts. Official neoliberal discourses around the state had to be reworked to justify this dramatic state intervention in the 'free' market and explaining this sudden *volte face* required some deft ideological footwork. The politics of austerity conveniently obliged (Callinicos 2012; Allen and O'Boyle 2013). Every state needs a functioning banking system, so the argument ran, thus banks needed to be propped up with public money to function again, no matter what. (The fact that this same banking system had just spectacularly failed appeared not to matter.) The state proceeded to hand over huge sums of public money to the banks, which required a sharp reduction in public spending. In some cases, like that of Ireland, this policy move resulted in one of the most serious economic contractions in modern history. The Irish bank bailout, whose cost to the state may amount to as much as to €90 billion, led to a reduction of €28 billion in public spending over the first five years of the recession, with more reductions to follow (Allen and O'Boyle 2013: 24–25). Such a drain from the public purse effectively enacted what neoliberals had sought for a long time, but the moment of crisis was the excuse for its full-blown implementation. The bailout marked the beginning of a period of extreme uncertainly and 'uninterrputed disturbance' which swept away customary ways of thinking, and allowed a revamped neoliberalism to make its mark (Fraser et al. 2013: 48). Austerity measures, selectively applied, became the means of recreating the conditions under which the market, and those who gained from it, could flourish again.

This neoliberal repositioning *vis-à-vis* the 'free' market became articulated in public discourse in various ways. In the earlier days of neoliberalism, market rule made itself felt through business language 'colonizing' hitherto unrelated fields. The 'semantic stretching' of market terms allowed business thinking to migrate to all social activities, and to map the consumer-in-a-market trope onto every social experience (Fairclough 2010; Hasan 2003, Kelly-Holmes and Mautner 2010). Post-crash, financial markets have dominated public discourse in new and surprising ways, as the next section will show.

Markets personified

Ideology involves a systematically organized representation of reality, and given that metaphors creatively interpret that reality they play a large part in bringing ideologies to life and making them seem real to people. They are not just literary embellishments but modes of reasoning about social life and politics and lead us in directions which privilege one understanding of social reality over another (Chilton 2004: 203; Hart 2008; Hodge and Kress 1993).

The influence of financial markets on public policy came to be expressed in language through certain metaphorical representations of financial markets. The 'speaking, thinking markets' have entered public discourse with extraordinary political force (Jones 2011: 134).[1] In newspapers, we find markets have acquired the status of living, breathing humans, for example:

36 *Markets, metaphors and neoliberal ideology*

Governments need to hear what the markets are saying.

The financial markets have seen through what the Government is trying to do.

Mr Noonan [Irish Finance Minister] insisted the Government's decision to go for a clean exit from the bailout programme had been approved by the markets.

Governments have been doing what markets understandably expect.

When leaders of government and the central bank say they will do what is necessary, then financial markets need not worry.

If the financial markets are pricing in a sharp rise because they think in the past every time the economy was growing quickly the banks raised interest rates, they should think again.

Governments had to show their seriousness by inflicting pain on themselves, only then could they regain the markets' trust.

The passage of the bill was met with a huge sigh of relief in the markets.[2]

Financial markets are presented as humans. Markets *say* things and should be *listened* to. They *respond to* or *approve* what governments do. They *need not worry*. Sometimes they need to *think again*. They *heave sighs of relief*. The personification process extends to include the subtlest of human qualities: they may not *have trust* in governments and they *see through* things. The financial markets become living and breathing beings, omnipotent, adversarial, autonomous, intensely unpredictable and in a position to dictate at will what should happen and what exact policies should be adopted:

The Markets registered their dislike over recent events in Greece.

Financial markets tried to persuade the government to privatize social security.

Their influence has become unquestioned and their power arbitrarily dispensed, rather like that of a tyrant in the ancient world:

The international markets do not have the appetite to fund the state for a year.

Why have the financial markets turned so bitterly on their saviours?

Occasionally in this personification process markets are presented as frail humans in ill health, and in need of special attention:

Financial markets were in intensive care.

An excerpt from an article in the *Financial Times*, reproduced on the next page, is one example of this elaborate metaphorical representation of financial markets. In this piece, the journalist, Martin Wolf, is presenting a more Keynesian interpretation of what the markets are telling us to do, namely that their message to governments might be to spend rather than cut back, nevertheless the ultimate authority upon which his argument rests is the wisdom of the markets.

We must listen to what bond markets tell us

They are saying: borrow and spend, please. Yet those who profess faith in the magic of the markets are most determined to ignore the cry

By Martin Wolf
September 6, 2011

What is to be done? To find an answer, listen to the markets. They are saying: borrow and spend, please. Yet those who profess faith in the magic of the markets are most determined to ignore the cry. The fiscal skies are falling, they insist.

HSBC forecasts that the economies of high-income countries will now grow by 1.3 per cent this year and 1.6 per cent in 2012. Bond markets are at least as pessimistic: US 10-year Treasuries yielded 1.98 per cent on Monday, their lowest for 60 years; German Bunds yielded 1.85 per cent; even the UK could borrow at 2.5 per cent. These yields are falling fast towards Japanese levels. Incredibly yields on index-linked bonds were close to zero in the US, 0.12 per cent in Germany and 0.27 per cent in the UK.

Are the markets mad? Yes, insist the wise folk: the biggest risk is not slump, as markets fear, but default. Yet if markets get the prices of such governments' bonds so wrong, why should one ever take them seriously?

(Wolf 2011: 15)

Here markets are presented as people, an authority with a will, a supernatural being with a deep knowledge of things. Even unexpected opinions imputed to markets do not shake our belief in their oracular status. Markets need to be *listened* to. They *say* things, they *insist*, they express pessimism, they *fear* things, they do things wrong; sometimes, like people, they should not *be taken seriously*. But even these reservations are expressed within the metaphorical frame that financial markets are a freestanding agent. The accompanying cartoon conjures up the quaintness of a market stall, but only to illustrate how the markets today pull all the strings. As Campbell Jones aptly points out, 'finance is the master narrative and the market is the master in finance's master narrative' (Jones 2011: 132). Markets are a cohesive whole, an invented single subject, which can compel governments to act in accordance with their wishes.

The figure by which speech is attributed to abstractions not normally considered able to speak is known as prosopopoeia. When the markets are said to have *spoken* or *given their response*, or when it is said that the markets need *to be listened to*, prosopopoeia of the markets is happening (Jones 2013: 1). When other human characteristics are attributed to the markets – as in their experiencing feelings of *bitterness*, or *dislike*, or *not having the appetite* for something, or *trying to persuade* – it is a process of metaphorical personification which is occurring.

Sometimes, it is one section of the financial markets which is the subject of metaphorical personification. In Ireland, it has been the bond markets which have been the enduring point of reference for the political class steering its way through the recession. Bond markets are represented in public discourse as a force to be *heeded*, to be *listened to*, and their yield ratio – the Bond Equity Earnings Yield Ratio to give it its full title – the pivot upon which economic policy turns. 'Strong austerity programme implementation was reflected in the improvement in Irish government bond yields' was the connection made officially by the European Commission (2012b) and this dominant narrative saw bondholders elevated to core public policy drivers.

Bondholders are presented, as in the excerpt below, as a tightly cohesive body, with the actual identity of the bondholders seldom given. Kieran Allen and Brian O'Boyle reveal, in the case of those who hold Irish government bonds, that they can be found in the asset management sections of some of the major world banks – BNP Paribas, Aviva, Axa Paris, Deutsche Investment and Goldman Sachs (Allen and O'Boyle 2013: 21). They remind us that it was the bondholders, not the Irish people that were bailed out, and that the Irish government, once it had decided that bondholders should be excluded from any burden-sharing of their own debts, had to convince its own population of 'the need to bail in the taxpayers' (2013: 21). A key component of this project, as the text here from the *Irish Times* demonstrates, was to convince the general public that bond markets were neutral social arbiters.

Ireland's bailout exit of huge significance for Europe

Suzanne Lynch
Last Updated: Thursday, November 14, 2013, 14:11

... Ireland's exit from the bailout is not only a momentous moment for Ireland, it is also of huge significance for Europe. Ireland's achievement in keeping to the terms of the bailout programme, and seeing its bond yields fall to 3.5 per cent, will be seized upon by euro zone leaders as proof that the much maligned policy of austerity is working.

> The first inkling that Ireland could exit unaided came last month. Michael Noonan's suggestion at the Fine Gael annual conference that Ireland could exit the programme unaided can be seen as a testing of the waters. Having opened the Pandora's box, the Government waited to see the market reaction.
>
> (Lynch 2013)

Bond markets here are personified by having a *reaction*, as we have seen above. They are essentialized as a collective *expert* to whom governments must unquestioningly, defer. They are the accepted financial barometers whose reactions to government initiatives will ultimately adjudicate on the rightness or wrongness of these decisions. Bond yields as referred to in this excerpt count for everything and their performance is the *proof* that the *policy of austerity is working*. Here we note that the market-as-agent has the function of not only guiding government policy but an external agent which can convince ordinary folk that what the government is doing is right.

The personification of financial markets in all their forms, so casually enacted in public discourse, raises issues about how and why human attributes should be applied to markets and the ideological implications therein.

First, attributing human characteristics to financial markets as if they were collective entities covers over the actual complex and competing transactions of financial markets. Financial markets are arenas of fierce aggression, dominated by large corporate players, whose participants win and lose on a large scale. The imagined unity of personhood does not exist in the lived reality – and mayhem – of financial markets. By presenting markets as speaking with one voice, their relentless competition dissolves into a unified subject and, at the same stroke, the substance of financial market activity – the trading huge sums of money at a flick of a switch – is tamed into a human subject with feelings and emotions that we are asked to identify with. The conversion through speech of a socially highly complex activity into a unified human-like entity helps to naturalize their existence and convince us that the markets, being the same as one of us, speak as if impelled by the natural instincts of human nature. Paul Chilton argues that use of the metaphor in this way hurries us along a certain political reasoning: '[m]etaphorical mappings, which are usually unconscious, are used for reasoning, reasoning about target domains that are ill understood, vague or controversial ... [S]ource domains are intuitively understood and have holistic structure, so that if one part is accepted other parts follow' (Chilton 2004: 52). The source domain of the human person brings familiarity to the complex workings of financial markets in such a way as to make us believe that they are as natural and as unfathomable as human behaviour.

Yet, given the casual personalization of financial markets, it is worth reminding ourselves of the activities that are said to constitute 'markets': Who carries them out and for what purposes? They encompass all manner of speculative activities which take place in the cavernous, screen-filled halls of Wall Street, of Frankfurt, of Tokyo, of London and of Shanghai; the capital markets, the commodity

40 *Markets, metaphors and neoliberal ideology*

markets, the foreign exchange markets, and the bond markets. These are the physical and virtual spaces where equities, bonds and derivatives, commodities and 'futures contracts'[3] are traded in highly intricate ways in pursuit of money making more money. In Ireland, due to the calamitous fallout of runaway speculation, the public has come to learn rather a lot about the exact nature of present-day financial market intricacies. The trial of the three directors of the now defunct Anglo Irish Bank, the subject of the most spectacular bank default in modern times, was one such occasion. This bank was once the lender of choice for property developers, and rated by financial experts as 'the best bank in the world' due mainly to the size of the fortunes being made by its share-holders (Steen 2013). At the trial, which took place six years after the state bailout, the University College Cork academic Séamus Coffey was called upon to explain to the jury how the bank's dealing in financial derivatives (in this case Contracts for Difference) worked. He described them as 'a bit like placing bets on horses'. The person placing the bet did not own the horse but he had an interest in the horse's performance and if the horse won he would benefit. Similarly, the court was told, if a share price rose, the owner of a CFD would make a profit based on 'the difference' between the starting price and the increased price. But also, if it fell, he would not make a profit and either the investment would be closed and he would take the loss or he could continue with it. If he wanted to continue on with the investment he would need to give the CFD provider more money. This additional payment was referred to as 'the margin call'. It was also explained that CFDs, being private contracts, were not recorded by the Irish Stock Exchange, unlike when a person purchases shares and their name is recorded and is visible publicly (Gartland 2014).[4] This web of dealings, in other words, amounted to complex deviations from earlier forms of financial speculation and was spun outside the mechanisms of public scrutiny. The derivatives may have amassed hefty returns for those that worked them, but they involved, as this court case heard, possibly illegal actions and ones which, if they had been made more public at the time, would have certainly been regarded as unacceptable. Yet it is these financial markets which have come to be the revered personages of public discourse.

Finally, anthropomorphizing financial markets transforms events themselves into subjects which erases the specific social agents involved. This metaphorical process can be described as an act of reification in which financial markets are transformed into powerful super-beings, while appearing to act independently of humans, and yet which govern people's lives. The activities on financial markets are only possible because of the social relations of capitalism which allow money to be traded in this way. Reification makes social relations appear as given, static phenomena thereby shrouding their existence in mystification. Georg Lukács, the Hungarian Marxist philosopher, described reification as a distinctive feature of modern capitalism, the upshot of a system which 'continuously produces and reproduces itself economically on higher levels' and whose 'effect progressively sinks more deeply, more fatefully and more definitively into human consciousness' (Lukács 1971: 93). He labelled this acceptance of things as they seem as the 'reified mind', a 'form without content' (1971: 94) a formulation which could be taken as including language as central to consciousness. Financial markets are recreated through metaphorical means as an inverted reflection of human beings which, in turn, freezes them as an essential thing, beyond the realm of critique and also, paradoxically, of human intervention.

In sum, the metaphorical representation of markets as independent self-propelled entities subtly confirms neoliberal ideology. It deletes the social aspects of financial markets – the specific actors, the players behind bond markets, the amount of money gained – and pastes in human characteristics which, like the weather, are ultimately unpredictable. The ideological intent of this discursive device is to forestall critique. How exactly a metaphorical figure of speech can have such ideological force, however, needs to be examined more closely and this is the subject of a later section of this chapter.

Market – the master narrative

Alongside the personification of financial markets, the market metaphor has expanded into many other human and social activities. This market stretching has resulted in some stark conceptual shortcuts. For example we may hear that:

> Rheumatoid arthritis is a competitive market.
>
> Kelly Martin, CEO Élan, as reported on Irish radio 2010

Rheumatoid arthritis, we should remember, is an auto-immune disorder which affects the joints of the body and brings with it many painful symptoms. Stiffness, serious movement problems, severe pain, aching muscles, warmth and redness of skin and incapacity are just some of these. Yet in a metaphorical identification between the disease and those seeking alleviation from the pain of it, and the subsequent identification of those people constituting a market, the disease itself fades behind its money-making potential.

The market metaphor finds expression not only in the field of disease, but also more and more commonly of education:

> In education, Africa and Latin America are new growth markets.
>
> British Council Report

> A new market for preschool English instruction is emerging, and showing great growth potential.
>
> Chinese English-language newspaper *China Daily*

> Overseas students who come to Britain to study is a market which has grown sharply in recent years, but competition from other countries is intensifying.
>
> UK Government International Education Report

42 *Markets, metaphors and neoliberal ideology*

Each situation – disease, education, language learning – is described as a market. The metaphorical device employed in these examples to identify each human condition or activity or condition more closely with the market is metonymy. In this figure of speech, one word or phrase is substituted for another with which it is closely associated. Within metonymy, theorists identify synecdoche as a separate trope, which draws attention to how terms can stand for each other in terms of part of a whole for a whole, or vice versa (Chandler 2007: 132). When we say a *glass* for a glass of wine, *plastic* for a credit card, the *Crown* for the UK monarchy, or when, as here, *rheumatoid arthritis* for those suffering from rheumatoid arthritis, *Africa* or *Latin America* for people in these places, or *education* for those who study, the metaphorical substitution of a part for the whole is being deployed. Uses of metonymy are very common in everyday language, and they rely for their acceptance on shared cultural and social knowledge and experience.

Because so much of ideology is expressed subtly and in an indirect fashion, because it often involves associating one idea with another, and because it appeals to shared common experience, metonymy is a figure of speech rich in ideological potential. When rheumatoid arthritis is said to be a competitive *market*, when education, pre-school English instruction, or overseas students who come to Britain are described as a *market* or *markets*, the social space of the market envelops other social phenomena – disease or education – not normally classified as market activities. In the expanding field of the market, we daily hear the metonymy in which a part speaks in the place of the whole and serves to silence others (Jones 2011: 141). With its capacity to short-circuit between one field and another, metonymy persuasively presents one category as naturalized within another, in a seemingly common sense way. As Campbell Jones points out, the market has a remarkable ability to expand metonymically so as to stand in the place of the entire public sphere (Jones 2013: 53).

The market metaphor stretches to the world of knowledge and ideas. Jimmy Wales, founder of Wikipedia, sees his online encyclopaedia as a 'marketplace of ideas', an information-sharing project which is both 'charitable' and 'humanitarian' in its endeavour to 'distribute a free high-quality encyclopaedia to every single person on the planet' (Wales 2008). The market metaphor naturally articulates Wales's conception of knowledge. Wikipedia, we are told, acts like a market of freely engaging individuals, 'committed to reason and the non-initiation of force as fundamental organising principles for a free world' whose exchange of ideas and objective facts helps to remove conflict from the world (2008). The *marketplace of ideas*, through a process of natural market selection, engages contributors to Wikipedia who are significantly 'more educated than average'; market principles make it likely that a flawed argument or conclusions made on faulty premises will be challenged and corrected. Here effectively the market is presented as a supreme 'information processor more powerful than any human brain' (Mirowski 2013: 55), a view held by the Austrian ordoliberal Frederick Hayek, who Wales quotes approvingly. Hayek advocated the 'superiority of appropriate (market-like) aggregation mechanisms for information' (quoted in

Mirowski 2009: 423), which allows the creation of objective knowledge. A similar principle guides Wales's philosophy for Wikipedia, for it sees knowledge as the disembodied accumulation and dissemination of information among decentralized users.

Knowledge as *the marketplace of ideas* is a metaphor which makes questionable assumptions. Wikipedia, just like markets, may not be quite as free nor as democratically constituted as is claimed. Wikipedia works in tandem with a giant multinational, Google, with Wikipedia articles very often showing up on the first page of Google searches. Wikipedia can be financially successful because, like other very profitable website such as Facebook, its garnering of free information can be repackaged in formats that allow 'the creation of "derivatives" that can themselves be marketed' (Mirowski 2009: 424). The naively imagined 'commons' of net information clashes with the reality of Wikipedia practices: working according to a strict editing hierarchy; heavy-handed editing procedures which freely undo the activities of participants at lower levels (2009: 422); high quality articles are often rejected as they are perceived to be too technical; entry selection operates, despite claims to the contrary, like any other encyclopaedia. What is different about Wikipedia, as Mirowski observes, is that it captures what passes for common knowledge produced by participants on the Internet at some specific point in time. But the Wikipedia view rests on a model of truth and knowledge which is inherently market-based. As Mirowski puts it:

> The conviction that truth 'emerges' from the random interactions of variously challenged participants in the precinct of the Wiki-world (sometimes retailed in the popular press as the 'Wisdom of the Crowds') only holds water if we are allowed great latitude in the definition of 'truth'. Neoliberals have great faith in the marketplace of ideas; and for them the truth is validated as what sells.
>
> (Mirowski 2013: 424)

Mirowski's warning, acts as a reminder against the received wisdom that the market-driven Wikipedia is a new means of democratizing knowledge acts as a reminder of the degree to which the market model has penetrated common ways of valuing things in social life. The metaphorical representation of the market in language – in fields hitherto considered external to the market – is a symptom of the dominance of neoliberal ideology. How such conceptual metaphors contribute to the intuitive articulation of neoliberal ideology is the subject of the next section.

Metaphors and mind

The rhetorical device which draws the analogy between financial markets and humans, as I have shown, is a personifying, or animating, metaphor. It involves thinking of one thing, what metaphor theorists call the topic (*financial markets*) as though it were another, the source (HUMAN BEINGS).[5] This process is called metaphorical mapping. This mapping is common in literature, as in 'All the

44 *Markets, metaphors and neoliberal ideology*

world's a stage', between *life*, (the target or topic) and ACTING (the source), or as in Robert Frost's poem 'The Road Not Taken', when *life* is thought of as A JOURNEY. Sometimes, in everyday metaphors, this mapping may simply be a novel or subjective way of describing things, as in mouse for a computer device or miserable for an afternoon. But some metaphors, it has been argued, form the basis of abstract thought, and as such constitute conceptual metaphors. It is these that are of interest to us here for conceptual metaphors map social events and processes on to familiar categories which allow us to make sense of the world. George Lakoff and Mark Johnson (2003) identify different kinds of conceptual metaphors. Some are based on orientation, for example 'up' and 'down' for things that are not spatial (e.g. *more* is UP and *less* is DOWN, *louder* is UP and *softer* is DOWN, *happy* is UP and *sad* is DOWN). Other conceptual metaphors represent the (target or topic) concept in terms of another (the source or the conceptual domain from which we draw metaphorical expressions). For example, *arguments* or *economic competition* is WAR; *life* can be A JOURNEY, though also a DREAM or A LONG HEADACHE IN A NOISY STREET. Some conceptual metaphors, like those which map market events on to human behaviour represent *markets* as HUMAN BEINGS are ontological, in that they present things as entities which they are not in real life. An ontological metaphor is one in which the topic is an abstraction, such as an activity, emotion, or idea, and it is represented as, or draws its metaphorical source from, something concrete, such as an object, substance, structure, or person. The economy is often described in human terms, as in AILING *economies* needing fiscal REMEDIES for them to RECOVER. So fundamental are some of these metaphors to the way we see the world that we are barely aware that we are in fact using metaphors at all. This impression created by metaphors, as Andrew Goatly (2006, 2007) points out, makes them an important vehicle of ideology and a subtle way of bringing meaning to the service of power. The reference point which makes any particular mapping seem apt, however, is not a settled question but one susceptible to change, interpretation and adaptation, as I discuss below.

Lakoff and Johnson (2003: 83) were among the first theorists to highlight the force of metaphors in their ability to classify our experiences, a classification that we need in order 'to comprehend, so that we will know what to do'. Behind 'conceptual metaphors', Lakoff (2008) argues, is a political and moral narrative, or framing, whose reasoning is activated and reinforced through the structures of the brain. In a crime story in the newspaper, for example, we take for granted the victim–hero structure; in a feature profile of a wealthy American, we may accept the American myth of the rags to riches story. The more these frames are repeated, the more the associative chain is strengthened. He explains successful mapping through physical neural binding, a process identified by cognitive scientists as being crucial to coordinating different neural responses in the brain to produce an integrated whole. He believes that a similar process governs narrative structures, or frames, in language. His claim is that the power of metaphorical framing has been seized upon by conservative politicians to put their message across and his aim is to expose the political wrongheadedness of their metaphors (2008: 3–15).

Markets, metaphors and neoliberal ideology   45

The metaphorical and ideological dimensions of the market figure extensively in Lakoff's writings. He describes how, as we have noted, the market is metaphorically constructed and personified as a legitimate authority which makes rational decisions. The imposition of this metaphorical frame becomes a way of 'imposing market discipline and punishing the lack of it'. Presenting markets as working like human beings 'rationalizes' their irrationality, allows us to accept their unacceptable behaviour, and compels us to act in their shadow (Lakoff and Johnson 2003: 65). Prosperity becomes the reward for obeying the discipline of the market, while poverty is evidence of lack of discipline, and thus deserving of nothing. In this frame, state expenditure becomes labelled 'anti-market' and social welfare provision stigmatized as confirmation of an individual's failure to work in the market system. Lakoff explains the hold of the dominant metaphorical frame through its appeal to morality, which rests on the myth of the American Dream, conceived around the traditional family and individuals working to better themselves. If source domains are intuitive, the imparting of a characteristic onto an unfamiliar target domain allows an understanding of something new in terms of something old. Deference for the self-made man, Lakoff claims, is a remnant of 'old enlightenment thinking' as propounded by Smith and Burke, which held that rational choice, under the invisible hand of the market, would lead to an optimal division of wealth (Lakoff 2008: 206). Lakoff's overall thesis is that 'what we learn from cognitive science applied to current-day American conservatism – is that the source of authoritarianism is the mode of thought itself' (2008: 65). His plea is that right-wing conservative morality, and the metaphorical frames that structure its 'political unconscious', should be replaced a more progressive moral frame, motivated by 'empathy, responsibility, protection and empowerment'. If metaphors are fixed in the structures of people's brains, then 'to change minds you must change brains' and new metaphors need to be found. Thus, he argues that we need to change the way we refer to social phenomena. The metaphor of relief as applied to taxes assumes the conservative credo of less government; if we thought of taxes in a more socially responsible way, we could give them another name (like social contributions) which expresses more accurately their role in the provision of services for the public (2008: 234–40). Conceptual metaphor theory, as propounded by Lakoff and Johnson, has been influential in framing theory and critical discourse analysis and has been a source for analysing the political and ideological effects of metaphor in public discourse (Chilton 2004; Hart 2008).

Stephen Pinker, in his book *The Stuff of Thought* (2007), builds on Lakoff and Johnson's insights but takes their observations further down the brain structure route, insisting that metaphors gel through cognitive structures and mechanisms which are wired into the human brain. Conceptual metaphors, for Pinker, uncover the nature of cognitive development and how people deal with abstract ideas. 'The atom is a solar system' or an 'antibody is a lock for a key' are not just explanatory metaphors, he claims; they are mechanisms for the mind to understand otherwise inaccessible concepts. 'Our powers of analogy allow us to apply ancient neural structures to newfound subject matter, to discover hidden

46   *Markets, metaphors and neoliberal ideology*

laws and systems in nature ... to eff the ineffable', as he puts it (Pinker 2007: 276–77). According to his model, thought is a form of computation out of which rational inferences occur, which individuals can use to test and scrutinize their merits and their fidelity to the structure of the world. He develops Lakoff's notion that metaphors are the vestiges of cognition and incorporates it into a functionalist, evolutionist schema, seeing their function as giving order to our universe, discovering hidden laws in nature and amplifying the expressive power of language itself. Metaphors are part of our human toolkit which make the brain fitter for purpose, more adept at conceptualizing, and thus help to provide evolutionary advantage or, in his words, to 'escape the cave' (Pinker 2007: 427). Conceptual metaphors, for Pinker, constitute part of the 'cognitive niche' in evolution and natural selection and they operate within cognitive processes straightforwardly as the 'stuff of thought'.

Pinker's neuro-theory locates consciousness within the individual human organism, rather than across inter-subjective and socio-historical contexts. His mapping of highly complex social phenomena onto localized brain functions does not distinguish between cognition (mental processes) and consciousness (awareness which evolves and changes according to social context), and thereby he disregards the role that the latter plays in human behaviour, thought and language. The mind-as-machine that Pinker presents to us, is autonomous and self-driven, an entity which works irrespective of society.[6] Pinker is fond of saying that 'language is a window into the way the mind works' as if the minds works according to pre-existing patterns, rather like a computer with its own ready-made component parts and structure. He appears to provide a practical explanation of how metaphors serve an existing human rationality but he discounts the changing aspects of historical, social or ideological dimensions of human thought and consciousness. Free will appears only fortuitously and inexplicably, to correct the excesses of 'harmful' genetic behaviour. This has been called, with justification, 'a sky-hook approach', or a kind of fictional apparatus plucked out of nowhere to escape the cage of biological determinism constructed by an overreliance on genetic explanations on their own (Rose 1999: 257). Like many functionalist views of genetic coding, whether for language or human behaviour, Pinker's attaches little importance to socialization in thought processes and metaphorical constructions in language.

His assertion is that metaphors are natural products of the way everyone's mind works and that metaphorical framing depends on the rationality test for it to be accepted (Pinker 2007: 260–66). However, metaphorical frames are confirmed, strengthened, weakened, configured and reconfigured throughout our lives by our interactions with our social environments. Financial markets likened to human beings connects to our imagination because they wield so much power in society. A disease described as a market, or a patient or student described as a customer are the 'natural' metaphors of a society which is run according to market rules. Pinker's assumption that where we are in evolutionary terms is where we should be, and that metaphorical thinking is a collection of stepping stones along this evolutionary progression, represents a timeless view of humans who are judged in terms of the present devoid of history or change. Metaphors, in this reading, are merely rational and practical instruments for everyday living which, as Deborah Tannen concludes, simply save 'the individual the trouble of figuring things out anew all the time' (Tannen 1993: 21). This kind of bland functionalism excludes social and ideological dimensions from metaphorical mapping, and sees the use of metaphor as one rung on an evolutionary ladder. Pinker, furthermore, situates contemporary US society very near the top of that ladder. As an example of how we have 'escaped the cave' with language, he cites the fact that 'we have managed to achieve the freedom of a liberal democracy' (Pinker 2007: 435). Goatly notes that Pinker goes as far as to argue that principles of evolutionary psychology are expressed in the US constitution, citing these as 'the right to life, liberty and the pursuit of happiness', including (in a breezy unawareness of his own ideological leanings) 'the prioritisation of trade as evidence of reciprocal altruism' (Goatly 2007: 32). Violence and dominance across human societies and the battle between men and women are two further examples given by Pinker (2002) as evidence of the unchanging nature of the human genetic make-up. His unthinking assertions in these matters undermine the objectivity of his claim that human nature is genetically programmed or that metaphors are simply functional to humans coping with life.

Metaphors, ideology and 'common sense'

Placing cognitive processes at the centre of explanations about how the mind works is attempting to answer questions that mental processes alone are not able to answer. Acceptance or non-acceptance of a metaphorical frame depends less on neural binding in the brain or innate mental structures than on the social reality within which these judgements are possible and without which development of individual consciousness is impossible (Rose 1999). The human mind cannot be reduced to a cognitive, information-processing machine as minds do not just deal with information, but with decisions, opinions, and emotions, and all of these in specific social situations. This is what distinguishes minds from computers and also what transforms information into meaning (Rose 2006: 102).

To grasp the power of metaphors, we need to look outside the realm of 'pure' thought and outside a 'morality' of the brain (Lakoff 2008: 93). We have to see that metaphors mainly owe their existence and efficacy not only to the mind, but to society (Wee 2005: 223). Metaphors are created and received as part of social experience, social processes, and some in conjunction with ideological and political strategies. Metaphors are particularly susceptible to ideological invention because, binding together two normally distinct ideas or contexts, they inherently invite comparison and synthesis. To understand the ideological significance of metaphor, we have to understand internal cognitive or linguistic structures in combination with the external context of social being, and how conceptualization is also an aspect of social consciousness. Lakoff's model may claim that if we want to change minds, we must change brains, but this kind of cognitive voluntarism is not very convincing. One of the reasons why *taxes* are unlikely

48 *Markets, metaphors and neoliberal ideology*

to be replaced by more positive-sounding labels is that, because they have a social reality; *taxes* have a denotational meaning about which there is broad consensus, rather than just an arbitrary meaning. *Taxes* may have also acquired a certain ideological connotation which particular social forces may make hegemonic, but to change that will require more than moral pronouncements or prescribed cognitive re-mappings.

Personification of the market makes sense to people, less for its self-standing rationality than for its connection with our lived world. Markets seem to dominate every aspect of our daily lives. Prices confront us when we shop for bread, for meals, our groceries in the supermarket, our take-away coffee in a café, a meal in a restaurant, on the bus or the train station when we pay our fare. When we go online to pay for a book, for a flight, for a 'special offer' hotel or holiday, when we search the ads for a car, when we look for somewhere to rent or somewhere to buy, when we want to acquire anything at all, prices, in competition with each other, inform our decision on whether we can buy this one, that one, or whether we can buy one at all. We partake in market transactions many times in a single day. Important decisions that we make in our lives about where we live, about education, about vital medical treatment, will be determined by sums of money set around market dictates. At a less immediate level, our experience of work, which gives us access to the wherewithal to buy all these things, is as an endlessly competitive market. Being taken on or laid off depends on the job market and the level of pay often determined directly or indirectly by the skills market. Our wages and salaries are set according to 'the going rate', and the work that we do must be ever more efficient, more flexible and more 'value for money', as measured against an imagined other worker somewhere else who appears to be constantly outperforming us. Employers are also subject to market pressures. Intense competition puts companies and employers in do-or-die conflicts: if they fail, factory closures and/or relocation to cheaper production sites are the result. Therefore, the metaphor that makes the market into a powerful autonomous power is not just a cognitive creation or even a political mind-set, but reproduces for us a reality that we are part of everyday.

When we are told, therefore, that *the markets know best*, this fits with our immediate experience of the social world. But the power of the market, whether by metaphorical personification or metonymy, as discussed earlier, adds a new twist: it bestows market activity with internally driven behaviour; it naturalizes its existence and makes it appear as if it were a force occurring according to the eternal laws of nature. The ideological charge of the metaphor resides in its ability to convert the appearance of things into a fixed essence. This transformation involves a number of distortions of social reality. It removes people as the active agents which determine market outcomes. This simultaneously hides those who play the markets and who stand to gain from them – the banks, investment companies, the speculators – and compels those that lose from them – tax payers and the general public – to accept the outcomes of market activity. Governments entreat us *to listen to what the market is saying* to assist them in the driving through of austerity programmes, presented now as 'rebalancing' and restoring the natural equilibrium of the market.

Metaphors play a role in the ideological representation of existing social relations. Stereotyped or ritual forms of expression, according to Pierre Bourdieu, represent the 'ritualised strategies for the symbolic struggles of everyday life' which 'imply a certain claim to symbolic authority as the socially recognised power to impose a certain vision of the social world' (Bourdieu 1991: 106). The Italian Marxist Antonio Gramsci, who also studied the philosophy of language, describes the ideological role of metaphors in language in more dynamic and changing terms as symptomatic of the porous and unstable nature of social authority. The role of metaphor in language, which Gramsci understands at different levels, can capture a moment of social praxis because it is an expression of social subjects and classes in their historical setting:

> Language is transformed with the transformation of the whole of civilisation ... And what it does is precisely to absorb in metaphorical form the words of previous civilisations and cultures. ... The new 'metaphorical' meaning spreads with the spread of the new culture, which furthermore also coins brand-new words or absorbs them from other languages as loan-words giving them a precise meaning.
>
> (Gramsci 1971: 451–52)

Gramsci stresses that language is 'metaphorical with respect to the meanings and ideological content that words have had in preceding periods of civilisation' (1971: 450). The process whereby words come to stand for things not hitherto normally identified with them and the degree to which this forged meaning becomes naturalized, and understood as 'common sense', Gramsci sees as part of how language changes and evolves. Language is metaphorical in two ways: it creates a metaphorical link between the word and something outside language but also language, through metaphor, attaches ideological meanings to words. Over time and in different contexts, awareness of the metaphor slips into the background but the meaning conjured up by the metaphor remains. For example, disaster, whose original metaphorical link to astrology (the misalignment of stars) has long since faded; similarly, Gramsci notes, 'even an atheist can speak of "dis-grace" without being thought to be a believer in predestination' (1971: 452). This account of metaphor lies at opposite poles to the abstractions of cognitive and structuralist views and proposes, instead, a view of language which sees meaning as part of history and society, and in a continual process of being made and remade. His focus was on how dominant world views in society inform the metaphorical process but how these later can interact with the spontaneous making of language from below which inject it with new meanings, which may depart from the original. His subtle understanding of the historical and social basis of metaphor underscores how metaphorical meanings are never socially neutral and can tell us something of dominant views in the societies from which they emerge (Ives 2004). Gramsci saw that in language there is

50 *Markets, metaphors and neoliberal ideology*

contained a specific conception of the world, and that 'from anyone's language one can assess the greater or lesser complexity of his conception of the world' (Gramsci 1971: 325). In a similar fashion here, the language invites us into a totality of determined notions, what Gramsci referred to as 'an entire system of beliefs, superstitions, opinions, ways of seeing things and of acting which are collectively bundled together under the name of folklore' (1971: 323) which he also refers to as 'common sense' (1971: 323).

Representing the market as a person is a metaphor whose symbolism lies in aggrandizing and mystifying with all the force of folklore. When we read that:

> The Irish Prime Minister is seeking to reassure the markets that his government is serious about tackling its budget deficit.

it is clear that the markets are being enlisted for a political project. The folkloric mystique embedded in the metaphorical device leads us away from the market actors themselves, or why they would have such an opinion, what the consequences of this particular 'opinion' might be, or whether they actually merit deference from elected governments. The figure of speech creates a sympathetic abstraction of financial markets, which blurs what they actually do and thus blocks off interrogation of these truths.

Conclusion

This chapter has sought to highlight how the metaphorical personalization of the market is one way of articulating neoliberal ideology in language. It is, as David Zimmerman notes in his discussion of the portrayal of the market in literature, 'a discursive realm which is fought over by more or less self-conscious social factions seeking to normalize their interests and justify their mission or struggle' (Zimmerman 2006: 13). The metaphorical representation of the financial markets as free-standing human agents bestows them with an authority to which all must bow, an interpretation which has its political uses. In the Irish case, the bolstering of the power of the markets was an indispensable ideological tool in the austerity narrative. It allowed the government to claim that it was implementing only what outside forces dictated and underlined, as Irish government debt soared as a result of the bank bailout, that it was a crisis situation imposed by powerful forces which could not be controlled. 'Doing what the markets told us to' thus became the powerful imperative to continue with the cutbacks to public spending and austerity.

The market metaphor in other social domains also serves as an invented outside force commanding conformity. Lakoff sees this as a result of a conservative mind-set which 'progressives' need to challenge through their own conceptual metaphors. This cognitive emphasis tends to seek to redress this ideological bias through alternative metaphorical language and framing rather than linking linguistic forms to social change. The highlighting of the ideological aspects of metaphor which has been central to Lakoff's work tends to become collapsed into questions of linguistic presentation, thereby leaving the social basis of the questions untouched.

Economic crises shake up these dominant narratives and put their common sense status to the test. Amid the turmoil and economic dislocation of a deep recession, the smooth articulation of representations of the market can be disrupted. Unravelling the ideological mythology of the market and the significance of its metaphorical representations, as this chapter has shown, requires a critique of political economy – a theme to which we shall return in the next chapter when we examine the market as a metaphor for language.

Notes

1 There is a long history of markets being represented as being living beings: John Maynard Keynes in the 1930s spoke of a spiralling optimism that people who work the markets have, what he called the 'animal spirits' set of motivations (Jones 2013: 2). But the adoption of the human metaphor for markets takes this theme much further.

2 The examples here and throughout this chapter, unless otherwise stated are taken from British and Irish daily newspapers *The Financial Times*, *The Irish Independent*, *The Irish Times* and *The Irish Examiner* from between 2009 and 2013.

3 An agreement, made on the trading floor of a futures exchange, to buy or sell a particular commodity or financial instrument at a pre-determined price in the future.

4 Séamus Coffey explained that CFDs were complex in nature and the level of complexity was bounded only by the imagination of those working in the financial markets. 'And they have vivid imaginations' was his view (Gartland 2014).

5 In this section, when referring to the topic of the metaphor I use italics, and when referring to the source I use block letters, to make the process of metaphorical mapping stand out clearly.

6 See Goatly (2007: 276) for a critique of Pinker's biological reductionism, which he sees as deriving from Chomsky's emphasis on linguistic universals and language as an innate, genetically determined faculty.

4 Language and the market metaphor

Metaphors can be so deeply embedded in language that the topic and the source may be conceptually difficult to disentangle. Personification of the market and other metaphorical representations have become so commonplace, as was shown in the last chapter, that it is often unclear whether they are intended to be taken literally. Metaphor re-describes reality and, in the process of linking one thing to another, generalizations about society are made and remade, and ideologies created.

Language has also been mapped onto the market as a way of understanding both its internal and social workings. Because languages and markets are both deeply social processes, the similarity between them might seem obvious. But the metaphor of a 'linguistic market', or an understanding of language operating according to market dictates, leans towards neoliberal assumptions about the market being a pure form of exchange. Recourse to the market metaphor for the social workings of language(s), it should be noted, occurs also in accounts that position themselves in opposition to neoliberalism, another indication of the widespread common-sense acceptance of the market as a universal truth. Providing a political economy dimension is essential to a critique of these issues. A critical investigation of the market metaphor as applied to language, as it has been interpreted in both linguistics and sociology, also uncovers important themes in neoliberal ideology. Thus, a theoretical engagement with the market as metaphorically representing language, as employed by Saussure and by Bourdieu, including the latter's influence on contemporary readings of the market–language analogy, are the subject of this chapter.

Structuralism, language and the market metaphor

The market metaphor has been widely deployed in relation to language and languages. In the early days of linguistics, Ferdinand de Saussure reasoned that languages worked like economies and linguistic value could be compared with market value. For Saussure, the market provided the natural metaphor for how signs acquired meaning and served as an apt description of the differential interconnection between signs which, like different goods on the market, were 'exchanged' across the language system. The value of signs, he claimed, was arbitrarily determined on the basis of their difference from other signs within the system. Thus language shared the same 'paradoxical principle' which characterized money. He expressed it thus: 'Value systems, even those outside language, are always constituted on the basis of (1) a dissimilar thing which can be exchanged for a thing whose value is to be determined and (2) similar things which one can compare with the thing whose value is to be determined' (Saussure 1971: 159). Saussure illustrates this in the following way: 'The value of a 5 franc coin depends on knowing (1) that it can be exchanged for an agreed amount of something different, for example bread, and (2) that it has a similar value within the same system, for example as compared to a 1 franc coin, or with a coin of another system, for example a dollar. In the same way, a word may be exchanged for something else which is not the same – an idea. It may also be compared with something of the same nature – another word' (1971: 160).[1] Words were like coins which had a value that was constituted in relation to other signs within the system and an exchange value which operated with other sign systems.

Saussure's metaphorical mapping was premised on the market being a pure form of exchange as represented by money. Market exchange, in Saussure's model, is abstracted from the social aspects of prices, currencies and commodities and language, when likened to money in this kind of market, is also abstracted from its social roots and recreated as a system of signs whose meanings are constructed internal to its own structures. For Saussure, as David McNally points out, the 'world of signs [was] constructed much like the world of commodities' (2001: 49) – or at least as this world appears to be – with both systems being constructed on the basis of items of purely differential, relational values. McNally argues that presenting value thus, Saussure made some over-simple assumptions: that commodities have no intrinsic value, that value is a purely differential relation, representing only exchange value and that money is the expression of the relational value of a commodity. McNally observes that 'Saussure thus starts us off in a fetishized world dominated by money and commodity exchange which are naturalized as the general forms of all economy' (McNally 2001: 50). When this world of commodities is applied to the world of signs, these too are defined relationally by their presence in a system, outside of which these units are without value and meaning, and denote nothing. Signs function, in Saussure's model, like commodities seen in the neo-classical perspective, not through any intrinsic value but through their relative position, not through use values but exclusively through exchange values. The pure form of language – the language system or *langue* – 'floats detached from speech and discourse just as the pure form of exchange – money – remains disconnected from the rudimentary elements of economic life', and 'the concrete particularities' of social life (McNally 2001: 52).

Mapping linguistic 'exchange' onto economic 'exchange' also depends on a very loose understanding of exchange. Even as a representation of language, Saussure's market metaphor mapped onto language ignored the fact that it is not just *difference* but *relevant difference* which is crucial within the language system. Commodity exchange in capitalism may indeed overlook the relevant

54   *Language and the market metaphor*

differences between the uses of cotton or copper, lamb or laptops, milk or magazines, because 'capital is indifferent to the concrete character of the commodity and its capacity to satisfy particular needs' (McNally 2001: 50), just as it overlooks the connection of the value of commodity to the human labour that went into it, as we saw in the last chapter. But we can only make sense of signs if we apply the principle of relevance in our understanding of how one sign stands in opposition to another. For example, the signifieds 'chair' and 'three' are not opposed terms in any meaningful sense, whereas 'hot' and 'cold', 'Tuesday' and 'Sunday', 'male' and 'female' are (Holdcroft quoted in McNally 2001: 50). What makes the binary opposition meaningful is our ability through knowledge of things external to the system, to establish whether it constitutes a relevant difference. David Graeber (2001: 15) argues that equating linguistic 'exchange' to market exchange makes no sense at all, as it represents a meaningless flattening out of the concept of value. Even 'dog' is only interchangeable with 'cat' in an abstract sense as its difference does not involve serious effects in the way that, say, 'money' for 'bread' does (Graeber 2001: 15). Saussure's purely relational economic categories applied to language serve to endorse *langue* as a self-referential and self-sustaining system, subject to determination by form rather than content which separates language from any social point of reference. It for this that Saussure's enclosed non-social view of *langue* has been categorized as abstract objectivism (Vološinov 1973: 77). McNally argues that the failure of later post-structuralists to critically interrogate Saussure's market-identification is the start of an entrapment within the language system which leads to the severance of language from social reality. Taking signs and commodities as equally self-referential, merges, according to McNally, a post-modern view of the economy with a post-structuralist model of language, with the 'hyper real' supplanting the real in both cases (McNally 2001: 65).

Sociolinguists have expanded on Saussure's mapping of language onto the economy, with more functionalist overtones. Florian Coulmas's claim, for example, that '[e]conomy principles permeate the linguistic system on every level' leads to him to conclude that 'the pervasive influence on language of the Principle of Least Effort' makes 'time a scarce resource' in language as well (Coulmas 1992: 258). Principles of economic efficiency, especially when articulated through this new management prism, overlook not only the 'useless' expressive dimensions of language but also the long literary chunks of it which simply ignore any such preoccupations (see Holborow 1999). More recently, the language–economy parallel has been drawn through mapping English rather too neatly onto the process of market globalization, through the 'stunning metaphor, Globish' (McCrum 2006, 2010). Thus 'Globish' presents the destiny of English as hitched to the unstoppable process of globalization, with the implicit conclusion that the linguistic future in whatever subtle manifestations, belongs to English. The fact that the impacts of English and globalization are being experienced simultaneously does not make them mutually dependent. Over-simplistic metaphorical mappings highlight, as Andrew Goatly notes, why we should be wary of taking metaphors as logical and obvious when they often contain a hidden ideological dimension (2006).

Similarly, likening the workings of language to the economy entails neoliberal presuppositions about how the market works.

Bourdieu's linguistic market – a hidden metaphor?

Sociologist and cultural anthropologist, Pierre Bourdieu applies the market metaphor to language somewhat differently to Saussure. For Bourdieu the *linguistic market* structures speakers' expressions and thus enables the social and hierarchical positioning of speakers. The linguistic market, also referred to by Bourdieu as a *field*, determines the manner in which speakers choose to adapt their language to the general laws of exchange which obtain within a market. His account of the social structure of linguistic exchanges relies heavily on the market metaphor: '[T]he constitution of a *linguistic market* creates the conditions for an objective *competition* in and through which the legitimate competence can function as *linguistic capital*, producing a *profit* of distinction on the occasion of each social *exchange*' (Bourdieu 1991: 55, my emphasis). So embedded is the notion of the market in relation to language in his book *Language and Symbolic Power* (1991) that the *linguistic market* appears less of a metaphor than a theoretical premise; it can be seen as part of Bourdieu's wider purpose, to incorporate economic terms into sociological description and to extend an economic metaphor to coin a new word (Grenfell 2011: 51) and a new sociological concept. Bourdieu himself insisted that his use of *cultural and linguistic capital*, was 'not a metaphoric usage' (Bourdieu 1998, quoted in Beasley-Murray 2000: 101) and that, more generally, he did not accept that his incorporation of economic terms into his socio-cultural theory was metaphorical (McGill 2013: 89). I would like to argue here that Bourdieu uses *linguistic market* and related market terminology in a way which alternates between the metaphorical and the theoretical, constituting thus a deeply embedded conceptual metaphor, not without its own ideological significance. Because this overlap gives rise to ambiguous understandings of the *linguistic market* in later Bourdieu-inspired accounts, I shall examine this in some detail here.

Bourdieu's market metaphor applied to language, although relying substantially on structure, has little in common with the abstract, relativistic system of Saussure's *langue*; indeed he is at pains to distance his approach from Saussure's.[2] Bourdieu's linguistic markets are emphatically socially constituted spaces in which social hierarchy is reinforced through possession of different forms of capital: economic, cultural or symbolic. He constructs a sociology of language which replaces Saussure's abstract sign differences in a language system with 'sociologically pertinent linguistic differences' within 'structured systems of social difference' (Bourdieu 1991: 54). The structure of the market, or field, for Bourdieu, represents a certain state of the distribution of the specific capital which, accumulated in the course of previous struggles, orients subsequent strategies. Linguistic capitals circulate in these markets with some stamped with social legitimacy, although this recognition derives from something resembling a 'secret code' (1991: 51). Agents who are established in a market determine

56 *Language and the market metaphor*

what linguistic capital pertains, creating thus a state of *doxa* in which the established norms are generally not questioned. These dominant agents will struggle to defend their monopoly and to exclude competition from any newcomers attempting to alter the structure in their favour. For Bourdieu, market mechanisms and a 'unified market' are crucial to understanding how language or speech is recognized as legitimate and how social authority becomes entrenched. He is explicit about the market-nature of this process: he writes, '*the laws of the market* are more favourable to the products offered by the holders of the greatest linguistic competence' (Bourdieu 1991: 69, my emphasis); or again, '*the more formal the market*, the more it is dominated by the dominant and *market mechanisms* guarantee that the reproduction of legitimate linguistic products receive their *full value* and confer social prestige' (Bourdieu and Boltanski 1975: 1, my emphasis).[3]

For Bourdieu, the market, through such laws as 'scarcity of supply', serves as a means of explaining how some forms of linguistic capital come to dominate. But this market, like the 'pure market' of the neoliberal economists, is not a 'free' market (1991: 56). The market that Bourdieu draws on to explain how language works is based, not on the neoliberal idealized version in which every individual is free to do as he or she likes, but on the real, existing market with its 'monopolies and oligopolies'. Bourdieu's linguistic market constitutes not 'a relativistic universe of differences capable of relativizing one another, but [one] with a hierarchical universe of deviations with respect to a form of speech that is (virtually) universally recognized as legitimate' (1991: 56). Other social fields determine the value of linguistic capital: the education system, for example, which has 'the monopoly in the large-scale production of producers and consumers' reinforces the social value of the recognized forms of linguistic competence in the formal markets (1991: 56–57).

Bourdieu's subtle analysis of how cultural attitudes and accumulated knowledge infuse social class opens a window onto the linguistic symbols of inequality that pervade our societies. The symbols of social distinction that he describes acquire almost material proportions, and become, like other material social products, language products in a market exchange framework. He recognizes that the market is neither free nor endowed with distributive efficiency and therefore takes a critical distance from dominant market orthodoxy. But this does not give him cause to consider the appropriateness of constructing a theory of social difference in language – as well as culture – based on a notion of market value in which various capitals acquire prestige. The market/language analogy, indeed, becomes crucial to Bourdieu's theorization of the social recognition of privileged forms of discourse, which he explains through market distribution mechanisms. He tells us that possession of assets – *cultural capital* and *symbolic capital* (including linguistic capital) – empowers certain agents to dominate their market in the specific field, and that these assets are 'convertible, in certain conditions, into economic capital' (Bourdieu 1986: 243). From the historical observation that the creation of a unified national market also created or imposed a unified language, Bourdieu extends the parallel to making linguistic phenomena behave like economic phenomena. He notes how the creation of the nation state allowed 'the conditions for an objective competition in and through which the legitimate competence can function as linguistic capital, producing a *profit of distinction*' (1991: 55, emphasis in the original). He perceptively describes how a homogeneous national market was not only the historical condition for the birth of a unified language but also for socially distinctive forms of language, including style, as indicators of social power. But the institutionalization of this social difference was not primarily political through social agents controlling the state, but culturally imposed through an independent distributive mechanism that mimicked commercial exchange. The value of a linguistic product, Bourdieu explains, is determined by its confrontation on the market with products which are recognizably different because of their social distinctiveness and the perceived conditions of production determine 'the law of price formation that obtains in a particular exchange'(1991:67). The view of language as a market also extends to Bourdieu's wider view of 'structural sociology' which he sees as an enterprise to 'bring together structured systems of sociologically relevant linguistic differences to equally structured systems of social differences', a coming together of the economic and the linguistic which enables him to characterise language as 'fetishised' (Bourdieu and Boltanski 1975: 4;[4] see also Thompson 1984: 49–52).

The market and market distribution are axiomatic to Bourdieu's account of the symbolic power of language, as his repeated use of market terms attests. Symbolic relations of power can be the subject of negotiation and the market can be manipulated through powerful players turning market rules to their own advantage and thereby extending their monopoly in that market. Bourdieu's key term, *habitus*, is defined in relation to the market also. The *linguistic habitus*, thorough knowledge of which enables those from the upper class to work the linguistic rules with ease, is a disposition formed on the basis of recognizing the demands of the linguistic market. In contrast, working class people are 'whose conditions of existence are least conducive' to the acquisition of this linguistic *habitus*, have 'linguistic products [which] are assigned, by themselves as well as others, a limited value' as noted by Thomson in his introduction to *Language and Symbolic Power* (Bourdieu 1991: 21). Rules are often broken but only in terms which the overall linguistic market can accommodate. One example given by Bourdieu are expressions such as 'if I may say so' or 'if you'll pardon the expression', 'off the record', etc., which may mark a departure in the accepted routines but, as Bourdieu points out, are themselves evidence of linguistic capital being exploited with flair and confidence, usually by those higher up the social hierarchy, in possession of a larger stock of greater linguistic capital, and in a position to bank a *profit of distinction* in this particular market (1991: 71).

At this point, and in relation to our theme of neoliberalism, it is worth pointing out that the market metaphor in Bourdieu's description of symbolic power is not the enduring reference point that one might have expected from one so consistent and passionate in his stand against the neoliberal market. For example, in his uncompromising polemic against neoliberalism, Bourdieu asks:

58 Language and the market metaphor

What is neoliberalism? A programme for destroying collective structures which may impede the pure market logic ... And it is achieved through the transformative and, it must be said, *destructive* action of all of the political measures ... that aim to *call into question any and all collective structures* that could serve as an obstacle to the logic of the pure market ...

The corporations themselves have to adjust more and more rapidly to the exigencies of the markets, under penalty of 'losing the market's confidence', as they say, as well as the support of their stockholders ...

Neoliberalism tends on the whole to favour severing the economy from social realities and thereby constructing, in reality, an economic system conforming to its description in pure theory, that is a sort of logical machine that presents itself as a chain of constraints regulating economic agents.

(Bourdieu 1998, emphasis in the original)

Indeed, Bourdieu was one of the first to launch a counterattack against neoliberalism which he saw as no less than an attack on civilization. His pamphlet, *Firing-back: Against the Tyranny of the Market* (Bourdieu 2003), which first appeared in French in 2001, marked a break with the ivory-tower intellectualism that had dominated French academia since the 1970s, and confirmed the return of the intellectual-activist, thereby 're-legitimizing the speech of resistance' (Callinicos 1999: 87; Calhoun 2002). Bourdieu was the public face of demonstrations, strikes and resistance against the neoliberal order and the source of inspiration to many in the emerging anti-capitalist movement. How is it, then, that an uncompromising attack on the neoliberal market appears side by side in his work with a seemingly uncritical use of the market metaphor in his description of the deployment of symbolic power? Bourdieu's critique of the neoliberal 'pure market', it is true, emerged in the late 1990s, after his earlier work on the linguistic market, but this does not adequately explain the apparent paradox (see Calhoun 2002).[5]

Part of the explanation can be found, I would argue, in Bourdieu's interpretation of neoliberalism. His opposition to neoliberalism was based, not on a critique of the capitalist market *per se*, but of the neoliberal project to *extend* the principles of neo-classical free market economics across all social fields. This political project was objectionable to Bourdieu because it represented the 'methodical destruction of collectives' through an effective 'withering away of the state' (Bourdieu 2003: 40). For Bourdieu, market rule neoliberal-style was an instance of symbolic capital in the form of neo-classical economic theory, colonizing all the structures of society. For him, neoliberal economics owes its allegedly universal characteristics to the fact that it has become immersed or embedded in society and that its beliefs, values, ethos and moral view of the world have extended into the 'social and cognitive' structures of the social order. The transition to neoliberalism takes place in an imperceptible manner, 'like continental drift'. As he puts it:

The neoliberal utopia tends to embody itself in the reality of a kind of infernal machine, whose necessity imposes itself even upon the rulers. Like the Marxism of an earlier time, with which, in this regard, it has much in common, this utopia evokes powerful belief – the *free trade faith* – not only among those who live off it, such as financiers, the owners and managers of large corporations, etc., but also among those, such as high-level government officials and politicians, who derive their justification for existing from it. For they sanctify the power of markets in the name of economic efficiency, which requires the elimination of administrative or political barriers capable of inconveniencing the owners of capital in their individual quest for the maximisation of individual profit, which has been turned into a model of rationality.

(Bourdieu 1998)

This invasion of every social field explains how the market has secured the status of economic common sense, *l'idée fixe* and 'the strong discourse' of our times (Bourdieu 1998).

This leads us to a second dimension: the nature of Bourdieu's social theory and its avoidance of political economy analysis. His thesis is that symbolic structures have 'an extraordinary power of *constitution*', a power which he rebukes both neoliberal theory and Marxism for failing to understand. Bourdieu is 'uncomfortable' with according too much weight to the economy and wonders, in a reassertion of the cultural over the material, if 'today's social structures are not yesterday's symbolic structures' and whether social classes are not the product of 'theoretical effect' (Bourdieu 1990: 18). His well-known notion of *habitus* builds on the perceptions and expectations that people have and, while some reference is made to economic capital, this is not the lens through which Bourdieu sees people's position – or at least their legitimized position – in society. His focus is on the culturally constraining features which give an implicit or practical sense of what can and cannot be reasonably achieved, or what does or does not fall within particular historically and culturally determined horizons, and is something which is internalized mentally rather than externally conditioned.[6] *Misrecognition* by those that suffer symbolic domination and *recognition* by those that systematically impose it, are the silent structuring powers 'which can be exercised only with the complicity of those who do not want to know that they are subject to it or even that they themselves exercise it' (Bourdieu 1991: 164).

For Bourdieu, the tyranny of the market is not so much an economic fact, or indeed a struggle over economic wealth, but the unwarranted (and unexplained) expansion of economics beyond its normal field and its entry into other social structures; market domination 'is part of the undisputed rule of the economy and economic powers' (Bourdieu 2003: 9). Questions about whether the economy has not always influenced all social structures or about whether economic interests – specifically the interests of capital – lie at the heart of the neoliberal market project are not raised. Bourdieu's intention is to reassert the force of the cultural and the symbolic, including language, over and beyond the economic.

60 *Language and the market metaphor*

Indeed, as noted by Craig Calhoun (2002: 36), Bourdieu goes further and doubts, in relation to the economy, whether 'any such object existed with the degree of autonomy from the rest of social life that conventional economics implied'. In effect, Bourdieu's distrust of what he saw as economism led him away from any economic analysis at all. Of course, he was acutely aware of the material costs of neoliberalism, to which his memorable account of human suffering in *The Weight of the World* (1999) bears witness, but the roots of neoliberalism he describes as primarily socio-cultural. Ironically, for all his weaving of economic terminology into the cultural domain and his 'materializing' of culture and language as 'capital', along with his theoretical reliance on market metaphors, actual economic analysis or critique is noticeably absent from Bourdieu's account. As is pointed out by critics and admirers alike (Callinicos 1999: 95; Calhoun 2002: 36), he offers no account of capitalism as a distinctive historically specific system of production which produces its own form of market exchange.

Yet any critique of neoliberalism must explain how it came to be adopted wholesale by governments and corporations at the time that it did and for what reasons. Its arrival in the midst of a long-term crisis of over-accumulation and profitability as a means of overcoming this crisis is surely relevant. The response from capital was to seek ways of forcing up levels of exploitation and eliminating unprofitable capital, both of which would require considerable restructuring and reorganizing of capital (Harvey 2010a). As Alex Callinicos observes, 'neoliberalism represents the political and ideological framework in which such restructuring has occurred' (Callinicos 2010: 54,). Disillusionment with Keynesian demand-management frameworks via state intervention, which had proved inadequate to recharge the system, along with what seemed to be a stronger labour movement able to maintain wage levels, and the global recession of 1979–82, helped to force an economic contraction which allowed Reaganism and Thatcherism to take hold. The US and Britain in this scenario became driving forces of financial liberalization involving the lifting of exchange controls, the deregulation of the City of London, and legislation in the US separating investment and commercial banks and protecting a rapidly expanding derivatives market from any form of regulation.[7] Neoliberalism, contrary to its own mythology, was ushered in not in counter-position to state intervention, but extremely reliant on it. This was no mere cultural or symbolic readjustment but one that developed from economic pressures to restructure in the interests of profit stabilization and growth. However, Bourdieu, in the absence of any critique of capitalist political economy, or of the process of financialization and developments in the global economy (elements which are seldom missing from neoliberal narratives) allows symbolic dominance to take the lead role in establishing and reproducing the prevailing neoliberal social order.

The market frame adopted by Bourdieu for discourse, paradoxically echoes, from a distance, some strands of neoliberal thinking. It removes the core social role from economic relations and grants causative powers to social structures. Bourdieu's linguistic market model presents speaking agents as subjects who accept or reject legitimate ways of speaking according to market mechanisms of distribution and value within a framework of a social structure made to the benefit of already dominant parties. The social valorization of language in Bourdieu's model becomes thus structurally streamlined within a notional linguistic market. His reliance on the structured aspects of society, and the structuring effects of field which mould linguistic capital produces a partial, and misleading, description of language. In reality, however, language is far less ordered than Bourdieu would have us believe. Social reproduction in the form of speech is, as Thompson aptly notes, 'rather less of a concert and more of a cacophony' (Thompson 1984: 62). Bourdieu does lay much emphasis on practice as potentially transforming society, but without incorporation of economic relations as a social dynamic, political practice appears only as operating within the confines of existing social structures.

In *Distinction*, Bourdieu stresses the structure-based nature of both mental and physical behaviour. 'The cognitive structures which social agents implement in their practical knowledge of the social world are internalized, "embodied" social structures. The practical knowledge of the social world that is presupposed by 'reasonable' behaviour within it implements classificatory schemes (or "forms of classification", "mental structures" or "symbolic forms" ...)' (Bourdieu 1979: 466–67). These schemes of perception are in turn the product of social classification by age, group, gender and social class and these principles of division make possible the production of a common-sense world. This structuring of subjects underestimates the fact that people may conform rather less wholly to structuration than Bourdieu's model would have us believe. Speakers, as Terry Eagleton notes, may be in the more complicated position of being critical of those values and beliefs *even while* they continue to conform to them in their speech (Bourdieu and Eagleton 1992). Furthermore, Bourdieu's emphasis on the structuring and classificatory processes, including the market structures that condition discourse, has little to say about meaning and content, as opposed to structure and form. Park, however, rightly notes that Bourdieu does have much to say about 'socially and politically determined meanings such as a speaker's anxiety or confidence' even if this is 'referential meaning' (Park, personal correspondence, 5 May, 2014). But, in spite of his sensitivity to social perceptions which official accounts of legitimate language ignore, Bourdieu connects meaning mainly to linguistic and social structures and sees them as predictably conforming to social norms. Speech in real life is rather more messy and ill-defined than a product flung to the imagined four winds of the market. It is fundamentally, an occasion of expression, laying claim to a meaning with 'content', however defined but including experience, knowledge, impressions, opinions and ideologies, unpredictable outbursts, passing notions – and nothings – in a heterodox mix which cannot be packed tightly into the confines of form, nor can it be ever sufficiently stable to constitute a reliably legitimate form of 'exchange' within a linguistic market (see Thompson 1984: 65–66). Bourdieu reaches for the market analogy because it provides a normalizing structure, which seems to explain the fixing of what is permissible and legitimate. Socio-economic differences are referred to but only as a backcloth. Emphasis on the distribution and regulating powers of the

62 *Language and the market metaphor*

market allows economic relations to be included as a given, not as a problematic. Linguistic capital, as a matter of fact, is a rather hybrid, intangible entity which cannot, like goods, be somehow stocked and restocked in permanence.

Bourdieu's intention is to provide a counterbalance to neoliberal attempts to 'economize' everything. This leads him to stress how society needs to keep economics contained within its own allocated field. One of the functions of the state, in the interests of the common good, Bourdieu argues, should be to oversee a strict demarcation of fields. A reason that Bourdieu gives for the US being the homeland of neoliberalism is that its state is 'weak' (Bourdieu 2005: 10) and that economics has been able to expand across all social fields. The logical rampart against this development, Bourdieu suggests, is a strengthening of the state, nationally or supra-nationally, to curtail the excesses of the market (2003: 48–52). A strengthened state would, Bourdieu argues, constrain the expansion of the market and confine it to matters economic. Bourdieu, following the Hegel–Durkheim view, endows the state with the structural potential to represent the social collective, an 'authority with a responsibility to act as the collective will and consciousness and a duty to make decisions in keeping with the general interest and contribute to promoting greater solidarity' (2005: 11). The creation of such bodies, whether at a transnational level of EU institutions or nationally as the 'social state', which Bourdieu sometimes refers to as the 'left hand of the state' (2003: 35), would have 'a remit to control the dominant economic forces and subordinate them to genuinely universal ends' (2005: 232). Bourdieu seems to take it at face value that neoliberalism equals a hands-off state, something which, as we have noted, was hardly the case even when he was writing and certainly, much less today (see also Harvey 2005; Holborow 2012c; Klein 2007; Mirowski 2013).

Bourdieu's emphasis on fields tends to define structurally the market–state separation, while conceding that the market mechanism works across the social fields. As a result the market, as it is described in Bourdieu, is paradoxically both savaged and strengthened. One version of the market – the extreme neoliberal view which allows retrenchment of inequality – Bourdieu subjects to unrelenting critique. But another version is a market which structures language and social values and which is an efficient conduit of social reproduction, emerges unscathed. One example of the latter can be seen in a description by Bourdieu of the social world as a space of social differentiation which are:

> ... powers or forms *of capital* which are or can become efficient, like aces in a game of cards, in this particular universe, that is, in the struggle (or *competition*) for the appropriation of *scarce goods* of which this universe is the site. It follows that the structure of this space is given by the *distribution of the various forms of capital*, that is, by the distribution of the properties which are active within the universe under study – those properties capable of conferring strength, power and consequently *profit on their holder*.

> (Bourdieu 1986: 3–4, emphasis in the original)

Language and the market metaphor   63

The market is so embedded in his description that there is little here (despite Bourdieu's assured protestations to the contrary) that would offend the Chicago school of human capital. This is no doubt why David Harvey finds Bourdieu's treatment of human endowments as forms of capital 'confusing if not perverse' (Harvey 2014: 186). By placing economic capital alongside cultural capital, and other forms of social and symbolic capital, Bourdieu fails to make the key distinction that human capital needs to be put to work to create value, whereas economic capital as a property relation can increase its value (even when it is not gaining profits in a production process that it owns) through interest. In a similar way to human capital theorists, Bourdieu, once he has taken the market as a neutral processor of social value, also ends up flattening out the conflicting social relations pertaining to the different kinds of 'capitals' and making them seem equivalent.

The capitalist market itself reflects capitalist social relations. A specific social arrangement that emerged at a particular point in time, it is a vast network of spatially and institutionally disparate connections, set in motion by capital and skewed towards the interests of capitalist enterprises (Harvey 2010b: 162). All markets, whether for the exchange of goods or money, are supremely insecure and subject to crisis, and are part of the 'the restless, never-ending process of profit-making', socially created and socially conditioned (Marx 1974: 152; see Harvey 2010a: 85–92). People are compelled to surrender the fruits of their work to its dictates, with their interests secondary to those of capital which extends and exacerbates social polarization. 'There is no such thing as a neutral market', Žižek says; 'market configurations are always regulated by political decisions' (Žižek 2009: 16). The political question regarding neoliberalism, he goes on to say, is the struggle to put aside the notion that there are neutral zones in society and resistance to neoliberalism must involve defining the basic 'apolitical' coordinates of our lives. When the market system runs into crisis, which it regularly does (although Bourdieu does not take this into account) it charges the state of whatever political colour with recreating the conditions within which it can flourish again. Since the 2008 market crash, this has meant, as Harvey notes, forcing people to surrender many of their rights and their hard-won asset values, in everything from housing to pension rights, and to suffer serial reductions in their living standards (Harvey 2010b). Given the capitalist market's starkly unequal effects, which in the wake of the Great Depression so many people across different countries have come to see with their own eyes, it seems strange that language too must be submitted to its dictates. Even if this is done with a view to explaining the unequal distribution of linguistic resources, it nevertheless constitutes something of a theoretical sleight of hand, seeming to signal another concession to the authority of the market. Bourdieu did not live long enough to experience the effects of the economic upheavals caused by the most serious market crash since 1929; perhaps had he done so, he might have reworked the notion of *linguistic markets* in a different light.

More significantly, Bourdieu's extension of the market to include a *linguistic market*, his use of the market terms *distribution, capital conversion, profit,*

64 *Language and the market metaphor*

exchange, whether metaphorically or theoretically, has the effect of blurring the distinction between goods on the real market and things such as language and culture which communicate and interact between people qualitatively differently. Although Bourdieu's aim is to highlight the social inequalities that affect culture and language, his recourse to the market metaphor, and recasting language as capital, paradoxically makes concessions to the neoliberal's 'endless utopia' (Bourdieu 1998), of redefining every aspect of human endeavour in economic terms. Indeed many of Bourdieu's terms – *social capital*, *cultural capital* and various forms of *markets* – have been re-appropriated by neoliberal positions and policies, so that we are now confronted by a 'plethora of capitals' in a plethora of neoliberal markets, woven together in a theoretical amalgam 'twixt Bourdieu and Becker' (Fine 2002: 18, 23). None of these multifarious 'capitals' in multiple 'markets' take into account the fact that capital in its economic form is an expression of unequal social relations and that markets are economically constrained, stacked in favour of big players, and the opposite of free. Bourdieu is not responsible for the adoption of his theoretical framework by his opponents, but the claim that symbolic capital can be converted smoothly into economic capital, alongside his reliance on market logic, allows for an interpretation which makes the individual, rather than society, responsible for this 'convertibility'. At the very least, notwithstanding Bourdieu's proven record of activist resistance to neoliberalism, his failure to provide a political economy critique of the capitalist market, of which his metaphorical mapping of the market onto linguistic exchanges is a symptom, leaves an important strand of neoliberal ideology uncontested.

English, profit and linguistic markets

Bourdieu's market metaphor in relation to language has been taken up widely in the context of globalization, English and language ideologies. Duchêne and Heller, for example, propose that, in the expansion of capital in late capitalism, language has come to be tightly linked to markets. Whereas in the era of national states language was connected to identity – to 'pride' – it is now reconfigured as 'profit', a technical skill to be sold on globalized markets (Duchêne and Heller 2012: 8). The authors claim that this shift is characterized by four interconnected processes: the *saturation* of markets, *distinction* (or added value) by which is meant the adding of material or symbolic value to products, *tertialization* by which is understood the strong growth of the information, services and 'symbolic goods' sector, and finally *flexibilization* or the greater need to source cheaper labour (2012: 9). These developments are seen to have destabilized the ability of nation states to regulate markets. States must now adapt to the new conditions by implementing neoliberalization and by 'pulling back' from regulation to facilitate global circulation. In this process, language is 'corralled into the branding effort', and represents the deep insertion of language into the market (2012: 10).

Bourdieu's theoretical framework is present in Duchêne and Heller's volume. Duchêne and Heller note that Blackledge and Creese's chapter shows 'how

Language and the market metaphor 65

heritage language education in Britain is torn between older discourses focusing on linguistic and cultural reproduction, and newer ones seeing it as a source of capital distinction'. (Duchêne and Heller 2012: 17). This seeks to extend Bourdieu's description of social distinction and linguistic resources to suit super-diverse, transnational societies, to move beyond the categories of ethnicity and class to describe 'complex interrelationships of constantly changing neighbourhoods' (Blackledge and Creese 2012: 121). The authors build on Bourdieu's notion of *profit of distinction*, although they apply it, not to its marketability, but to differences of ethnicity and caste among their cohort of schoolchildren (in this case the socially more prestigious Bengali language and the socially stigmatized rural variety of Sylheti). More generally, language as a resource competing on markets provides the thematic unity of this collection of essays. Drawing on Anthony Giddens' notion of the social market as 'the complex articulations and processes constraining contemporary social markets and the life trajectories of social actors', Duchêne and Heller identify *social actors* as predominantly *market actors* (Duchêne and Heller 2012: 14). These may be institutional or individual actors, but they are, in the case of Swiss football fans described in the paper in this volume by Del Percio and Duchêne, 'actors positioned favourably on modernist markets' who 'attempt to maintain the value of their capital by resisting its appropriation by other actors' attempts at commercialisation' (2012: 16). Other examples in the volume describe market actors attempting to 'appropriate the "profit" trope in the interests of maintaining their position as workers in new market conditions' (2012: 14, 17). In the case of Basque linguistic minorities, and of French speakers in Canada and Welsh speakers in the UK, the emergence of tensions between a language as a cultural category and language as a labour category is described from different perspectives as part of the extended globalization process, tensions which can be summarized as older identity notions of language as 'pride' and language now recast as 'profit'.

The 'materializing' of language in the form of linguistic capital or language resources and the 'profit' which language resources can accrue (or not, as the case may be) would seem to owe much to Bourdieu's theoretical framework. Their theme is that language plays an increasingly important role under the conditions of late capitalism, and this allows linguistic resources to be integrated into economic markets. Markets play a crucial role in the dispensing of value and the branding of languages: varieties of language are 'marked as local in positioning around the marketization of authenticity'; amassing forms of linguistic capital help in 'navigating access to multiple market[s]' (Duchêne and Heller 2012: 16). Sociolinguistics can provide a special window into the new role of language in late capitalism, since sociolinguists can 'track the circulation of discourses and practices ... in the chains of production and consumption' and note how value is attributed to them in the market in which we are situated ourselves (Duchêne and Heller 2012: 18).

It is not always fully clear whether these chains of production and consumption of 'linguistic resources' constitute actual markets or contrived or imagined ones. One might be sceptical, as Kenneth McGill is, about whether heritage tourism

66 *Language and the market metaphor*

can be accurately described as constituting a functioning market in minority language production when in Catalonia high levels of state intervention sustain linguistic heritage tourism (McGill 2013: 85). McGill also questions whether language skills can be considered as an identifiable component of labour which command their own wage premium, or whether, as is more likely, they are subsumed in the general exploitation of human qualities which have been a feature of labour for centuries (2013: 85). The main defect that McGill sees in ascribing market value to linguistic capital is that it blurs the distinction between metaphorical framing and reality. His claim is that the case for language skills being able to command material benefits is not convincingly made in 'language markets' accounts. Without firm evidence, it is not possible to say with any certainty that language skills do in fact reap material returns, either as part of a 'language industry' or for the 'language worker' herself. He emphasizes the need to distinguish metaphor from reality and that 'economistic rhetoric does not itself constitute language as a regular form of economic value' (McGill 2013: 92) and that political economy analysis is necessary for this distinction to come to light. The ideology of the market, including repackaging skills as a marketable commodity, while on the surface seeming convincing, is a distorted version of events, which, McGill claims, those who have those skills are only too aware of since the possession of language skills in reality seldom delivers what is promised for it. In defence of Duchêne and Heller, however, they do refer to language-as-profit as a 'trope', and recognize that treating language in primarily economic terms is discursive device (2012: 3). They also indicate that this discursive treatment can act as a legitimizing process for neoliberalism (2012: 6). But, at the same time, they appear to cede to the authority of the market frame when they claim that late capitalism has accorded a 'new centrality of linguistic form and practice in economic production' and that the markets attribute 'value' to linguistic resources (2012: 18). Again, it is not quite clear whether the 'value' here is literal or metaphorical.

Bourdieu's metaphor of the linguistic market has been taken up by other studies. Joseph Sung-Yul Park and Lionel Wee's extensive study into the 'markets of English' is founded on Bourdieu's understanding of the linguistic market to show how different types of resources, positions and policies are evaluated socially (Park and Wee 2012: 26). Their argument is that language is a type of practice which receives value according to particular systems of 'price formation' in a given market. They note that standard varieties are given more value compared to vernacular varieties and in this sense 'language varieties, linguistic utterances, accents and their embodiments are all like commodities on a market – the linguistic market' (2012: 27). They argue, following Bourdieu, that certain linguistic resources are recognized, or *misrecognized*, as having social prestige and that legitimized linguistic capital can be converted into economic capital. The linguistic market that they describe is based not on straightforward supply and demand but on 'practical relations of social power', which determine laws of price formation. They recognize the structural and social agency limitations of Bourdieu's market analogy, but nevertheless see the notion of the

Language and the market metaphor   67

linguistic market as capturing the geographical scale of how language becomes socially marked. For them, languages and varieties of language are like contending capitals within a market and the metaphor, they claim, captures the cross-over between the linguistic and the non-linguistic (2012: 30). As they put it, 'the notion of market' allows them 'to move relatively seamlessly across various phenomena at different scales, while still capturing the complex interconnections between them' (2012: 32).

Bourdieu's conception of *habitus* they recognize as a countervailing tendency to his overall structuralist view of legitimation, and for its ability to focus on 'subjectivity'. They claim that *habitus* involves 'practice' as much as 'structured dispositions', and amounts to a subjective way of attuning oneself practically to the structured 'linguistic market'. Habitus is subjectivity or a 'sense of knowing the place which one occupies in the social space' (Bourdieu, quoted in Park and Wee 2012: 35) and allows an individual to recognize what is 'appropriate', 'good', 'correct' and 'polite' on the basis of one's own judgement. Conceived in this way, the linguistic market is a two-way process, a structural force which is relatively stable but also one which 'derives its meaning entirely from speakers' own everyday practices of dealing with and using language' (2012: 36). To this linguistic market framework, Park and Wee add three other dimensions drawn from sociolinguistics: language ideology or the way language users attribute social meaning to linguistic forms; indexicality, or the property of language that points to its context of usage through the three-way relationship of sign, object and interpretant, which form a multi-meaningful indexical field; and inter-discursivity or the interconnectedness of different types of discourse in different sites (2012: 38–39).

In their chapter on 'English as Capital', they show very convincingly that English as a neutral entity, affecting all members of a community and discriminating against no one, is an ideological construct which conceals social tensions. One example that they give is three areas of San Francisco in which the language used in signs assists in the ideological creation of social space. In the working class and unemployed area of the Tenderloin, the signage is genuinely multilingual, which reflects its ethnic diversity; in the Chinatown district the multilingual signs are mainly in its main lingua franca, Cantonese, though they also cater for tourists from European backgrounds; in the main commercial Union Square area all signage is in English and would be perceived to be ethnically non-indicative or culturally neutral. Here English works not as a neutral medium but as a marker of social prestige, as part of the use of the official dominant language of the US. As the authors rightly conclude: the value of linguistic capital in these three social spaces is not established on a free market but on an already divided social one (2012: 15).

Joseph Sung-Yul Park (2011), in another study, captures more roundly the ideological dimension of the market and linguistic capital. He describes how, in the Korean context, the linguistic capital of English is a matter of social inter-pretation and is judged by market rules set by the large corporations. English language skills, as evaluated in Korean society, at the mercy of capitalist market

68 Language and the market metaphor

criteria, have a fluctuating value and grow ever further from the reach of those that seek to acquire them. He shows how the huge multi-business conglomerates, *jaebols*, of which Samsung is one, dictate what the English standards are and their criteria are constantly shifting. Initially, the US Test of English for International Communication (TOEIC) is adopted by the *jaebols*, encouraged by the government's 'English frenzy', and declared the only measure of competence in English with the result that TOEIC experiences a veritable boom. Then, once young Korean graduates have met the demands of TOEIC, there is a brusque change of tack: corporations set the bar higher and begin to disparage the test for not being a good measure of English competence. From initially having represented the best measure for what was good English, TOEIC is suddenly demoted, and derided for testing 'mute English' (2011: 450). The corporations then switch their preferred means of testing English and introduce new tests and higher standards. Park's account reveals the myth of a linguistic market in which revisions act as a constant recalibration of the market in favour of what suits the interests of the corporations. Not only is this market skewed irrevocably towards those with the resources to enter it, but it is run on the terms of those who benefit from it. As Park puts it, 'the only ones who are guaranteed to gain in the circular pursuit of the promise of English (besides the English language teaching industry) are the corporations themselves, who get precisely what they wanted in the first place – workers with better English language skills' (2011: 452). And this at no cost to themselves, as the cost of the training, encouraged by a strategic government focus on poor standards of English, falls on individuals. Park goes on to draw out the dangers of the deep naturalization of the logic of the linguistic market: it acts as a buttress to neoliberal thinking. The 'neoliberal worker' is expected to display initiative, flexibility and responsibility – including the responsibility to pay for English tuition – in which 'the constant raising of the bar becomes the mundane fact of work' (2011: 453). But by illustrating how in the Korean case the promise of English is an illusion, how the rewards of English language skills are forever deferred, Park *de facto* explodes the myth of the linguistic market. He notes that internalization of the logic of the neoliberal workplace may be a source for further accommodation to neoliberalism. However, the evidence he presents would seem to point to more nuanced understandings. By exposing the seemingly objective criteria for defining linguistic resources as tools in the hands of the powerful corporations, Park's study serves to undermine the supposed objectivity of corporations in matters of standards. Following a series of government–*jaebol* corruption charges, Park's exposure of the corporations' cynical manoeuvres with regard to standards of English gives further expression to a general malaise regarding the unduly powerful role of the corporation-government nexus. 'The struggle of the worker in the neoliberal linguistic market', as the title of this study indicates, injects a dynamic of social agency and change into the frenzied and unfulfilled 'promise' of English in South Korea.

Linguistic capital appears sometimes in Park and Wee (2012) to be taken at face value. They assert that linguistic value is determined by the 'linguistic market', which, despite their pointing out that this market has a metaphorical use in Bourdieu (2012: 27), seems to identify linguistic value in unproblematic market terms. They note that 'just as capital in the economic sense means money that can be used to make more money, the point about linguistic capital is the other kinds of profit it can bring' (2012: 142). A more robust political economy based critique, for both sorts of 'capital', is required here. Capital 'being used to make more money' promulgates a further neoliberal myth, namely that capital possesses miraculous powers of self-expansion. Capital may seem to valorize itself independently, but through the way it absorbs living labour power, it remains the expression of 'a social relation' which rests on exploitation (Marx 1974: 1007; Harvey 2010a). As one political economist has succinctly put it 'owners of capital can choose to exploit in one way or another but they cannot choose not to exploit at all' (Harman 2009: 37). To ignore this dimension entails a submission to the law of the market in its neoliberal version, which claims that capital is a value that requires only the market for self-expansion.

Furthermore, the ability of language skills to be convertible into capital is, on Park and Wee's own admission, not guaranteed. The belief that English under all circumstances 'will serve as linguistic capital with maximal convertibility' is an ideological myth promoted in neoliberal discourses to encourage potential employees to invest in their own future, take sole responsibility for the learning of English and 'bear all the burden of failure in the market' (Park and Wee 2012: 142, 161). But in order to fully unravel the self-entrepreneurial myth which depends so much on accepting the logic of the capitalist market, the capitalist market itself must be interrogated. If this is admitted, then to what extent does the theoretical framework of the 'linguistic market' blur the reality of underlying social inequalities and perpetuate the neoliberal myth that skills can be converted into human capital for individual gain?

Conclusion

For structuralist views of language, such as Saussure's, the market becomes the obvious metaphor. But likening signs to money allows a detachment from social developments in relation to both systems. The metaphor used in this way, I have argued, severs the ties of *langue* to social life and abstracts money and commodities from their use values and their origins in living labour. By taking the market at face value and devoid of social relations, the language–market analogy tends to rest on similar assumptions about the market as those in neoliberal ideology.

Bourdieu's recourse to the market metaphor is motivated by different concerns: to bring questions of social power into the workings of language. Bourdieu's metaphorical materializing of language as linguistic capital operating in a market is an attempt to present a holistic view of society in which language is marked by inequalities. But in his use of the market metaphor for language – which he claimed constituted his theoretical premises – Bourdieu appears to support the notion that individual interest drives conformity within 'economies of practice', a theme which overlaps with the neoliberal view of the autonomy of the market and the need for individuals to conform to it. Bourdieu's reliance on the market

70 *Language and the market metaphor*

metaphor, particularly in the absence of a critique of how the market functions in capitalism, acts as an obstacle to clearly making a connection between the market and capitalist production for profit.

Bourdieu's notion of the linguistic market when applied to the role of English in the world is a valuable tool for identifying the social inequities which access to English both confirm and entrench. It enables a convincing critique of the neutrality of English, and the notion of English as linguistic capital provides a means of explaining how English holds the promise of material and social power. However, to develop a sustainable critique of the ideological dimensions of this false promise, the ideological dimensions of the 'linguistic market' need to be fully teased out. Neoliberal commodification, part of which is transforming language into an acquirable skill and framing the value of language in narrow economic terms and as a means to material gain, contributes to obscuring and reproducing class-based inequalities of power. The 'linguistic market' is a metaphorical invention that misrepresents how language actually works. While it may point to how language is part of the political economy, uncritical use of it may, inadvertently, repeat the economistic vision of the social world inspired by neoliberal thinking.

Notes

1 My translation.
2 Bourdieu is critical of Saussure's semiotic analysis, which remains internal to the language system or text, for not taking adequate account of socio-historical factors (see J.B. Thompson in his introduction to *Language and Symbolic Power*, Bourdieu 1991: 4).
3 My translation.
4 My translation.
5 Calhoun (2002) gives a comprehensive view of the continuity of Bourdieu's work.
6 See Lane (2000: 194) for a succinct account of this aspect of *habitus*. When describing the dominance of a legitimate language Bourdieu invokes the silent compliance of the process of symbolic domination: 'It is inscribed. ... in dispositions which are impalpably inculcated through a long and slow process of acquisition, by the sanctions of the linguistic market, and which are therefore adjusted, without any cynical calculation or consciously experienced constraint to the chances of material and symbolic profit ... ' (Bourdieu 1991: 51).
7 See chapter 1 in Callinicos (2010) for a useful summary of this process, and also Harvey (2010b), who characterizes the neoliberal project as being a collection of policies to restore and consolidate capitalist class power (Harvey 2010b: 10).

5 The neoliberal reinvention of *entrepreneur*

Raymond Williams's core proposition in his study of ideological keywords (1985) was that words change their meaning over time in relation to changing social, economic and political pressures. For Williams, keywords were a range of terms which carried different meanings depending on where you stood in the social structure, and usually represented clashing views of the world. They were words which were recognizably politically charged, brimming with social friction and, in the post-war upheavals of Williams's time, as much about meanings contested as they were about meanings established. The words he selected – *ideology, nationalist, progressive, reactionary, realism, revolution, taste, underprivileged, welfare, western*, and many others – represented the linguistic-ideological hubs of his time, some calling up political positions at their very mention.

Williams sensed that these keywords stood for wider social meanings; they carried 'the explicit but as often implicit connections which people were making ... [and ways] of seeing many of our central experiences' (Williams 1985: 15). They contained 'a history and complexity of meanings; conscious changes, or consciously different uses; innovation, obsolescence, specialisation, extension, overlap, transfer; or changes which are masked by a nominal continuity so that words which seem to have been there for centuries, with continuous general meanings, have come in fact to express radically different or radically variable, yet sometimes hardly noticed, meanings and implications of meaning' (1985: 17). The extension, variation and transfer of meanings highlighted the 'difficult relations between the general processes of sense and reference' which stretched beyond language rules 'to social norms which both enable sense and reference to be generated and in some large degree to control them'. These problems of meanings were 'primarily embedded in actual relations', 'within the structures of particular social orders and the processes of social and historical change' (1985: 22).

His observations about 'sense and reference' are remarkably apt for the cluster of neoliberal keywords (Holborow 2012a) which, mutually self-reinforcing, are part of the ideological glue of the neoliberal narrative. Today's neoliberal keywords, however, in different times and ways, are less politically explicit than Williams's original keywords. Arguably, the persuasive power of neoliberal keywords lies precisely in their apparent non-ideological character and their matter-of-fact, common-sense status as mere pointers to adaptation and

72   *The neoliberal reinvention of* entrepreneur

advancement in market society. These keywords have an air that echoes Slavoj Žižek's observation about the advocates of neoliberalism, namely that they 'imagine that [they] do not "really believe" in [their] ideology while continuing to practise it' (Žižek 2009: 3). In one sense, neoliberal keywords are so much part of the dominant ideology that they almost pass unnoticed. However, as we shall attempt to show, their meanings are in flux and disputed, as was highlighted in Williams' account. This chapter draws out this tension by analysing the uses, intentions and contentions surrounding one neoliberal keyword, particularly rich in ideological significance: *entrepreneur*.

The age of the *entrepreneur*

Entrepreneur, entrepreneurship, enterprise, entrepreneurial are repeated unendingly and in a dizzying array of contexts. These words flit seamlessly across websites, brochures, articles, blogs and, as we shall see, have put their stamp on language with a strident super-uniformity, making them the subtle bearers of thought control undreamed of by earlier makers of dominant ideologies, east or west.

Originally the meaning of *entrepreneur* was a person who sets up a business or businesses, taking on financial risks in the hope of profit. Standard synonyms are given as *businessman, businesswoman, business person, business executive*, with some further synonyms given as *enterpriser, speculator, tycoon, magnate, mogul, dealer, trader, dealmaker* and *promoter*. The *Merriam-Webster Dictionary* describes *entrepreneur* as 'a person who starts a business and is willing to risk loss in order to make money'; the *Oxford English Dictionary* 'as a person who sets up a business or businesses, taking on financial risks in the hope of profit', adding specific uses, such as 'a promoter in the entertainment industry'. The *OED* definition also includes informal meanings of *entrepreneur* such as *wheeler-dealer, whiz-kid, mover and shaker, go-getter, high flyer, hustler, idea man/ person*, highlighting the expanding range of meanings of the term. The related word, *enterprise*, which can be used for projects outside money-making, or can simply mean an undertaking, and 'especially a bold or complex one', allows *entrepreneur* by association to adopt these extended meanings. *Entrepreneur* is an ill-defined concept but an instantly recognizable one: it is about inventions geared to commercial ends but also implies operating in a society of entrepreneurs operating at different levels and scope. The social significance invested in *entrepreneur* makes it a pivotal neoliberal keyword, one which, following Williams's definition, acts as a complex hub of sense and reference. It encapsulates a social imaginary in which individuals are centre stage, wealth is understood in individual terms and wealth-seeking individuals are the role models. *Entrepreneurs* are the social icons of our neoliberal age.

Today, *entrepreneurship* has entered unexpected social activities and domains. Medical journals describe how, for example, dentistry and surgery are 'entrepreneurial in nature' and how *medical entrepreneurs* can now help patients monitor their recovery. In nursing, one 'nurse-entrepreneur' (and New

Jersey Businesswoman of the Year) tells us, while business itself may be foreign to many nurses, nursing is full of entrepreneurial potential. She enjoins her colleagues to become entrepreneurial because, after all, nurses are really just salespeople in another guise, as this extract from her website insists:

> Nurses have what it takes to be successful in business. We're smart, think on our feet, have excellent communication skills, are good listeners, and are versatile and adaptable. We're hard working, ethical, and totally customer-service oriented. We're even good salespeople. Every time you have to convince a patient to adhere to a regimen or follow up on some tests, you're selling! We also possess a great body of knowledge and experience that is marketable, valuable, and in demand.
>
> (Cardillo 2014)

An *entrepreneur* is the necessary complement to the now ubiquitous *customer*, in a new understanding of social relationships which, in whatever domain, are defined by the money transaction. Professionalism, skill, care, judgement and the concept of a public good or welfare fades under the assumed notion that what drives both parties in the relationship is the amount of money spent or received during the encounter. All manner of social activities – from care work to personal coaching, organizing family events and weddings, sessions on getting fit – present the opportunity to practice entrepreneurship. Bringing this ethic to family, leisure or home activities is what Arlie Russell Hochschild sees as the encroaching 'marketization of time' which has developed over recent years (Russell Hochschild 2003, 2012). Business magazines note how 'entrepreneurs are eager to respond to the time crunch, creating businesses unimaginable just a few years ago' (2003: 36). House cleaners, wedding planners, surrogate mothers, nannies, household consultants, elderly-care managers, life and love coaches are offering services to fill the gap in home and personal care caused by the increase in the numbers of women working. It has led to a cascading invention of jobs, projects and responsibilities to be bought, some of which – such as spying on babysitters' behaviour – exist to monitor another expanding set of service providers (Russell Hochschild 2012). *Entrepreneurship* is stamped on this vast industry of 'outsourcing of the self' and is claimed as the motivating quality for both sides of the transaction: those who are entrepreneurial enough to brand their services to sell, and those who are entrepreneurial enough to take stock of their busy lives and deal with the services they need to buy in.

Entrepreneurship received its badge of respect in the early days of neoliberalism; Thatcher is sometimes cited as the entrepreneurs' prime minister, and Reagan saw entrepreneurs as 'a special breed', the real leaders of American society (Reagan 1983). Later, Third Way social democracy, according to one its main advocates, would also set its sights on *entrepreneurialism* and rewards for individual effort (Giddens 1998). Following the convergence of the traditional right and left on economic thinking, *enterprise* and *entrepreneurial* became, in

74 *The neoliberal reinvention of* entrepreneur

the 2000s, the buzzwords of governments of all hues, as they sought to privatize public services. With the public sector increasingly branded as stubbornly *unentrepreneurial* and sclerotic, the state, in the name of greater efficiency, customer satisfaction and lower labour costs, prioritized the outsourcing of services to private 'entrepreneurs'. Entrusting the running of government services, social security and schools to private corporations *with strong entrepreneurial capacities*, raised *entrepreneurship* to a highly prized social trait; it was the engine of all things creative and innovative and the hidden spark to ignite economic growth. From Australia to Scandinavia, partnership with *enterprise* would produce both the right policy and the right approach, whether for transport, energy, communications, the environment, health, community services or education (Marttila 2013). The hovering presence of privatization would force the public sector to be more market-sensitive and, in imitation of the private service providers, infuse its employees with the spirit of competitive *entrepreneurship* – even if it was difficult to imagine how entrepreneurialism played out behind a desk of forms to process, at the bedside of the sick and elderly or in front of a class of children. No social field was exempt from the entrepreneurial cure. Even the trade union movement was not adverse to 'promoting and supporting entrepreneurship' (Irish Congress of Trade Unions 2011). Behind its eclectic use was the foundational belief that individuals, alone and rugged, were the prime movers of societies. In an extraordinary act of obliteration of the social dimension of human lives, core communal and societal activities – from birth, raising of children, formal and advanced education, provision of leisure activities, to hospital care, health, leisure, education, care for the elderly – became fragmented into individual life-choices (even though the choices people made turned out resembling everyone else's). This creed of radical individualism dissolved the divisions imposed by standing and wealth and drew an imaginary direct line between Joan or Joe Bloggs who might be thinking in an innovative way about bettering their life, and the wealthy CEO, the hedge fund manager, the owner of capital, the millionaire. Such terms as tycoon, media baron, captain of industry, industrial magnate, financial speculator, or boss were dropped in favour of *entrepreneur*, now seen as the benign improver of society and the kind of person we could all aspire to being.

Irish official circles have always had a special relationship with *entrepreneurs* and *entrepreneurship* and, in recent times, they have enthusiastically embraced it as their defining theme. It was an Irish banker in the eighteenth century, Richard Cantillon, as it happens, who first popularized the meaning of entrepreneur as risk-taker (McNally 2010). His name still features as the title of a regular economics column in *The Irish Times*. Entrepreneurs figure in prime slots on Irish radio and TV. The Irish version of *Dragon's Den*, a TV programme featuring entrepreneurs pitching their business ideas in front of a panel of venture capitalists, is sponsored by Ireland's leading bank and has a well-known TV presenter as its host. The rags-to-riches ideal, a notion implied in *entrepreneur*, has a special place in Irish mythology, bolstered by the Irish emigrant dream of

The names of entrepreneurs – such as those of billionaires Tony O'Reilly and Denis O'Brien – adorn library buildings and university departments, head up Irish charities at home and abroad, and figure

the success story abroad, of the US as the land of opportunity, and of following in the footsteps of the Kennedys, from rural poverty to wealth and fame. Today, it is indigenous Irish entrepreneurs who are held in high regard. Bill Cullen, an Irish businessman, is repeatedly feted over the Irish airwaves and held up as the entrepreneurial model against what he calls the 'mollycoddled youth' (Allen and O'Boyle 2013: 5). The names of entrepreneurs – such as those of billionaires Tony O'Reilly and Denis O'Brien – adorn library buildings and university departments, head up Irish charities at home and abroad, and figure frequently on lists of honorary doctorates. Even the statues which commemorate the Irish famine – five bronze tragic, emaciated figures which stand on the quayside of the River Liffey in Dublin – have to include a plaque to Norma Smurfit, ex-wife of a well-known Irish entrepreneur. The irony is that the social conscience of Ireland's entrepreneurs barely extends to remaining taxpaying Irish citizens: when Irish rock star Bono moved part of his business out of Ireland to the Netherlands to avoid paying higher taxes, he claimed that being 'tax innovative' was part of the creative and inventive culture upon which Irish entrepreneurship was built (Fridell and Konings 2013: 19). Irish entrepreneurs have close connections to Irish politicians. One study found that 'Ireland's elite "Golden Circle" consisted of a tight cross-over between "entrepreneurs" and politicians, with just 39 individuals holding more than 93 directorships in top Irish state and private companies during the Celtic Tiger years' (Clancy et al. 2010).

The economic crash has tightened, not loosened, the Irish government's ties with entrepreneurship. Amid the wreckage of the effects of austerity policies, *enterprise* was reborn to become *the* main plank of economic policy. The Department of Labour was renamed the 'Department of Jobs, Enterprise and Innovation'. 'Championing the enterprise agenda' through 'evidence-based approaches, influence and advocacy' was part of making 'Ireland the best small country in which to do business', a project for which 'the widest possible support within and outside government' needed to be mobilized (Department of Jobs, Enterprise and Innovation 2014). Jobs growth would occur through 'the development of a strong, indigenous enterprise base, the attraction of foreign direct investment and the development of cross enterprise networks' (2014). *Enterprise Ireland* became the obvious name to give to the Irish government organization responsible for the growth of Irish companies in world markets; included among its other priorities, was overseeing the establishment of business start-ups, based in Ireland's publicly funded 14 university and college campuses (see www.enterprise-ireland.com). There could be no official government policy document without several mentions of *entrepreneurship*; no public speech could fail to stress the need to bring things closer to 'the needs of enterprise' (Department of Education, Ireland 2014). A small excerpt from the *2014 Action for Jobs Programme*, reproduced below, illustrates just how many times, in a short text, *enterprise* and its coordinate parts are used. The Department of Jobs, Enterprise and Innovation summarized its priorities thus:

> Transforming Ireland's entrepreneurship and start-up culture through the rollout of 31 Local Enterprise Offices supported by a Centre of Excellence in *Enterprise Ireland;* reviewing tax based schemes for entrepreneurs with a view to supporting an increased level of entrepreneurship; and launching a €2 million fund to help identify and support the best entrepreneurs in each county in the country.
>
>
>
> (Department of Jobs, Enterprise and Innovation 2014)

Presumably, the thinking is that the more you repeat, the more the culture of enterprise sinks in. The use of *entrepreneurship, enterprise, entrepreneurs* (alongside the inevitable *centre of excellence* that Enterprise Ireland would house) is seen as having no need for explanation; the point is driven home self-referentially and by dint of repetition. As public deference to *entrepreneurship* has grown, so too has its field of use. From the original meaning of *entrepreneur* as 'someone who undertakes business ventures' or founds 'a business enterprise' it has been semantically stretched to become an umbrella term for anyone who is able to link any ingenious and imaginative thinking with making money. As with any metaphorical extension, the original association remains, as evidenced in the casual alternation between *enterprise* and *business* or *industry* in official documents. But it has become the 'official' word to replace business, now seen as too banal, and able to capture the brave new world of invention, individual energy and motivation. Marttila notes the elasticity of *entrepreneur*, but also how it is always used against the business–economic backdrop:

> To deal with problems actively and find solutions, to run ideas into actions or to be entrepreneurial in general – these are some characteristic traits of an entrepreneur … It can be at school, on construction sites, in health care at university of anywhere else. Some start businesses. Others mobilise their entrepreneurial potential at work as employees. Others develop ideas on improvements and innovations. They all contribute to welfare and growth.
> (NUTEK policy paper, quoted in Marttila 2013: 5–6)

In other words, whether you are a school principal, a teacher, a carer, a graduate, a trainee, an unemployed person, a company manager, a cleaner, a supervisor, a council worker, a university lecturer, an intern, a mother, even a primary school child – *entrepreneurship* is the means to maximize your chances, in employment and in life. With breathtaking simplicity amid the growing maze of social problems in the Ireland of today (and despite the limit on the number of

The neoliberal reinvention of entrepreneur   77

successful entrepreneurs that there can realistically be) the *entrepreneur* has become what everyone should aspire to being.

The *entrepreneurial* individual and economic crisis

Although being entrepreneurial is about the direction of government policy towards privatization and commercialization, it is also about much more than that. It is about a totalizing life-world which centres on the role of the individual and her place in society. Shorthand for having a positive approach to life and what it means to be a modern person, its appeal lies in its beguiling 'can do-ism', with the promise of material benefit into the bargain.

Michel Foucault (2008) was one of the early commentators on the role of the entrepreneurial individual in neoliberalism. Long before others, Foucault noted how neoliberal market-centred societies were requiring people to see themselves differently to the citizen models of the past. Individuals needed to become mini-replicas of corporations; each person should be 'a sort of permanent and multiple enterprise' (Foucault 2008: 241) with the different sides to their identity and personhood reinforcing, on a micro-level, compliance to market society. Foucault identified the generalization of the *enterprise* form to the individual as an extension of 'the economic model of supply and demand and of investments-costs-profit' to 'a form of relationship of the individual to himself' and to 'those around him, the group, and the family' (2008: 242). As we shall see later, his account of the energetic, disciplining power of entrepreneurship over individuals accepted the neoliberal narrative as reality, thereby more than meeting neoliberal ideology half-way. However, Foucault's description of the neoliberal self as an individual enterprise, constructed as a collection of identity parts, each with its own consumer needs and potential market fulfilment, identifies something significant about the archetypal neoliberal person. This new, entrepreneurial individual is expected to be 'equipped with promiscuous notions of identity and self-hood', is surrounded by 'simulacra of other such selves' and constitutes a fragmented self (Mirowski 2013: 92). Philip Mirowski provides a graphic description of the intended effects on the human subject that this self-fragmentation takes:

> [The individual] ... is not just an employee or student, but also simultaneously a product to be sold, a walking advertisement, a manager of her résumé, a biographer of her rationales, and an entrepreneur of her possibilities. She has to somehow manage to be simultaneously subject, object, and spectator. She is perforce *not* learning about who she really is but rather provisionally buying the person she must soon become. She is all at once the business, the raw material, the product, the clientele, and customer of her own life. She is a jumble of assets to be invested, nurtured, managed and developed: but equally an offsetting inventory of liabilities to be pruned, outsourced, shorted, hedged against and minimised. She is both headline star and enraptured audience of her own performance. These are not effortless per-sonas to be adopted but roles to be fortified and regimented on a continuous

78 *The neoliberal reinvention of* entrepreneur

basis ... The *summum bonum* of modern agency is to present oneself as eminently *flexible* in any and all respects.

(Mirowski 2013: 108, emphasis in the original)

The neoliberal persona has forever the potential for transformation and reinvention: a multi-faceted entrepreneur, she is the risk-taker who takes charge of herself by embracing change in every dimension of her life.

The other side of the infinite potential for change is that a crisis for an individual is interpreted as a personal failure, an unwillingness to take risks, an inability to self-reinvent or simply the result of making bad choices. The individual is wholly and independently responsible for the world they inhabit. Barbara Ehrenreich, writing about the effects of unemployment on white collar workers after the burst of the dot.com bubble of 2001, noted how, in their attempts to find jobs, these discarded workers encountered a particular mind-set which went something like this:

> You must recognise that *you alone* are the source of all the conditions and situations in your life. You must recognise that whatever your world looks like right now, *you alone* have caused it to look that way. The state of your health, your finances, your professional life – all of it is your doing and no one else's.
>
> (Hernacki 2001, quoted in Ehrenreich 2006: 81–82, emphasis in the original)

Ehrenreich's study, entitled *Bait and Switch: The Futile Pursuit of the Corporate Dream*, was written as an undercover reporter among recently laid-off middle class employees and revealed in stark detail the growing sense of insecurity of this social layer. They were vulnerable to an 'insidiously manipulative culture' (Ehrenreich 2006: 226) which held that there was no external world of any consequence and that we alone are responsible for everything that happens to us. The jobless employees turned in desperation to coaches and counsellors, training manuals and self-help courses, only to find that all of them repeatedly emphasized that circumstances count for nothing compared to the power of the individual will. Having the right 'attitude' – that of an upbeat, good 'team player', a 'cracker-jack PR person' and someone who had an 'absolute and unreserved identification with their potential employers' – was the only way to get on to the job ladder again (2006: 234). The encouragement of attitudes of self-blame and of acquiescence to the corporate model, Ehrenreich concluded, exonerated those in power who had led people into this predicament, but also served to perpetuate belief in the system, even though it patently was not delivering.

Ehrenreich's observations are of relevance to the present upsurge of *entrepreneurialism* in official discourse. After the more severe economic crash of 2008 brought down many much-hailed entrepreneurs, one might have expected the fortunes of *entrepreneur* to abruptly wane – especially in Ireland, where the

The neoliberal reinvention of entrepreneur   79

crisis was the most severe. In the immediate aftermath of the crash, some Irish *entrepreneurs* did become something of a public embarrassment and were quietly removed from the much publicized Entrepreneur of the Year webpages (Holborow 2012a: 53). But a couple of years into the recession, *entrepreneurship*, as Ehrenreich had found with her subjects, came to have its uses. As evidenced by its persistent presence in official Irish documents, entrepreneurship soon bounced back into public discourse, if anything with more vigour than before.

Social entrepreneurship and 'fixing Ireland'

Entrepreneurship was stretched to include being *entrepreneurial* towards social issues. *Social enterprise* is a term that first found its way into official discourse in the early 2000s mainly among academics and policy makers in the fields of business and management studies (Teasdale 2012). It stands for an eclectic mix of approaches and activities, from official social policy to entrepreneurial ventures in local communities. This semantic binding represents how two concepts not normally associated with each other, can merge to reinforce, with considerable ideological ingenuity, a neoliberal view of society. One Australian account describes *social enterprise* as the reconstruction of welfare by building social partnerships between the public social and business sectors (Cook et al. 2003). Another British account sees the project as closely aligned to New Labour's embrace of the term the 'social market', which accepts the market as the basic organizing feature of the economy but which argues that the market can be 'socialized' by state regulation on the one hand and that it can enable 'business solutions for social problems' on the other (Teasdale 2012). One of the leading, non-profit social entrepreneurial networks in the United States describes social entrepreneurs as 'individuals with innovative solutions to society's most pressing social problems' (Ashoka 2014). Their priority is to bypass the state and business sectors, to provide start-up financing, professional support services and 'activate multi-sector partners across the world that increasingly look to entrepreneurial talent and new ideas to solve social problems'. In Ireland a recent phenomenon, social enterprise is defined as 'an enterprise that trades for a social/societal purpose, where at least part of its income is earned from its trading activity, is separate from government and where the surplus is primarily reinvested in the social objective' (Forfás 2013: 2). Bringing together *enterprise* and social services and welfare certainly required some deft semantic manipulation, and confirmed the foisting of neoliberal thinking on all hitherto publicly provided services.

Pre-empting the criticism that business is just about greed, *social enterprise* attempts to neutralize the self-seeking aspects of entrepreneurialism, as one advocate of social entrepreneurship on the Forbes website explains:

> The concept of social entrepreneurship is centered not just on mission, but on entrepreneurship, making a social benefit-focused organization become more like a business. The idea is that nonprofits can benefit from the focus

of for-profit businesses – effective planning, efficient operations, and financial discipline. Hopefully the social entrepreneur focuses as intently on excellence in all of these as any back-to-the-wall for-profit entrepreneur. For them, as perhaps it should be for all of us, success is social value.

(Dees 2012)

This logic, as we shall see, has an ideological effect but is not without its own contradictions.

Since the Irish banking crisis and the ensuing social dislocation, the idea of tying entrepreneurship to social issues has been strongly supported by the Irish government. Official government policy advocates 'a strong Social Enterprise base in Ireland' which needs to be developed and encouraged (Forfás 2013). The emphasis in a state agency report on social enterprise is that 'social enterprises are in general not seeking additional State funding' as they have 'self-reliant business models' which can shift the community sector 'towards the commercially oriented model'. Social enterprises, the report notes, can 'provide key supplements to public sector services' (Forfás 2013: 3–4). This last stipulation shows how social enterprise has been embraced by the government as a necessary complement to its radical austerity policies pursued since 2008, which have stripped many social services of large amounts of funding. The umbrella body, Social Entrepreneurs Ireland, has as its slogan *Think Big, Act Now, Change Ireland* and suggests that:

In order to solve some of Ireland's social and environmental problems, we need innovative thinking and new solutions. We need to challenge the status quo and try new things. We need to focus on effectiveness and on impact. We are lucky to have people all over Ireland who are developing new solutions to our societal problems.

(Social Entrepreneurs Ireland 2014).

The following text, an interview with newly formed Irish *social entrepreneurs*, confirms the arrival of *social enterprise* to Ireland. It is interesting for the ideological dimensions to *entrepreneurship* which it contains and for its articulation of some of the post-recession features outlined by Ehrenreich. In April 2014, *The Irish Times* interviewed five social entrepreneurs who were affiliated to the umbrella group Social Entrepreneurs Ireland. The excerpt contains responses from Colman Farrell (co-founder of the School for Social Entrepreneurs), John Fitzsimons of Camara (which uses technology to improve education in disadvantaged communities), Michelle O'Donnell Keating (whose Women for Election movement inspires and prepares women for political candidacy), and Lucy Masterson of Hireland (a company which encourages small businesses to create employment). I have selected the part of the interview (reproduced below) which deals very directly with the interviewees' understanding of *social entrepreneur*.

How you can help fix Ireland

In a meeting room in the offices of *The Irish Times* five social entrepreneurs affiliated to Social Entrepreneurs Ireland tweet their location, joke about having Bono's phone number (none of them actually has Bono's phone number) and chat about their experiences.

Can individuals change society for the better? What stops people?

Farrell: One of the most positive things about working with *Suas* [Educational Development][1] is working with young people … Instead of thinking it's grand, or blaming someone else, they take on huge personal responsibility. Our summary of what happened in the Celtic Tiger is often 'It wasn't me, it was someone else.' I think we mix up responsibility and blame.

I believe there's a lack of entrepreneurship in the country. It's still left to the elite and those with university degrees … Forty per cent of our under-45s in Europe operate in a part-time capacity. If the job for life is gone, how do people create a job for themselves? Kids need to be taught how to run a business and how to take risks.

[In the same way] social enterprises can provide models for new approaches that may grow to replace existing ones … It's about government being flexible and open, and where the lines between what's provided by the state and what's provided by third parties can shift.

Your advice for people who want to make a change in society?

Fitzsimons: The Nike answer. Just do it.

O'Donnell Keating: Don't complain about things and then go home and watch *EastEnders*. If it affects you it affects someone else, so get a group together, talk about it and then see what you can do.

Farrell: Just start it. Think of the smallest thing you could do: a letter, a phone call, something that makes you think, well, I could definitely do that. There's no point worrying about the big stuff. Just choose what to do next: the next word you say, the next action you take or don't take.

Masterson: George Boyle [another social entrepreneur, involved with the Fumbally Exchange] always says, 'You can't eat an elephant in one sitting.' It's a whole lot of little bites.

O'Donnell Keating: It isn't just about being Hillary Clinton. It's also about the person making sure there are adequate provisions for the library services or that the local playground isn't a heap of rust. Yes, geopolitical issues are important, but when you talk to major political figures, [you find] they often started with the rusty playground.

(Freyne 2014)

82   *The neoliberal reinvention of* entrepreneur

The extract brings together some of the themes represented by *entrepreneurs* as applied to social issues in general, and illustrates its role as a core keyword in neoliberal thinking. First, the reference to the pop group U2's lead singer, Bono, at the beginning of the text is significant. According to one account (Browne 2013), no one person represents more succinctly what it means to be an entrepreneur and philanthropy advocate than this world-acclaimed 'celebrity humanitarian'. Bono stands for a particular set of discourses around global poverty one of which is 'selling the idea that powerful people and institutions are genuinely committed to making the world a more just and equitable place' (Browne 2013: 2). Bono has popularized the idea that the problem-solving approaches he advocates are merely practical solutions to practical problems and somehow apolitical, as well as entirely in keeping with his accumulation of massive personal wealth.

A similar belief informs some of the responses given by the social entrepreneurs in this interview and this sheds light on how *social entrepreneurship* melds with neoliberal thinking. Above all, as Farrell states at the beginning of the extract, *social enterprise* is about avoiding succumbing to the 'blame culture' and embracing the responsibility of determining your own life. It is a get-up-and-go attitude to social problems, a way of applying business methods to social deprivation. The attitude 'it wasn't me, it was someone else' is dismissed by Farrell as unhelpful; although, despite Farrell's reservations it is worth noting that the reference to a vaguely defined 'someone else', still manages to obscure the identity of those who were responsible for the economic collapse, while simultaneously deflecting the focus back to the individual and the neoliberal rejuvenation of personal responsibility. Farrell's comments express the same self-blame culture that Ehrenreich observed among her group of office executives so devastatingly affected by an economic downturn. The broader issues which explain the increase of social marginalization – referred to in this interview as 'big stuff' and 'the geopolitical issues' – are seen as unimportant compared to you, 'the rusty playground', your immediate problem and the only place to start. This emphasis on the present within your reach, on your own personal initiative is encapsulated by Fitzsimons's appeal to the model of the Nike *Just Do It* slogan. She feels no need to elaborate: it symbolizes, significantly via a corporate advertising slogan, the spontaneous, self-motivated creativity to go and fix the problem yourself.

Commentators on neoliberal austerity policies have noted that the main ideological focus of both the US government and European Commission post-crash has been to deflect the crisis away from those responsible for it (Peck 2014; Fridell and Konings 2013; Blyth 2013). They echo Ehrenreich's observation that when economic crises occur there is an overarching 'bait and switch' strategy pursued by those in power. The boom model is built on run-away speculation and then when that collapses the state puts all that debt on its balance sheet in a 'bailout'. Then as public debt rises to mammoth proportions, we are told that everyone has been overspending and that now we all need to cut back. The notion of social enterprise, knowingly or not, upholds the same fraud. People are lured into solving the effects of the crisis because things have become so bad, but by

The neoliberal reinvention of entrepreneur   83

assuming responsibility for this they are perpetuating the myth that the crisis is no one's responsibility. They end up repairing themselves their enforced deprivation.

In this extreme individualism, social conditions barely figure. The social entrepreneurs interviewed here, although dismissing deeper structural social causes of poverty, are forced to allude obliquely to class, but in terms of attitude rather than material circumstances. Farrell regrets that entrepreneurship has hitherto been left to 'the elite and to those with university degrees', and wants to change what he perceives as the victimhood culture of the working classes, symbolized for him by the passive watching of soaps such as *EastEnders*. Social entrepreneurship is about shrugging off social determinations and making one's mark. It is above all, as O'Donnell Keating later remarks, about 'doing something', not becoming bogged down with finding the deeper causes of social marginalization, unemployment or the underrepresentation of women. Just forget about the causes of the financial crisis, it's not worth spending time on them. Take action now, use to the full your own initiative. In imitation of the celebrity-humanist of the Bono type, this is the super-individual, a sort of 'hyperagent' (Fridell and Konings 2013: 18), one who has the capacity, with the business ethos that appears to work so well elsewhere, to do essential things far better than anyone else.

The interviewees are confident that their emphasis on 'entrepreneurial social doing' is part of being 'flexible and open' and the 'new' way of doing things. They accept unquestioningly that the for-profit motive can be redirected towards good causes. Getting a group together and talking about the problem becomes the can-do activism ushered in through the individual initiative of social entrepreneurship. Social division and causes for marginalization fade around getting things done. 'Fixing Ireland' is about everyone fixing their own social problem and getting out of the social rut is about having the 'right attitude'.

But, however much *social entrepreneurs* choose to ignore the underlying reasons for poverty, social marginalization and the deeper causes of the economic crisis, it is material deprivation that sets limits on what *social enterprise* itself can achieve. Not everyone has the same opportunities to become a social entrepreneur as becoming one requires having some material wherewithal to start with, sometimes even a considerable amount, as the group of business leaders interviewed here show. *Just doing it* is not possible if social disadvantage curtails the range of choices open to you.

Furthermore, the assumption that 'nonprofits can benefit from the focus of for-profit businesses' rather misses the obvious point that what actually creates the focus for success is, in point of fact, profit. Separating *entrepreneurialism* from its money-making drive unravels the mind-set upon which entrepreneurial thinking rests. A successful entrepreneur is unlikely to be content with being poor. Stating that 'success is social value' passes over the fact that society judges success in material terms. Also, linking social issues to the corporate way of doing things is not without its own structural anomalies and ones which are apparent to the community supposedly being helped. Grossly inflated remunerations for corporate style CEOs in the community sector, especially in times of austerity, are resented and seen as inappropriate payments for those working in

84 *The neoliberal reinvention of* entrepreneur

the social sector. This simple transposing of the corporate ethos to the community is not always well received, as has been shown to be the case in recent scandals over highly paid executives in the charity sector in Ireland.[2]

The interviewees take for granted that the changes advocated by neoliberal thinking have already been fully implemented, thereby embroiling themselves further in ideological stances. 'A job for life is gone', therefore people have to think about creating jobs for themselves; 'the line between services being run by the state and what's provided by third parties can shift' and social entrepreneurs must fill the gap. As critics of social entrepreneurship have pointed out, this amounts to accepting the erosion of rights based on eligibility to universal welfare services and to being resigned to the fact that no such social justice will ever be delivered (Cook, Dodds and Mitchell 2003: 67–68). Social enterprise initiatives bolster the departure from rights-based welfare provision and continue the neoliberal trend towards making individuals responsible for social problems. At a deeper level, rather like what Fridell and Konings call a genre of 'capitalist faith in action' (2013: 10), social entrepreneurship rests on an unwavering confidence in the ability of existing institutions and business mind-sets to actually deliver inclusiveness and empowerment.

This assumption is blind to the reality of widening social inequality which has taken hold over recent decades. It also stubbornly refuses to recognize the awkward fact that it was excessive entrepreneurialism, exercised on the stock markets, that worsened the social symptoms which social entrepreneurs now seek to cure. *Social enterprise* in proposing to solve social problems with the same mind-set that created them carries contradictions that are never very far from the surface.

Naomi Klein claimed, before this depression, that social crisis was the preferred field of action for neoliberals, since it provided further leeway, amid the fear of social collapse, for introduction of bold experimental 'reforms' (Klein 2007). Others have also noted that the 'personalisation of poverty' (Mirowski 2013: 116) and its sequel of self-help and *social enterprise* acts as a convenient diversion away from the real forces at work in the creation of inequality. On this count, *social entrepreneurship* can be judged as a logical extension of the neoliberal project and contributing to the concerted ideological offensive against the public provisions of services and social welfare. The use of the term *social enterprise* shows how social crisis offers new ways to expand neoliberal ideology.

'Governmentality' meets neoliberalism

The subtlety of neoliberal entrepreneurialism, with its emphasis on the individual, has been seen by some to constitute a novel hegemonic regime, infinitely capable of spreading itself in different forms throughout society (Rose 1996) as both an 'out there' and 'in here' phenomenon (Peck and Tickell 2002: 383). Neoliberalism is understood as a regime exercised through 'a profusion of shifting alliances between diverse authorities in projects to govern a multitude of facets of economic activity, social life and individual conduct' (Rose and Miller 1992: 174), as a system

The neoliberal reinvention of entrepreneur   85

of diffused power (Hardt and Negri 2000) and even as an extreme individualism which has eclipsed the social altogether (Rose 1996).

These interpretations build on the observations of Foucault, who, as noted above, was one of the first to describe the distinctive aspect of the neoliberal individual as entrepreneur. This formed the central theme of his lectures in the Collège de France given in 1978–79 under the title of 'The Birth of Biopolitics', which were constructed as a genealogical account of the emergence of neo-liberal politics in the US and 'ordoliberalism' in Austria and Germany (Foucault 2008).[3] The lectures mark an important landmark in the analysis of neoliberal-ism. Foucault's account presents a distinctive understanding of the power of ruling ideas which is worth analysing in some detail, given both its influence across the social sciences and cultural studies, and its focus on the notion of the entrepreneurial self and its connection to neoliberalism.

In the lectures, Foucault makes the distinction between the classical economic liberals and the neoliberals who enact a different form of government. Neoli-beralism, he notes, should not be seen as a continuation of *laissez-faire* classical economics, for modern day neoliberalism, in both its Austro-German and North American incarnations, is concerned with a highly vigilant and intrusive form of government which above all seeks to shape society according to market dictates. Foucault notes that this development requires a new form of rule, a new 'art of government' which he sees as a 'technology of government' or 'govern-mentality', whose origins date back to classical times but to which modern neoliberalism has given a new twist. The linking of the words, 'government' and 'mentality' allows Foucault to merge governing with modes of thought, rule with rationality. Governmentality is taken to mean the representation or discourse which delineates and rationalizes social conduct; it is an art of government which seeks to demarcate legally areas of responsibility and activity for the individual, as opposed to the government, and engender compliance on the basis of 'what must be done and what it is advisable not to do' (Foucault 2008: 11). 'The whole question of critical governmental reason will turn on how not to govern too much' (Foucault 2008: 13). Neoliberal governmentality, through its particular interpretation of political economy, appeals to the individual to regulate his or her own conduct (2008: 7),[4] to govern the self, the main part of which is to be *entrepreneurial*.

Foucault notes that this marks a departure from classical economics by entrenching the principle, as noted by Thomas Lemke, 'that the modern sovereign state and the modern autonomous individual co-determine each other's emergence' (Lemke 2001: 191). Governmentality, therefore, is the coming together of, on the one hand, of the rule of government and, on the other, 'the process of sub-jectification', or the assuming of responsibility by the individual for his own behaviour. 'Subjectification' in Foucault's social configuration extends beyond ideology to encompass the whole human body, creating a regime of 'bio-politics'. The entrepreneurial self as conceived by Foucault is the enactment of the submission of the person to the neoliberal regime and therefore lies at the heart of his notion of governmentality.

86 *The neoliberal reinvention of* entrepreneur

Both here and more fully elsewhere in his works, subjectification bears a resemblance to ideology, but he explicitly rejects ideology for being too closely identified with material interests (Foucault 2002: 119). Neoliberal subjectification, according to Foucault, is a controlling mechanism based on self-regulation, with the regime of truth enacted as mental and discursive narrative by the individual.

Foucault charts the neoliberal refocus from the social to the individual *entrepreneurialism* through what he terms a genealogy of political economy. The classical Smithian aim of political economy, starting from the production and circulation of wealth in a society, was to identify the method of government which could best procure a nation's prosperity and the organization, distribution and limitation of powers in a society. The state and government was central to political economy but, at the same time, government was to limit its interventions to what was deemed acceptable to the natural laws of the economy. In the modern era, Foucault claims, this notion of government comes to be defined, not around notions of justice and rights, but around the concepts of maximum/minimum intervention according to the needs of the economy. Foucault's thesis is that neoliberal governmentality extends beyond the principle of the appropriate level of intervention in the market to the state itself being modelled on market laws (2008: 131). Foucault's point is that his new level of market–government overlap shows how politics and ideologies exist 'decidedly not as errors or illusions as Marxists would hold', but 'are things that do not exist, and yet which are inscribed in reality and fall under a regime of truth dividing the true and the false' (2008: 20). Governmentality is no mere ideology; rather it is a 'regime of veridiction' (2008: 36), by which Foucault presumably means a social order with its own truth-giving categories.

It follows that the neoliberal *homo œconomicus* is a departure from the economic man of classical economics, whose role was social. He is a self-standing *entrepreneur*, 'being for himself his own capital, being for himself his own producer, being for himself the source of [his] earnings' (2008: 226). Foucault uses this observation to show how the regime of governmentality draws neoliberal rule down from the state to micro levels of the individual – the self-sustaining, entrepreneurial *homo œconomicus*. He draws extensively on the neoliberal understanding of human capital as a general index of defining action (2008: 104), and as a way of redirecting attention away from general economic categories to a focus on the individual, whose use of their human capital affects their entrepreneurship potential. He describes in detail the work of the neoliberal trailblazer, Gary Becker, and his grid of *homo œconomicus* for its inclusion of domains that are not directly economic and for its individualist implications regarding government. Becker's individual is someone who must be 'let alone', to be left to respond themselves to the social environment. The entrepreneurial self dissolves the distinction between producer and consumer and there is no preset hierarchy of resident personas, only a shifting cast of characters, depending upon the exigencies of the moment. These traits as defined by Becker make the new *homo œconomicus* infinitely 'governable' (Foucault 2008: 268–70).

The neoliberal reinvention of entrepreneur   87

Foucault's account of the Chicago school of economics narrative results in some shrewd observations on their ideal of the neoliberal person. But Foucault puts no critical distance between the object of his description and his own view. He appears to concede to a rethink of economic development in the terms that are proposed by Becker; he suggests that 'the problems of the economy of the Third World can also be rethought on the basis of human capital' (2008: 232). In places, he leads us to believe that Becker's world has effectively become his world. Foucault's neoliberal, plastic *homo œconomicus*, the entrepreneur vividly and engagingly described, is presented not as a neoliberal project, or the leitmotif of an ideology, but as actually existing. Neoliberal governmentality, Foucault tells us, has succeeded in mastering us as subjects, has already got under our skins. This claim is to make too many assumptions. In this connection, Žižek notes 'one should be careful to avoid the trap that makes us slide into ideology under the guise of stepping out of it'. He explains that once it is accepted that all we are dealing with is narratives and discursive regimes, and never 'reality', we enter into the realm of 'a slick postmodern solution' which, unable to maintain a necessary critical tension between different kinds of reality, tends to succumb itself to the ideology (Žižek 2012a: 17–18).

Others have shared similar reservations about what they see as the cul-de-sac of Foucault's position. Loïc Wacquant shows that governmentality as a process of fashioning of populations and people through 'a flexible conglomeration of calculative notions, strategies and technologies' (Wacquant 2012: 70) amounts to a power which is hard to pin down. 'Biopolitics is both nowhere and everywhere'. Because it occurs at the micro-level of a generalized normativity and rationality, it appears to wholly structure not only the actions of the governing but also the governed. Wacquant succinctly summarizes the fluid and indefinable nature of this regulative rule: 'governmentality seeps across society in different sites of self-production': the body, sexuality, consumption, education, urban space. As technologies of conduct 'migrate' and 'mutate', neoliberalism by this definition, Wacquant concludes, 'becomes all process and no contents; it resides in flowing form without substance, pattern or direction' (Wacquant 2012: 70).

The result is that there is no space outside of the regime, as Foucault defines it, to evaluate whether it does as it says it does; there is no position from which its workings can be questioned and its actual implementation assessed. As Mirowski notes, for all Foucault's insightful comments about the theoretical writings of American neoliberals or German ordoliberals, he was seemingly uninterested in how 'the dynamics actually played out at ground level' (Mirowski 2013: 90). This ambiguity steers Foucault closer towards the neoliberals than he might have envisaged. The fact that the individual entrepreneur may crash on the rocks of social realities, that she may flounder amid the fall-out of a market crash, or that she may discover that her entrepreneurial skills get her nowhere in the real world, does not enter Foucault's tableau. Equally, the possibility that people may not fully embrace the brave new world of the entrepreneurial regime – which after all is only an abstract concept – or that they may see it as one model alongside other different, or even conflicting ones, is not admitted. The result is

88   *The neoliberal reinvention of* entrepreneur

that Foucault's neoliberal world is one of smoke and mirrors from which there is no outside.

But crucially, Foucault's description of the entrepreneurial regime precludes ontologically any analysis of the functioning economy. 'Politics and the economy' Foucault writes, 'are not things that exist, or errors or illusions or ideologies'; they are 'regimes of truth' (2008: 20). In accordance with his relativist understanding of knowledge, for Foucault there is no provable demarcation between what happens in the sphere of the economy and the neoliberal regime of truth. The privileging of mentalities and technologies has the effect of severing the ideational from the material and excluding any discussion of political economy. This assertion, as seen through our eyes today, when the effects of the economic crash are possibly the single determining factor in people's understanding of their lived social experience, is misplaced. Foucault takes as given the smooth economic backdrop, emptied of crisis and implosion, and projects a new social existence which depends on the economy as the new *dispositif*, or knowledge structure, but whose nature is not discussed. The economy is an opaque '*milieu* which produces a number of combined effects bearing on all who live in it' (Tellmann 2009: 11), but which merits no analysis.

Likewise, the wholesale adoption of the notion of the self as a multiple *enterprise* concedes, by default, that the market has the power to mould us, and society, in its image. Indeed, Foucault admits the strong, regulatory power of the market, which he sees as 'an agency of veridiction' and a 'site of truth' (Foucault 2008: 30–35, 51). Mirowski claims that Foucault accepts the neoliberal premise of the market as the ultimate point of reference, and 'the boundary condition' for governmentality (Mirowski 2013: 98). Certainly Foucault circumvents rather than analyses the economy (perhaps due to his keenness to avoid what he sees as the overbearing economism of Marxism), with the result that in *The Birth of Biopolitics*, exactly how market entrepreneurialism has taken such hold is mysteriously absent.[5] This comes close to accepting the vital ideological plank of the exaltation of the entrepreneur: that the market commands blind submission to its rules of conduct.

Foucault's deferral to the truth of the market, it should also be pointed out, is also seldom raised in applied and socio-linguistics studies which touch on his view of discourse disciplining the self. The Foucault framework of discourse and power is often referred to (for example in Blommaert 2005; Pennycook 2001, 2007; Schieflin et al. 1998), but seldom with a discussion of the implications of his views for social analysis. Foucault's focus tends to reinforce the assumption, now widely held, that it is mainly culture and mentalities – in 'biopolitical' form – that shape subject formation. As Robert Albritton notes, this results in 'hardly a trace of the possible impact of capitalism on the making of subjects' (Albritton 2003: 60). A regime driven by 'entrepreneurialism of the self' thoroughly undermines any socially caused notions such as exploitation, surplus value or social class. In these conditions, the overall neoliberal imaginary of the entrepreneurial self appears to swell to self-sustaining proportions and render the social static and unchanging – a view which makes more than a few concessions to neoliberalism.

Entrepreneurialism as ideology

Foucault's construction of the individual entrepreneurial self is traceable to his understanding of discourse as the mobilizing feature of reality. Regimes of truth, adrift from their social moorings, and denied specific ideological dimensions which arise from their insertion in social relations, elevate the discourse of 'governmentality' as imbued by individuals to the status of a stifling imposition. Thinking outside its boundaries becomes impossible. Foucault was explicit that, for him, critique was not about challenging the basis of ideas but charting their genesis:

> A critique is not a matter of saying that things are not right as they are. It is a matter of pointing out on what kinds of assumptions, what kinds of familiar, unchallenged, unconsidered modes of thought the practices that we accept rest ... We must free ourselves from the sacralization of the social as the only reality and stop regarding as superfluous something so essential in human life and human relations as thought.
>
> (Foucault 1988: 151)

Poststructuralists have followed Foucault down this path and chosen to leave aside evaluation or judgement based on reference to an external reality. One Foucault-inspired analysis of the culture of enterprise in neoliberalism considers his role to be limited to one of 'deconstruction' only, of concern with the 'how and why of particular ideational systems'. The author states candidly that he has 'no intention to criticize the way entrepreneurship is being experienced and performed in contemporary society' (Marttila 2013: 205). Another writer on the neoliberal university, despite a round condemnation of the commercialization of British universities, referring to 'the impossibility of what I seek to defend' and (only half jokingly) to 'the neoliberal bits of my soul' (Ball 2012: 19) also gives credence to the idea that sustainable critique is an impossible task. This caution in matters of explicit criticism chimes with a wider one, that neoliberal ideas are too entrenched to be contested, that we cannot stand outside them, and maybe even that we have all succumbed to the 'entrepreneurial self'.

Yet a sustained critique of neoliberal ideology, in its post-crisis, revamped form, is what is required, both to challenge its seeming common sense and strengthen resistance to it. Such a critique of a ruling set of ideas requires direct reference to actually existing social and economic relations, not because these are seen as in some way 'sacralized' as Foucault claims, but because, without this, no 'challenge to unconsidered modes of thought' can be made. The merit of a focus on the use of keywords such as *entrepreneur* is that, by re-immersing such words in the social context upon which they tacitly expound, inconsistencies and ideological tensions

90 *The neoliberal reinvention of* entrepreneur

can be exposed. Decoupled from their usual, 'common sense' in official discourse, and analysed with reference to specific social actors and socio-historical contexts, their ties to dominant ideology can be identified.

Studies which have successfully uncovered the 'hidden' thread of dominant ideology have been those which, as part of their analytical method, re-immerse the discursive representation fully in contemporary class struggles. For example, Roland Barthes, in his early writings, stressed how connotation was determined by the battle of social forces and that this lay behind the construction of social myth. Basing his analysis on this premise allowed him to identify the ideological narrative of empire and its veiled elitism and racism in popular visual images, such as a black soldier saluting a French flag (1973). Despite the structuralist orientation of Barthes, early works such as *Mythologies* had the effect of pointing discursive representations outwards towards the social world, and thereby successfully highlighted the contradictions between the narrative and social reality.

Similarly, Stuart Hall, in an early, perceptive piece entitled 'The Problem of Ideology: Marxism without Guarantees', in drawing the connections between linguistic representation and economic power, pinpointed the unique role of ideology as a method of critique. He wrote that 'the languages, concepts, categories, imagery of thought and the systems of representations – which different classes and social groups deploy in order to make sense of, define, figure and render intelligible the way society works' are 'the mental frameworks of ideology' (Hall 1986: 29). He referred to the 'distortion of ideology', not in the meaning of 'false' but in presenting only half the picture, the one that suited the interests of the social class articulating it. Hall emphasizes how language is ' the medium though which ideology is generated and transformed' (1986: 33). The 'concepts and languages of practical thought' can 'stabilize a particular form of power and domination' through reconciling and accommodating 'the mass of the people to a subordinate place in the social formation' (1986: 29). He cites Marx's identification of the everyday consciousness of the capitalist entrepreneur who represents the working of the capitalist system in the way that someone of his class 'lives' them out (1986: 30). In redeeming the notion of ideology as explained by Marx, he shows how it was a method of identifying the political nature of bourgeois philosophy and constituted a vital and critical weapon against 'speculative mysteries' of vulgar economics (1986: 31). He speaks directly of the social project of ideologies stating that 'ideas only become effective if they connect with a particular constellation of social forces' and that in this sense, 'ideology is part of general struggle for mastery and leadership – in short for hegemony' (1986: 43). Ideology is not just power or hegemony, as is often loosely assumed, but a specific instrument in the struggle for hegemony.[6] Ideological struggles often take place over specific meanings of words in language, in what Žižek later called ideological 'nodes of discourse', which attempt to 'totalize' by means of the halting or fixing of ideological elements to become part of the structured network of meaning (Žižek 1989: 96). In the sense that *entrepreneur* attempts to 'fix' certain understandings of individualism, of wealth creation, it can be seen as a similar point of ideological contention in language,

The neoliberal reinvention of entrepreneur   91

an attempt to 'live out' a common sense view of capitalism, as 'practical bourgeois consciousness', as suggested by Hall.

The connections that Hall made between ideology in language and social class can be traced back to earlier writings on this theme. Valentin Vološinov centred his ideological analysis on the three-way interrelation between the sign, ideology and social forces. He argued that a word 'reflects and refracts another reality; it may distort that reality or be true to that reality or may perceive it from a special point of view'. As a result 'every sign is subject to the criteria of ideological evaluation' (Vološinov 1973: 10). But equally, a word's ability to fix meaning is dependent on social and political factors outside of the discursive structure itself. Ideology expressed in the specific use of words is not confined to discourse as it invites us to think about society and social order in a particular way and has the social means to make it become banal and accepted. The social agency aspect of words for Vološinov made up the 'social life of the verbal sign' (1973: 21) and contributed to the word becoming 'the most sensitive index of social changes' (1973: 19). He argued that language and ideology overlapped and that signs could not be separated from the economic relations of society. The question of what he called the 'basis and superstructures' was absolutely central to understanding how ideology and language were linked (Vološinov 1973: 17–18). He dismissed unequivocally mechanical causality in this relationship, since the two domains were interactive and in a state of constant change with each interaction dependant on a specific historical moment and form of expression. The social sensitivity of a sign is reflected in its 'multiaccentuality' (1973: 23), the intensity and variety of which is determined by the pressures of the conflict between social classes. As Hall noted, Vološinov's view of ideology as 'intersecting accents' based on the 'intersecting of differently orientated social interests' replaces 'the notion of fixed ideological meanings and class-ascribed ideologies with the concepts of ideological terrains of struggle and ideological transformation' (Hall 1986: 40). This is not to say that the ideological meaning of a sign cannot also be consciously imposed. The power of those at the top of society, can bestow on signs what Vološinov noted as a 'uni-accentual', fixed, eternal character which serves to naturalize, at that time, what are specific class positions. 'The ideological sign in an established, dominant ideology attempts to stabilise the flux of the social process and present its interpretation as the truth' (1973: 23–24). *Entrepreneur* carries something of this 'uni-accentual' character not only because it carries the imprint of the social class that promotes it but because it has the power and means to impart, through being able to dominate official discourse, what Vološinov characterizes as 'supraclass and eternal character to the ideological sign'. *Entrepreneur* can be judged as being one such 'ideological sign' or keyword, with a similar 'uni-accentual' character. It 'refracts' reality, in that it insists on the belief that individuals are at the root of wealth creation and that profit making should be extended into all social fields. The next section aims to show how the ideological content of *entrepreneur* consists of the presence of distortions which express, in uni-accentual fashion, the class interests of those who seek its promotion.

Entrepreneur, a neoliberal invention

Neoliberalism, despite the claim by its adherents that it was simply an economic theory, was from its beginnings a class project articulated on behalf of the interests of capital (Harvey 2005). It is an ideology in the sense that it claims that its view of society is universally true and universally applicable and desirable. That neoliberal policies will deliver economic recovery after the recession is a constant and reworked theme. If there is slow or no recovery, or greater economic hardship and greater inequality and social instability, then the ideological force of the doctrine is weakened, however much its credo appears to have been accepted by the population at large. The promotion of *entrepreneur* can be understood as a part of the neoliberal project in that it implies that its view is feasible and that it corresponds to how the world and the economy actually works. Identifying the divergence between the promise and the reality is therefore part of unpicking the ideological reasoning and challenging its official status. This last section aims to demythologize the assumptions behind the neoliberal invention of *entrepreneur*.

Reliance on the keyword of *enterprise* in its contemporary form proposes that *entrepreneurs* are drivers of the economy and that *entrepreneurship* must be prioritized in education, in the awarding of grants, and also, because of its capacity to create jobs, in receiving tax incentives. However the actual presence of entrepreneurial activity in the economy hardly warrants such special treatment. *Entrepreneurs*, taken to be people who start a business (White 2014) are actually a very small group in society. According to one Irish report, 2010 marked a significant decline compared to 2005, in those setting up a business, with fewer individuals intending to start a business, fewer actively planning and just starting a new business, and fewer who were owner-managers of new firms (Fitzsimons and O'Gorman 2010: 10). Even at its high point in 2005, only 4.7 per cent of the working-age population were involved in setting up their own business (2010: 12). Not surprisingly, given the sharp increase in unemployment since the crash, one-third of those considering starting their own business were doing so from 'necessity' rather than from 'opportunity' (2010: 11). Furthermore, counter to the myths about success and job creation, many start-ups last only a short time, with some never managing to create employment for more than one person and others finding themselves quickly being taken over by larger corporations (White 2014). Internationally the picture is no different. The average rate of those aspiring to start a new business across 15 European states is only 8.9 per cent. What is called 'early stage entrepreneurial activity' across different countries is even lower. Australia experienced a substantial decline in its rate of entrepreneurial individuals from 2006 (12 per cent) to 2010 (7.8 per cent). The United States (7.6 per cent) also showed a continued decline in 2010, following a more marked drop in 2009 from its 2008 rate (10.8 per cent). Where the debt crisis was most severe, entrepreneurs dwindled to very low levels, with Greece having no more than 5 per cent overall (Fitzsimons and O'Gorman 2010: 15). Based on these facts, the notion of entrepreneurs as the drivers of the economy, or that everyone should aspire to being one, is somewhat fanciful.

The neoliberal reinvention of entrepreneur   93

More broadly, the widening of the income inequality including the concentration of wealth at the top and greater impoverishment at the bottom of society does not appear to point in the direction of an upwardly mobile society in which the individual *entrepreneur* can flourish. In Ireland, income inequality in 2014 was four times the Organisation for Economic Co-operation and Development average with long-term unemployment having quadrupled in the four years to 2012, with record poverty rates. A 2014 Oxfam report estimates that of the €14.3 trillion held by individuals in 52 tax havens around the globe, almost 5 per cent, or €707bn, is sitting in Irish accounts (Reilly 2013), which would seem to indicate that entrepreneurialism where it exists, takes the form of maximizing returns in the money markets rather than investment in new firms. The trend in Ireland is the same internationally. Global inequality has increased, according to Oxfam's 2014 report, to the extent that the €1.2 trillion combined wealth of the world's 85 richest people is equal to that of the poorest 3.5 billion, or half of the world's population. Almost half of the world's wealth is now owned by just 1 per cent of the population, and seven out of ten people live in countries where economic inequality has increased in the last 30 years (Fuentes-Nieva and Galasso 2014). This report concurs with academic research which claims that growing inequality has been driven by a 'power grab' by wealthy elites. This is no economy poised for growth in which individuals stand a chance of joining the ranks of the well-off; rather it is a stubbornly unequal system in which wealth begets wealth, and one which seems to be returning, as regards income disparity, to the dark days of the nineteenth century rather than ushering in a smart bright future of an *entrepreneurial* economy. Thomas Piketty's account argues that inherited wealth or 'patrimonial capital' yields far larger returns than 'entrepreneurial' or productive capital. Inherited fortunes have produced a class of rentiers who dominate politics, with negative consequences for social mobility as well as creating a serious crisis for the system as a whole (Piketty 2014). Piketty's thesis may leave some questions unanswered about the nature of capital, but his data collected across different countries does highlight the stark reality that ever greater concentrations of wealth are held by a tiny financial oligarchy which is stymieing the potential for the magical *entrepreneurship* of the neoliberal account.

The hold of the *entrepreneurial* individual is claimed by neoliberals, and some of their detractors, to derive from a new political economy, one which has transformed social subjects into individual economic units driven by self-interest to invest and seek returns in a new, higher form of market capitalism. However the *entrepreneur* template, when viewed through the lens of a broader historical and political economy, seems rather less novel. As with other ideological formations, the one we live under always appears to be the exceptionally dominant one. Yet, despite the reach and influence of *entrepreneurialism* and despite its overwhelming presence in public discourse, it repeats, we should remember, the refrains of the powerful capitalist ideologies that have preceded it. For example, the self-made man, so dominant in early twentieth-century American capitalism, prefigures, both in content and message, the contemporary entrepreneurial theme. It, too, promoted a radical individualism across the boom and the bust of

94 *The neoliberal reinvention of* entrepreneur

the 1920s and 1930s, albeit in a language attuned to an earlier stage of production and markets (and couched in more sexist terms). The self-centred material dream, powerfully promoted by the US government at the time, was expressed in terms surprisingly familiar to us today. The catch-cry of Warren Harding, president during the 1920s, was 'less government in business and more business in government'. The motto of his successor, Calvin Coolidge, expressed a craven deference to business (even by our standards), claiming that 'the man who builds a factory builds a temple, the man who works there worships there'. Interestingly, the virtues of self-reliance and individual initiative were promoted for several years after the crash of 1929 and were considered by government to constitute a useful diversion from the impending social storm of the First Great Depression (Watkins 1993; Newsinger 2012). The hold that the American Dream had on the population at large probably appeared quite as tenacious in the minds of individuals as any self-regulatory entrepreneurial regime that might be invoked today, but this did not stop it from being undermined by the crises of the 1930s and world war, nor from it being ousted, after the war, by alternative more socially oriented narratives of the individual. From this perspective, *the entrepreneurial self* of today represents, less the irresistible legitimization of neoliberalism, than an ideological variation on a common capitalist theme.

Conclusion

Enterprise, entrepreneurial, entrepreneurship as appearing in official discourse constitute, this chapter has argued, an ideological keyword cluster in the narrative of neoliberalism. This cluster's use outside the field of economics and its effective status as the centrepiece of official government policy in Ireland for economic recovery points to a highly developed notion of *entrepreneurialism*, which attempts to place the individual at the centre of social life and economic activity and make her responsible for the economic conditions of her existence. The creation of *social enterprise*, in which the entrepreneurial spirit is applied to social issues of poverty, unemployment and marginalization, indicates how *enterprise* can be used as an ideological instrument aimed at neutralizing the political effects of social crisis.

The 'entrepreneurial self' as described by Foucault, stresses its role as a new form of 'governmentality', and sees this new form of self-regulation as the foundation of the neoliberal regime of truth. This focus excludes a sustained critique of neoliberalism as, in rejecting the existence of an objective social reality, it mistakes accounts of reality for reality itself. By contrast, when *enterprise, entrepreneur, entrepreneurial* are analysed as part of a keyword cluster in the articulation of ideology, and their assertions measured against economic and social realities, their distortions, inconsistencies and vulnerabilities emerge. Ideological evaluation allows a focus on the 'uni-accentual' nature of *entrepreneur* which consists of inviting us to unburden social crisis onto the individual.

Notes

1 Suas Educational Development is a movement 'dedicated to supporting high quality education in targeted under-resourced communities', with programmes in India, Ireland and Kenya (www.suas.ie).

2 In 2013 a scandal surrounding the top-ups and pension benefits of the head of the Central Remedial Clinic charity in Ireland led to a drop in donations and a questioning of the way money was being spent in all such charities. See http://www.irishtimes.com/news/ireland/irish-news/chief-executive-of-central-remedial-clinic-resigns-1.1622006 (accessed 15th December 2014).

3 Foucault's lectures appeared first in French in 2004 published by Gallimard-Seuil. Thomas Lemke provided a summary in English and interpretation of these lectures in 2001 (see Lemke 2001). A translation in English first appeared in 2008.

4 The translation, by Graham Burchell, uses 'his' throughout the text (although, in the French original, the use of this personal pronoun would not have carried the same exclusion of women that it does in English).

5 As Ute Tellmann notes for Foucault, as 'the mediation of power through money and objects drops from view' so the political perspective of 'governmentality', and the effective tying of political reason to the truth to the market as a court of veridiction, reinforces the liberal premise that the market is invisible (Tellmann 2009: 8, 14–15). This also means that the entrepreneurial self supposedly able to play the market, is also undertheorized.

6 Eagleton notes that ideology is often taken as hegemony or 'super-hegemony' and is understood as being only about power (Eagleton 1989: 171). Hegemony he defines as all the means by which a ruling order secures consent to its dominance, of which ideology is an essential sector.

6 Austerity and the entrepreneurial university

Reflecting on the fall-out of the Great Recession of 2007–8, David Harvey observes:

> What is so striking about crises is not so much the wholesale reconfiguration of physical landscapes but dramatic changes in ways of thought and understanding, of institutions and dominant ideologies, of political allegiances and processes of political subjectivities, of technologies and organisational forms, of social relations, of the cultural customs and tastes that inform daily life.
>
> (Harvey 2014: ix)

Perhaps nowhere, apart from Greece, have the social effects of the crisis been as deeply felt as in Ireland, a country which went almost overnight from boom to bust and whose government, on one of those nights, signed up to one of the most spectacular and expensive bank bailouts in world history (Burke-Kennedy 2011). A rescue package for private banks, courtesy of the government, was not easy to justify, especially after decades of neoliberal censure of state economic ineptitude. When ballooning public debt led to deep cuts in public spending and rocketing unemployment, the ideological dilemma for the government became more acute. The European Bank solution, compellingly articulated via debt bailout programmes and dutifully adopted by the Irish government, was austerity. The crisis was translated into 'sovereign debt' crisis, supposedly brought on by states that had been overspending, and the only way to balance the books was hefty reductions in state spending: the health budget to be pared back, social welfare payments to be reduced, state employees to receive less, taxes to be increased. The crisis started with the banks and could only end with the banks yet their role was camouflaged under a sophisticated ideological cover, what Mark Blyth (2013: 5) calls the greatest and most successful 'bait and switch' in recent history.[1]

Austerity thus amounts to 'a dangerous idea' (Blyth 2013). Proceeding from the logic of translating private debt into social debt, austerity socializes the crisis by calling on the whole of society to make cutbacks. Austerity reinforces a concealment of the original cause of the crisis, vividly illustrating the tight cross-over between ideology and language. Words operate in close connection with the conditions of the social situation in which they occur and some exhibit what Valentin Vološinov (1973: 20) termed 'an extraordinary sensitivity to all fluctuations of the social atmosphere'. Barely noticeable shifts and changes in meanings and connotations will, in a particular social conjuncture, 'accumulate into fully-fledged ideological products' (1973: 20). The process of 'ideological accumulation' within a linguistic sign is evident in the social role that austerity has come to play for neoliberalism.

Jamie Peck (2014) takes further Blyth's observations to note how austerity acts as a 'strategy of displacement' on behalf of neoliberal elites and is devised as a means of deflecting the social impact of the crisis. The strategy as pursued by the US administration, he argues, was the translation of the Wall Street crisis into a series of federal state crises which then became the means by which the costs of the economic crisis could be offloaded on to ordinary citizens. The rallying cry of 'austerity' placed the responsibility and blame for economic failure at the doors of federal state institutions and made others – the marginalized, those reliant on welfare, the public sector and the social state – bear the cost of the speculative excesses of the wealthy 1 per cent. The 'pushers of austerity' – identified in his account as the neoliberal elite but who might also be considered as the representatives of the interests of capital – employed two distinct but mutually dependent tactics in their displacement strategy. First, they transferred the actual costs, risks and burdens of the banking crisis onto subordinate classes and branches of government, thereby effecting social *redistribution* in favour of the already wealthy. Second, to justify this move, they employed a tactic of *re-narration* in the form of 'new homilies of state failure' (2014: 19–20). The displacement strategy described by Peck for the US has considerable relevance for the situation in Ireland. Irish 'austerity' policies, as pursued following the banking collapse of 2008, resulted in the same unequal redistribution of wealth, which like elsewhere, saw the richest in society accumulate more wealth. The top 10 per cent in Ireland increased their national income from 27 per cent in 1977 to 36 per cent in 2009 and the top 1 per cent increased from 5.5 per cent to 10.5 per cent (Taft 2011; see also Clark 2013; Cahill 2013).[2] But the re-narration of bank debt as 'sovereign debt' deflected the causes of the crisis from private interests to all citizens, with the added appeal of 'sovereign', in the Irish case, conveniently invoking the tried and tested theme of nationalism. The two Irish governments at the time of and following the crash,[3] both amid rising social deprivation and turmoil, drew copiously on these associations and implemented a highly effective strategy of displacement. As the Labour Minister for Public Expenditure and Reform succinctly put it, 'Austerity is not a choice; austerity is learning to live within our means' (Drennan 2013), implying that everyone had shared in the excesses of the boom and everyone should now pay.

98 *Austerity and the entrepreneurial university*

Peck's 'strategy of displacement' also provides insights into the connections between ideological/linguistic representations in official discourse and funding issues within higher education after the crash of 2008. The systematic adoption of specific neoliberal keywords – particularly the university as *enterprise* – re-circulated with new meanings during the crisis was an element of the strategy to re-narrate higher education. *Enterprise*, as circulated in official discourse, expresses an accumulation of meaning and connotations which, in specific social conditions becomes, following Vološinov's formulation, a 'fully-fledged ideological product' in the service of a neoliberal offensive, whose overarching aim is to justify the significant reorganization of higher education funding, from public to private sources. The themes and content of *enterprise* articulated through the privileged communications channel of universities, were defined by 'the social purview of the given time period and by the given social group' (Vološinov 1973: 21). It is an ideological sign which carries, as Vološinov noted, a 'refracting and distorting peculiarity' and acts as 'a most sensitive index of social change' and a repository for 'countless ideological threads' (1973: 21–23). In Ireland prior to 2008, unlike the UK, the neoliberalization of higher education was only in its early stages; the deep recession in Ireland provided the social moment to implement it more cogently and thoroughly. The Irish case thus provides a particularly strong example of how neoliberalism was revamped, an element of which was the enthusiastic adoption of *enterprise* and other neoliberal keywords in official discourse.

This chapter will illustrate the renarration of universities as *enterprises*. Following the account of the general ideological dimension of *entrepreneur* in the last chapter, it will examine the origins of the *university as enterprise* and how *enterprise* and *entrepreneurial* are used in relation to universities and students in official documents and to what effect. It will then describe how *enterprise* displaces the economic reality of reduced funding on to another plane with specific ideological intentions. It will trace the origins of this use of *enterprise* to international bodies and national states that have authorized *enterprise* in higher education for their own specific interests. It will conclude on the importance of an ideological critique of the neoliberal language in the university as part of a wider project of resistance to the neoliberal university.

Universities renarrated as *enterprises*

Ireland's official strategy for higher education was published in January 2011, two and half years after the banking crisis, although it had been in preparation for three years before. Its main emphasis was how higher education needed to radically change to meet the challenges of economic recovery and the 'innovative, knowledge based economy'. *Enterprise* is used 89 times in the 134 page report, the first ten examples of which-in the executive summary-are listed below.

Examples of the use of *enterprise* from the executive summary report of the Hunt Report (Strategy for Higher Education to 2030)

The economic importance of linkages between research and *enterprise*. (p. 5)

Ireland a country recognised for innovation, *competitive enterprise* and continuing academic excellence ... (p. 10)

Higher education institutions will have a strong engagement with individual students, communities, *society and enterprise*, ... (p. 10)

... many of these ideas will translate into the sustaining *innovative enterprises* of the future. (p. 10)

The structure and design of PhD programmes should incorporate generic skills and be formulated with direct engagement with *employers and enterprise*. ... (p. 11)

Higher education research will need to *connect to enterprise* and society in new and imaginative ways. ... (p. 12)

... a coherent set of higher education institutions with complementary and diverse missions that together meet *individual, enterprise and societal needs*. (p. 15)

a more responsive and open engagement with key *stakeholders*, particularly *students and enterprise* ... (p. 16)

Greater mobility of staff should be facilitated between higher education on the one hand and *enterprise and the public service* on the other. (p. 19)

To ensure a more effective level of *collaboration with enterprise*, funding agencies and higher education institutions should develop review mechanisms ... (p. 19)

(Hunt 2011: 1–20)[4]

Engagement with enterprise, linkages between research and enterprise, enterprise and innovation, PhD programmes and enterprise skills, enterprise and society, enterprises as stakeholders, flow between the public service and enterprise, applying private enterprise performance and funding models to the public service; these are the keyword clusters through which the notion of *enterprise* in the university is developed. The Hunt report noted the 'serious challenges' of 'funding and operational matters' and the need to find practical solutions to these (2011: 3). It referred to the need for 'a new contractual relationship or service level agreement between the State and the higher education institutions', as part of a wider strategic dialogue to 'ensure that that the requirements for performance, autonomy and accountability are aligned' (Hunt 2011: 14). The body charged with this oversight role was to be a 'reformed' Higher Education Authority (HEA), a state body whose functions traditionally were the awarding of degrees and an advisory role in matters of education, but which would now be empowered to monitor the 'financial sustainability' of institutes of higher education. This state agency, made up of politically unaccountable functionaries and whose chairman for the first time was from the

100 *Austerity and the entrepreneurial university*

corporate sector (a former CEO of a Swedish multinational),[5] was now to have the 'responsibility, on behalf of Government, for engaging with institutions to enable them collectively to meet national priorities, without wasteful duplication' (2011: 14). Hunt made clear that universities were now to be considered as self-standing, competing *enterprises* with 'funding decisions' being made 'in the context of the institutions' performance against identified and agreed targets as part of the service level agreement or contract' (Hunt 2011: 14).

A later report from the HEA takes Hunt's recommendations, including its own role in financial monitoring, to a new level of corporatization. Entitled *Towards a Performance Evaluation Framework: Profiling Irish Higher Educa-tion*, 'profiling' was in fact the 'financial profiling of the performance of the institutions of higher education' with a full 'quality assurance' dimension with a view to ensuring that they provided 'value for money' (Higher Education Authority 2014: 8). Profiling of the higher education institutions was understood in exclusively business-enterprise terms, as a means of 'evaluating institutional performance against performance indicators'. The report 'profiles' the balance between 'exchequer' and 'non-exchequer' sources of income – henceforth the two recognized official funding planks for universities – and sees the ratio between them as 'a core performance indicator', and those institutions with larger propor-tions of non-exchequer funding as performing better. The template for universities, in this HEA report, is the business *enterprise*, a term which occurs frequently (see box below).

Examples of *enterprise* in *Towards A Performance Evaluation Framework: Profiling Irish Higher Education*

The national strategy calls on higher education institutions to 'engage with the communities they serve in a more connected manner – identifying commu-nity, *regional and enterprise needs* and proactively responding to them'.
… increasingly the locus of innovation is dispersing and moving well beyond the campus, and the *interaction of institutions with enterprises and communities* offers significant potential for job creation as well as for social and civic innovation.
… higher education institutions have the potential *to innovate in partnership with enterprise and community groups and with cultural organisations locally, nationally, and internationally;* to inform public policy and practice; and to stimulate regional development
(Higher Education Authority 2013: 25, 181)

The national policy and the *enterprise* model has been transmitted, almost *verbatim*, to documents in each higher education institution, with *enterprise* now deployed with greater frequency. For example, in my own university, Dublin City University (DCU), the strategic plan singles out *enterprise* as the foundational theme for the university's future development. Its objectives revolved, almost exclusively, around making the university *entrepreneurial*, as its second strategic objective made plain (see box below).

> ## Dublin City University's Strategic Objective 2:
>
> To be recognised internationally as a leading University of *Enterprise*
>
> Our vision of a *University of Enterprise*, which sets DCU apart in the Irish Higher Education landscape, comprises two principal elements:
>
> First, we will create an environment that encourages creativity and fosters the development of *entrepreneurial and innovative thinking* in our students and staff. Consequently, many of our graduates will be stimulated to create their own future and to contribute strongly to Ireland's future prosperity.
>
> Second, we will *engage deeply with enterprise (commercial, cultural and social)*, both in Ireland and abroad. We will establish regular fora for dialogue with *enterprise* in order to inform our degree programmes and our research agenda.
>
> Furthermore, we will continue to develop *deep partnerships with Enterprise* that will provide mutually beneficial opportunities across a range of our activities. Industry–academic collaboration has been a substantial and distinctive element of our university's research profile since its establishment and this feature will be reinforced and enhanced in the years ahead
>
> (Dublin City University 2012)

The strategic plan advocates that *enterprises*, understood as both *industry* and *commercial enterprises* and also *cultural and social enterprises*, should be the driving force of the university's strategy and ethos, irrespective of academic discipline. In the twenty-one page plan, *enterprise* is used no less than 40 times, while *study* is used twice, *critical* three times and *analyse*, *investigate*, *reading* and *subject*, in the sense of subject studied, not at all. The text understands *enterprise* as a company but also as an innovative and creative way of thinking, which being beneficial to the individual is beneficial to economic growth and a dynamic economy.

In the year after the publication of this plan, in 2013, just at the lowest point of economic crisis, *enterprise* now secured the prized position of being part of the university's official title. Thus, on the opening page of DCU's website, it was announced as in the box below.

> ## Welcome to the University of Enterprise
>
> Dublin City University has forged a reputation as Ireland's University of Enterprise, through its strong, active links with academic, research and industry partners both at home and overseas.
>
> DCU provides a unique learning environment where students are encouraged to develop their creativity and skills as innovators. The focus

> is not solely on academic learning; students get the opportunity to spend time in real world professional environments as part of their studies, and they also get to work with innovators on their own ideas, setting up enterprises and exploring their own social and commercial ideas.
>
> And it's not just the students: researchers at DCU are also forging ahead, translating ideas and discoveries into new solutions in business, technology and society by spinning out companies and licensing technologies to industry (http://www.dcu.ie/university-of-enterprise.shtml, accessed 15 December 2014)

The opening pages of the website make repeated mention of enterprise, *enterprises* and *entrepreneurship*, within campus companies, start-ups, spin-offs, spin outs, and various hubs of corporate sponsorship. These pages market the university as a set of different units selling their own unique product to potential student *entrepreneurs*. For example, on one of the first webpages, the DCU Ryan Academy of Enterprise is described as a bridge between 'academia and entrepreneurial practice' and a 'unique partnership' between 'Ireland's leading young university, Dublin City University and the family of one of our greatest entrepreneurs, Tony Ryan'.[6] The university's *Enterprise Advisory Board* and a 'student accelerator start-up programme' – named *USTART* – figure prominently on the webpage. USTART seeks to encourage *entrepreneurship* among students, through the awarding of 'seed funding' to students. The programme offers 'an exciting student entrepreneur start-up competition' in which students are given the opportunity to present their 'great ideas for profit or for non-profit ventures' on an 'Investor Day' attended by 'venture capitalists and business angels', a term used for people who invest in start-ups.[7] Successful applicants will receive funding as well as the free use of university office space and facilities to help with 'the design and build of prototypes for the setting up of their new businesses'. It is to be noted that publicity for start-up companies and for various forms of *enterprise* takes precedence over information concerning faculties, courses or degrees, academic subjects or areas of research that the university offers.

Enterprise in this context is understood in two ways: as a corporate unit – in this case operating under the broader *enterprise* entity of the university – and as an attitude which involves new ways of thinking and creative means of making money. *Enterprise* and *entrepreneur* find their potential as neoliberal keywords in the fact that they sit semantically on the border between a business and an attitude, as discussed in the last chapter. Their extensive and indeterminate connotations make them the ideal language tokens for the neoliberal project: in the university context, *entrepreneur* can claim semantic associations beyond the greasy till of *commerce* and strike a bolder, more creative note than *business*.[8] This elasticity and ambivalence of meaning allows *enterprise* and *entrepreneur* to jar less when used within academic disciplines outside business. It is these shifting emphases in *enterprise* that make it, in the hands of certain social agents in specific social moments able to expand to signify the 'new spirit' of capitalism.[9]

Figure 6.1 Image on cover of booklet of Dublin City University – Ireland's University of Enterprise – Strategic Plan (available at http://www.dcu.ie/images/carousel/ DCU_Strategic_Document.pdf, accessed 15th December 2014). Caption reads: 'Our mission: to engage with enterprise for the benefit of our students'.

The *enterprise* élan is also translated into images, reproduced in various forms on the pages of the university website, in student brochures, in university documents and publicity material. One such, which appears in the university strategic plan and on the cover of a blue student booklet, is to be found in large inviting piles in the students' union, the library and communal areas around the university, with the aim presumably of keeping the students 'on message' while they are on campus.

The students shown in the photo are intended to capture the distinctiveness of students at this university, and what might be considered to constitute the *student entrepreneur* – eager, totally engaged, talented (Figure 6.1). Guy Cook in his discussion of 'PR language' in the university, identifies the 'hooray' character of words such words as *excellence, impact, sustainable*, which are so generally positive that everyone can agree that they are 'a good thing' to have as goals. 'Hooray words refer to concepts and goals with which everyone will endorse, until one gets down to the detail' (Cook 2012: 40). The entrepreneurial students, as represented above, extend the appropriateness of the 'hooray' tag to images. The subjects are too good to be true: many lecturers very possibly may never have encountered such undiluted fervor on the faces of their students. Cook's observations about PR language in the university highlight the exaggeration and overkill of such words and the same can be said for these images of *entrepreneurial* students.

DCU is not alone in the widespread use of *entrepreneur*. Entrepreneurship is deeply in vogue in the Ireland of today; entrepreneurial skill training now forms the necessary component of all subjects in university education (as well as for

104 *Austerity and the entrepreneurial university*

'life skills' for the population at large). State agencies sponsor plans to upskill lecturers so they can 'teach entrepreneurship' and 'give our children the toolkit they need to design their own future' (NUIG 2014). Announcements for special entrepreneur orientated seminars, workshops, conferences – or 'mojo' ('especially-magic-power-filled') conferences – fall almost daily into every academic's email for consideration. One such email sent on the internal mail in DCU in October 2013 began as in the box below.

> Dear Colleagues
>
> You may be aware that as part of the National Strategy for Higher Education to 2030, the HEA ... is supporting the development of *entrepreneurship education* and embedding *entrepreneurial learning* throughout partner institutions and the Irish HE sector in general ... As part of this initiative, our university, one of the project partners, will be delivering, on a pilot basis, the country's first module dedicated to supporting academic and non-academic staff in *embedding entrepreneurship and entrepreneurial learning* in their institutions. For this Level 9 module titled '*Enterprise and Entrepreneurial Learning*' we will provide 2 nominated participants, with a background in the policy, theory and practice of *entrepreneurship and entrepreneurship education* ...

Enterprise is seldom explained and its value to general education rarely discussed. Sheer dint of repetition, as highlighted in this email, is presumed to be enough to justify its relevance. Significantly, one Irish advocate of entrepreneurship, himself a former academic, explained the use of *enterprise* by quoting from former Chinese premier Deng Xiaoping's slogan 'to be rich is glorious', pointing out that it was *enterprise* that marked the Chinese turn to the market and the creation of an entrepreneurial class who would create both wealth for themselves and in trickle down fashion for society too (White 2014). The *student entrepreneurs* so glowingly portrayed on university websites, or the blatant repetition of all things entrepreneurial in the email correspondence above, carry something of the same onward and upward sloganeering of the former Chinese premier, although it seems strange to enlist this type of propaganda to the cause of education.[10]

In sum, the strongly repeated use of *enterprise* in the university has a purpose: to create a way of seeing the world which, aided substantially by the prestigious communication channel of the university, becomes naturalized as common sense. Its meaning stretches from a place of business to a go-getting attitude and both aspects, as we shall see, contribute specifically to the ideological composition of the neoliberal narrative.

Neoliberal think tanks and the standardization of keywords

The extent and uniformity of the use of *enterprise* across official documents in higher education draws attention to the role of social agency. National educational policies draw heavily on policy recommendations from international bodies, conservative think tanks and bureaucracies within the EU (Henry et al. 2001; Ward 2012). The influence of these institutions can be seen in the presence of *enterprise* in higher education documents in Ireland, as this section will show.

From the 1990s, discussion of education policy for Ireland had already begun to stray from the rather elitist Newman model of 'training good members of society' (Collini 2012: 46) which had served Irish universities since the foundation of the state. The language of catholic-inspired liberalism in the constituent colleges of the National University of Ireland was replaced by the language of globalization and partnership with industry. Higher education as a public good (until the 2000s, 85 per cent of funds for higher education in Ireland were state provided) began to be replaced with the idea that knowledge should be put to the service of states, companies and economies and sold on the market. Policy change in Ireland was tightly directed by the Organisation for Economic Co-operation and Development (OECD). In 2004, the OECD Examiners' Report on Irish Higher Education, ambitiously declared its terms of reference to be 'examining policy issues in all aspects of the system, including strategic management and structure, teaching and learning, research and development, investment and financing and international competitiveness' (OECD 2004: 5).

Based in Paris but led from Washington, the OECD has established itself as an influential policy maker in the EU and beyond, but in higher education its role in implementing the 'reform agenda' is pivotal. In the 1990s, it identified a 'crisis of performance' of institutions of higher education and demanded that universities acted as 'catalysts and organisers' in the 'dynamising of nation innovation systems' (Ward 2012: 142). Universities now needed to fully embrace the enterprise agenda which included competing on top ranking global university league tables, attracting high-flying academics and their 'world-class' research, seeing their main task (as laid out for each member state in the in the Lisbon Treaty) 'to contribute to making their national economies competitive and dynamic' (OECD 2004: 5). OECD policy was that universities now needed to be steered by their governments towards the commodification of knowledge or the packaging of knowledge to be sold on the market and aligning the activities of universities directly towards national economic development. The OECD became the powerful promoter for the idea that government, industry and university – what Ward (2012: 138) calls 'the triple helix' – should coalesce to drive the 'free' market agenda in education.

OECD reports, surveys, and policy recommendations, supported by a generous budget, represented the beginning of a document-producing process whose outcome is to replicate one neoliberal-inspired education policy across its 34 member states and its associate members (one of which is China). The process is explained by Steven Ward (2012: 140): a government commissioned a report on an aspect of education, the OECD researched it and listed recommendations for the country in question, and it was the OECD report which formed the basis of government policy, including the necessary 'reforms' to be implemented.

Spreading this policy involved using the same core neoliberal keywords, which were faithfully copied and pasted across to other policy-enacting texts – such as

106 *Austerity and the entrepreneurial university*

EU Treaties and the Bologna Declaration – and to local texts (Keeling 2006; Wright and Ørberg 2012). The policy was articulated with an extraordinary lack of local variation. In stark contrast to other contemporary speech forms, these documents converged in their use of keywords and phrases, producing a linguistic 'super-uniformity' (Holborow 2013). Whether in the English-speaking settings of Australia, New Zealand, the US or Europe, and in other locations where English is used in public discourse, university websites described their mission, their plans, their departmental activities in almost exactly the same words and phraseology (Collini 2012).[11] Completely disregarding local traditions and cultures, the neoliberal language of the OECD cemented a highly centralized and cohesive neoliberal message. It made a unified linguistic neoliberalism a reality. A poster for the Marshall Plan produced in the late 1940s had a picture of a windmill whose sails carried all the flags of its associated nation states and the slogan 'Whatever the weather we must move together'. True to this tradition, the OECD now achieves new heights of convergence in ensuring that, in educational policy, its member states move very much together and literally speak with one voice.[12] Through its generous budget, large research facilities and the annual profiling of educational systems of its member states, the OECD provides 'the lock-in of neoliberal policies' (Mirowski 2013: 62). The publication of OECD 'indicators in education' acts as a strong pressure to conform; or in OECD's words, it 'enables educational policy makers and practitioners alike to see their education systems in the light of other countries' performances' and, 'it supports the efforts that governments are making towards policy reform' (OECD 2011: 3). The OECD 'Education at a Glance' reports on individual countries frame their findings within neoliberal views of education and give currency to the favoured keywords such as the *entrepreneurial* university, *human capital*, the *graduate premium* and the *skills agenda* in the *knowledge economy*, creating over time a 'discursive taken for granted' (Henry et al. 2001: 162). Thus is effected a seamless language reproduction process in which local higher education institutions, for the most part, obligingly participate.

The standardization of neoliberal keywords was further strengthened by the official policy status that these expert reports, by-passing local policy interventions, quickly gained in the countries in the OECD fold (Ward 2012: 146; Wright and Ørberg 2012). This tight cross-over between report and policy makes the OECD, according to one study, exist 'simultaneously as policy instrument, forum and actor' (Henry et al. 2001: 174). In Ireland, OECD dictates were faithfully replicated. In 2004, the OECD Examiners' Report of Irish Higher Education in Ireland, as we have seen, saw fit to adjudicate on all areas of educational policy and ethos. (OECD 2004: 5). Ireland adopted this report in entirety, without amendment or parliamentary intervention, and all 79 pages of it became official policy (Holborow 2006a).

When the crash happened, the economic dimension of higher education became more important than ever, as OECD documents on Ireland made clear. 'Tertiary education policy is increasingly important on national agendas. The imperative for countries is to raise higher-level employment skills, to sustain a

Austerity and the entrepreneurial university   107

globally competitive research base and to improve knowledge dissemination to the benefit of society' (OECD 2008). The 2011 Hunt Report, itself relying heavily on OECD data, follows the trend and describes the mission of Higher Education as

> making Ireland a country recognised for innovation, competitive enterprise and continuing academic excellence ... If Ireland is to achieve its ambitions for recovery and development within an innovation-driven economy, it is essential to create and enhance human capital by expanding participation in higher education.
>
> (Hunt 2011: 10)

The HEA carries the same prioritization for innovation and interaction with enterprise:

> For the future, the education system must be the key driver of Ireland's competitive advantage ... Increasingly the locus of innovation is dispersing and moving well beyond the campus, and the interaction of institutions with enterprises and communities offers significant potential for job creation.
>
> (Higher Education Authority 2012b: 24)

Post-crisis, the institutions of the EU have added their voices to the standardizing of neoliberal keywords. The European Commission for Industry and Enterprise has played a lead role in prioritizing *enterprise* in higher education. These reports were framed in such a way that they confirmed official policy. For example, the 2012 *Survey of the Effects of Entrepreneurship Programmes in Higher Education in Europe*, written by the European Commission Industry and Enterprise states, with no further elaboration, that 'the primary purpose of entrepreneurship education at university is to develop entrepreneurial capacities and mindsets'. While 'the teaching of entrepreneurship has yet to be sufficiently integrated into university curricula', the study reaffirms its commitment 'to make entrepreneurship education accessible to all students as innovative business ideas may arise from technical, scientific or creative studies' (European Commission Industry and Enterprise 2012). *Enterprise* acts as a normalized point of reference upon which education performance is measured. The Irish HEA report (Higher Education Authority 2013) then takes up the pointers laid down at EC level to reaffirm the need for universities to interact with *enterprises* and quotes in confirmation the achievements of 'university-enterprise partnerships (UEPs) across Europe through their mapping and benchmarking' (Higher Education Authority 2013: 26) and the process becomes self-confirming. Figure 6.2 illustrates the transmission process from the OECD, via the EU Commission, to national institutions. It shows how *enterprise* and *entrepreneurial* appear in the same word clusters.

Linguistic authorship and social agency, crucial to identifying the social aspects of language, requires identifying the connections between speech acts, texts and text-types, words and social institutions. Mikhail Bahktin, in his

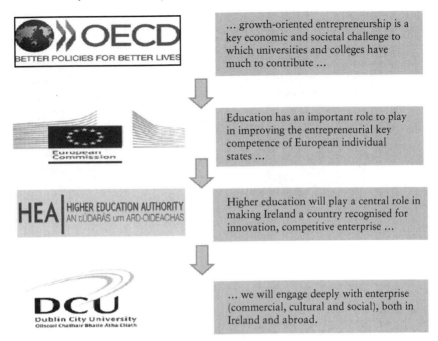

Figure 6.2 Standardizing keywords down the chain – from think tank to local university.

discussion of social voice, identified in recognized standard discourse, social agents at work in the creation of linguistic uniformity. These were 'centripetal forces that overcome the heteroglossia of language'; forces that serve to unify and centralize the verbal ideological world (Bakhtin 1981: 270). His observations mainly applied to the literary genre and in a national state context, but he also refers to 'the professional stratification of language' 'the language of the businessman, the politician, the public education' which has 'its own semantic nuances' and 'slogan words'. He noted that these concrete instances of language have the ability to 'infect with their own intention' and to carry 'specific ideological overtones' (1981: 289–90). His remarks have particular relevance to the transmission forces that I have identified here in the standardization of *enterprise*. The reproduction of keywords from OECD reports and policy recommendations, aided by local states, illustrates how powerful social voices can act as strong centripetal forces in language, 'infect with their own intention' and carry considerable ideological force.

Ideological significance of universities as *enterprises*

The OECD states that 'entrepreneurship education should not only focus on narrowly defined tools (e.g. how to start up a business, financial and human resources management) but also to broader attitudes (like creativity, risk taking, etc.)' (OECD 2009). It describes entrepreneurship as 'the development of one or more of a combination of attitudes, personal qualities, and formal knowledge and skills' and that education for entrepreneurship is concerned with 'the inculcation of a range of skills and attributes, including the ability to think creatively, to work in teams, to manage risk and handle uncertainty' and 'a group of qualities and competencies that enable individuals, organisations, communities to be flexible, creative and adaptable in the face of rapid social and economic change' (2009: 13). The OECD is surprisingly candid about the broad reach of the concept.

> Changing mind-sets is fundamental. Thus, an overarching goal becomes that of fostering the development of a mind-set which is conducive to entrepreneurship and to entrepreneurial behaviour. [This] broadens our perspective on what 'entrepreneurial' behaviour is about. It is not restricted to starting a business or running one's own enterprise. Individuals can act entrepreneurially within a wide range of roles. ... Moreover, they can do so outside the working environment – in non-work activities, such as voluntary work or the organisation of sports clubs, and in the domestic and social spheres.
>
> (OECD 2009: 14)

In the context of 'rapid social and economic change', *enterprise* carries a stronger specific ideological message. First, universities as *enterprises* represent the re-narration of universities as mainly income-generating institutions. Second, *entrepreneurial* as the model attitude to be developed in the individual student transfers economic risk from the system to the individual. It is to these two ideological aspects of *enterprise* to which I now turn.

Calls in universities for sources of income outside public funding – donations and sponsorship, increased student fees and registration costs, research grants for specific projects – have long become a feature of the higher education landscape in Ireland. Library and other capital facilities have benefited from philanthropic donations and it is estimated that between 2005 and 2008 private investment (including philanthropic) accounted for 50 per cent of total capital investment (Delaney and Healy 2014: 26). Academic commercialism has become a major part of what universities do, with campus companies and university–industry partnerships much in evidence across Irish campuses. Like elsewhere, possession of patents and intellectual property has become a pre-requisite for promotions and an accepted measurement of academic achievement (Washburn 2005; Ward 2012). Policy calls for increased enrolments of overseas students, who pay higher fees, have been made in Ireland, but so far this income source has remained smaller in Ireland than in other countries, such as the UK (Gu and Schweisfurth 2011; Whitehead 2011).

The 2008 crash has dramatically accelerated the trend away from public funding for higher education. The bank bailout, at one stroke, increased government debt from 25 per cent of its GDP to 118 per cent of its GDP, to an overall cost, according to some estimates of €90bn (O'Connor 2011) and one of the most expensive bailouts in world history. Such a huge debt burden on government

110 *Austerity and the entrepreneurial university*

affected all public spending and higher education has been particularly badly hit. Over the period 2004/05 to 2009/10 the number of full-time students increased by roughly 20 per cent while public funding per full-time student fell by 16 per cent (Hazelkorn and Massaro 2010; Higher Education Authority 2012b). Since then, government funding has been further reduced. All staff working in education – from academics, administrative staff and ground staff – have seen between 16 per cent and 25 per cent taken off their salaries,[13] measures which would have been inconceivable in Ireland just five years before. They have transformed the conditions of work in universities.[14] Most significantly, the contribution of the state through grants and fees is shrinking from 76 per cent of higher education income in 2007 to a projected 51 per cent in 2016 (Humphries 2014).

Universities as *enterprises* have been promoted in this context. Faced with severe cutbacks, *enterprise* becomes the means through which new private sources of funding are to be plumbed, in an economic crisis when enterprise is floundering on the rocks of recession and when competition for funding has never been greater. It meets an institutional funding crisis with more marketization (even though the crisis was caused by an excess of the market). The *entrepreneurial* university can therefore be described as a pragmatic response to reduced state funding within the parameters of austerity. From this perspective, it shares the characteristics of a 'strategy of displacement' (Peck 2014) for its effect is to divert attention away from the causes of decreased state funding and to strengthen commitment to the marketization of the public sector. A recent HEA report bears this out as it sees 'the decline in public funding' as providing 'heightened expectations' (Higher Education Authority 2013: 6) regarding performance evaluation and sourcing private funds.

Although seldom referred to in the ethos of *entrepreneurialism*, attracting funds from corporates or individuals involves competition at every level, which is infinitely more intense in times of recession. Competition on world table leagues, for university awards, for student intake, competition for research funding, competition for contracts, competition to secure the 'best' academics, competition over investment in state of-the-art buildings, campus attractions, student retention rates, employment prospects for graduates – post-crash, entrepreneurship is about cutthroat competition for scarce resources. Funding is the overriding concern for universities: academics are promoted on the basis of how much income they can bring in, sometimes over and above how many publications they produce, and students win awards for 'commercial ideas' and for securing seed funding.

Intense competition has an impact on text production and the type of language used. Greater rivalry between universities, for students, research projects, donations, and commercialization schemes, has resulted in the ballooning of marketing strategies, part of which involves an exponential growth in the production of texts – printed, electronic, on websites and social networks – aimed at selling the university to an ever-wider market (Osman 2008). Alongside these texts, in response to calls for accountability from government and 'stakeholders', there has been a profusion of internal documents listing and quantifying every aspect of what the university does (the writing of which, in an endless downward spiral of work begetting work, takes up more and more of the time of those working in the university). The proliferation of these texts mean there are more hand-outs, booklets, documents, posters, advertisements, which promote the university's 'brand' and ever more opportunities to promote the university's unique selling-point. *Enterprise* achieves its high profile through these channels. The process of creating brand images is built on repetition which further explains how key-words come to be repeated over and over again. There is a further pressure to repeat the buzzwords. *Enterprise* is picked up with enthusiasm by individual universities, in part, because adopting this linguistic style is taken as a good indicator that 'change' is under way – now a necessary condition to secure continued funding from the 'exchequer' source. Market competition, under the aegis of 'free' choice, is thus the impetus to a rigid linguistic uniformity. This grates with notions of academic freedom and invokes sometimes bitter responses from academics: 'hideous management speak' infused with 'indescribable grey philistinism' was a description given by one Irish academic (Garvin 2012).

Entrepreneurial as an attitude to engender in the student has deeper ideological significance. It is presented as an addition to the skills cluster judged necessary for an 'employable graduate'. The academic content of degree programmes, already steered toward specific learning outcomes and measureable skills, is no longer considered to be the most important aspect of university education. The aim now is to enhance 'human capital' for the employment market (Lo Bianco 1999; Park and Lo 2012; Holborow 2012b), one aspect of which is to build up a student's entrepreneurial skills. The *entrepreneurial self* as was described in the last chapter is at the heart of neoliberal thinking. However, its promotion in the university has a special function – to promote a neoliberal view of radical individualism, which is linked to a functionalist notion of education deriving from human capital theory. As already noted in Chapter 2, human capital theory drew strong connections between economic growth and levels of education, and argued, from the position of society and employers, that investment in skills acquisition and education paid off in terms of a 'premium' in income earned (Becker 1962). As the theory developed, the focus shifted to the potential economic gain for the individual. If the individual was willing to 'invest' in themselves (Ward 2012: 140) in re-training, up-skilling, including acquiring entrepreneurial skills, this would improve the individual's prospects for success on the labour market. Human capital theory in the 2000s moved centre stage in education policy and became the term which both seemed to complement the increasing emphasis on the 'knowledge economy' and justify expanding higher education. The 'age of human capital' (Becker 2002: 3) had arrived and higher education was targeted as its chief enabler.

The OECD single-mindedly endorses this view of education. In a candid piece, entitled *The OECD and Education: An Evolving Narrative of Human Capital*, it admits:

> From its inception, the OECD has stressed the importance of human competencies for economic and social development. The organisation [brought]

112 *Austerity and the entrepreneurial university*

> emerging theories of human capital then being developed by Gary Becker, Theodore Schultz ... centre-stage in the international dialogue. Hard evidence to substantiate these theories did not emerge, however, until the 1980s when work on endogenous growth theories ... formulated and tested ... the positive associations between growth at the national level and crude indicators of human capital, especially educational attainment.
>
> (OECD 2011: 16)

The OECD acknowledges its role as a trail blazer for human capital thinking and openly admits that its considerable resources can be mobilized to carry its message or, as it declares, 'international benchmarks can help make reform happen' (2011: 19). In the more competitive context of recession, the OECD states, 'countries can no longer afford to measure their education systems against national standards and today the Organisation is better equipped than ever to both track and support its role to match education with economic development' (OECD 2011: 20). The promotion of entrepreneurial talent has now become a pivotal term both in relation to economic recovery, and to the 'knowledge economy'. Possession of entrepreneurial skills is presented as the key to be able to compete favourably on the global labour market.

Being 'entrepreneurial' as the OECD suggests, is about extending entrepreneurialism to a wide range of roles and 'changing mind-sets'. Being on campus is not only about formally following degrees but is taken to include a range of 'co-curricular' activities which takes the life of an entrepreneurial student well beyond studies *per se*. For every entrepreneurial student once classes are over, as one promoter of campus entrepreneurial networks explains, 'there are coding languages to be learnt, jobs to be sought, and enterprises to be founded'. The entrepreneur mindset should mean students 'appreciating every minute that they have in college before it's too late' ... using 'free hours to learn how to code with HTML, CSS, JavaScript, and jQuery', be an 'an event planner working with companies to plan conferences', get extra jobs on campus, like being a 'social-media ambassador' or a 'special-events video recorder'. Students need to make use of 'the full 168 hours in a week to apply for jobs and focus on gaining new skills'. Crucially, 'entrepreneurship says you don't have to be looking for a job. You can be creating a job.' Advocates of campus entrepreneurship, the article shows, share this perspective: 'Acquiring the knowledge, skills and competencies (learning outcomes) required will support their entrepreneurial activity in employment including self-employment' (Humphries 2014) and partaking in entrepreneurial activities on campus can point the way to creating a job for yourself.

The merits of *entrepreneurship* in terms of actual outcomes for students living amid a deep recession are rather less obvious than these glowing accounts would suggest. First, and most disturbingly, a large number of Irish graduates, rather than finding or creating jobs in Ireland, emigrate. While 47% of Irish people aged between 25–34 hold a tertiary qualification of three years or more, 62% of recent Irish emigrants hold the equivalent qualification, suggesting that, following the crash, graduates are over-represented amongst those leaving

(Glynn, Kelly and Éinrí 2013). Furthermore, Ireland's high participation rate in higher education may actually have contributed to Irish graduates experiencing significantly higher levels of youth emigration than other Western European countries affected by the Eurozone crisis. As emigration researchers Glynn, Kelly and Mac Éinrí point out, it may be the possession of extra skills that makes Irish graduates choose emigration as an option more frequently than other sections of the working population (2013: 35). Such facts show that accounts which claim that student *entrepreneurship* can build the Irish – as opposed to the global – economy are very wide off the mark.

Second, entrepreneurial skills as a route to employment is misleading because it ignores how current economic conditions have affected employment for graduates. As indicated in the last chapter, people who set up their own businesses still constitute a small percentage of the population.[15] Phillip Brown and Hugh Lauder, in their research on the subject (2012), show that highly skilled graduates on the global jobs market are underpaid and are not using their knowledge and skills to the full; if and when they do find employment, they are being paid less than a graduate might have expected to receive two decades ago. Even OECD studies on graduate unemployment admit that a key current feature is the lack of progression in Ireland from education to work. One such study shows that graduate unemployment rose by 5 per cent to almost 9 per cent, compared with an OECD average of 7 per cent (OECD 2013), and this figure does not include those graduates who have emigrated.

Third, while higher levels of pay might reasonably be expected for more educated and skilled labour, this is not the same as equating those higher rates of pay with a proportionate return on the effort a student has spent on upskilling in general and acquiring entrepreneurial skills in particular. For the vast majority of graduates their skills are put to use in a context of work that they have no control over, let alone one which allows them to demonstrate an entrepreneurial bent – except, perhaps, in the sense that they will be required to flexibly adapt to their employers' needs. Apart from a thin layer of graduates who will end up in high paid managerial positions, the vast majority can only realize the higher value of those skills by working for capital under conditions of exploitation such that it is, in the end, capital that reaps the benefit from the employee's varied and extensive skills not the possessor of 'human capital'. The trend across the industrial world of labour's declining share of overall output (despite significant productivity increases) confirms how little highly skilled workers benefit from their more sophisticated skills (Harvey 2014: 185). Irish statistics show the same decline in the share going to labour (Sweeney 2013). In other words, the social relations within which employment takes place limits considerably any potential wage premium for the possession of higher skills or for the potential for *entrepreneurial* thinking.

These stark realities which run counter to the official themes of student *entrepreneurship* highlight their ideological nature. The neoliberal revival of this word has the intention of covering over the significance of class differences and making it seem that we, as individuals, are all responsible for whether we are employed or not, and how much we get paid. If a person has not made the

114 *Austerity and the entrepreneurial university*

choice to equip oneself with entrepreneurial skills then, so the narrative goes, she has only herself to blame if she finds herself in a poorly paid job or out of work. Promoting entrepreneurial thinking among students pinpoints individual talent as the primary explanation for securing better paid employment and thereby deflects the crisis in jobs away from social causes to individual ones.

Universities and ideology

If international think tanks play a role in standardizing neoliberal keywords such as *enterprise* and *entrepreneurial*, the university itself substantially contributes to giving currency and social standing to neoliberal keywords. Critiques of the neoliberal university often centre on economic aspects and transformations of the university – its increasing corporatization, its involvement in market-like behaviours, its production of knowledge workers for a knowledge economy, its replication of the social division of labour of capitalist production (Gill 2009; Harvie 2004; Rhoades and Slaughter 2009; Washburn 2005). But, as Panagiotis Sotiris (2012) points out, the entrepreneurial university incorporates both material and ideological factors.

> Education is not a factory – or it is not only a factory. University remains a hegemonic apparatus, a condensation of practices and rituals that has to do with social reproduction, practices and conceptions.
>
> (Sotiris 2012: 118)

Universities are privileged sites for the reproduction of dominant ideology in a variety of ways. They are managed and still considerably financed by the national state. Organizations such as the OECD may play an important role in the transmission of neoliberal keywords but the national state gives them the official *imprimatur*. The state is the chief enabler of the reform agenda and, in Ireland, as elsewhere, the marketization of higher education has been the result of state initiatives. Financial profiling, quality assurance, changes in accreditation and the skills focus, have all taken place under the direction and surveillance of the state or its advisory bodies. In Ireland, the monitoring role of the HEA is evidence of increased regulatory functions adopted by state agencies.

In the case of neoliberalism, university economic departments have played a powerful role in the promulgation of the ideology. The University of Chicago has historically been one of the most prominent, but Mirowski (2013) lists others such as the London School of Economics, St Andrews University, the Virginia School and George Mason University which have, at various times, given extensive public airing to neoliberalism. During this crisis, Mirowski (2013: 52) argues, many economic departments closed ranks to 'foster intellectual exchange' among neoliberal allies', and 'pursue stable objectives and repetitive arguments' which allowed neoliberalism to hold its unexpected strength in the current crisis. In Ireland too, economists in the academy, despite many of them singularly failing to see the crash coming, have continued to see their interpretations dominate public debate of the crisis, with some labelling economists as the 'new secular priesthood' of modern Ireland (Allen 2009: 125).

Sotiris argues that Gramsci's concepts of the 'integral state' and the notion of the 'hegemonic apparatus' offer the possibility to rethink the university not in an 'either educational factory or Ideological State Apparatus' manner, but 'as a complex site of struggles for hegemony, in all its aspects including the combination of leadership, representation, domination and consent' (Sotiris 2012: 119). Universities have always been important sites of ideological legitimization of prevailing ideas about education, class, national culture and language. Academics have easy access to the media and constitute important opinion formers. University education also serves to perpetuate existing social inequalities, through what Bourdieu (2000: 41) called 'scholastic enclosure' and 'academic elitism'. In Ireland 'scholastic enclosure' has been manifest in the traditional overrepresentation of the higher social groups in universities, a phenomenon which helped to cement the comfortable relationship between universities and the political class and the relative absence of independent-thinking public intellectuals (Clancy 2007; Corcoran and Lalor 2012).

More recently, as higher education has been opened up to wider social layers, the official ideological leitmotiv of Irish universities, championed by a new crop of CEO-style university presidents, is the unreserved endorsement of market capitalism. This belief is articulated less as a committed position and more as a practical and rational – and supposedly unideological – interpretation based on common sense, economic realities, a mere adaption to the new cash-strapped times. The process of ideological legitimization within the university is diffuse and, as Sotiris points out, can also be a product of the university's economic functions. A research project, financed by a private corporation is not only a step further towards the commodification of university research, 'it can also lead to the reproduction of a competitive, market-oriented conception of science, to the ideological justification of capitalist imperatives, to the establishment of more precarious labour relations within Universities' (Sotiris 2012: 120). Similarly, the opening up of university research to private corporations, and their logos prominently displayed on university buildings, embeds an entrepreneurial culture on campus. Rising fees for students, highly competitive applications for research grants, prizes for 'excellence' awarded for every conceivable activity, all have the ideological effect of promoting market competitive norms and radical individualism among students and academic staff. In this way the dominant ideology suffuses university campuses, determines the titles of modules and degrees, hangs in the air of faculty meetings and shapes the choice of language.

Universities, as institutions of learning and of social privilege, instil social styles and attitudes and ways of speaking which together constitute a powerful momentum towards conformity. *Enterprise* and *entrepreneurial* and other such neoliberal keywords take on what Andrew Vincent calls a 'magical conjuring status' which 'deployed in institutional academic discourse trumps all comers and demand verbal obeisance' (Vincent 2011: 335). Articulated with a new vigour after the economic crisis, against the backcloth of sharp reductions of public

116 *Austerity and the entrepreneurial university*

funding, this pursuit of ideological hegemony contains elements of Peck's (2014) characterization of a conscious strategy of displacement: it re-narrates universities as economically inefficient institutions in order to effect a redistribution of funds from public to private sources. The severe economic crisis creates a psychological climate which facilitates the imposition of neoliberal thinking, the effect and intensity of which resemble something akin to a 'shock block doctrine' (Mirowski 2013: 28). Fraser, Murphy and Kelly (2013) have described Ireland's 'deepening neoliberalism' as achieved through the never ending uncertainty created by the social effects of the crisis. The 'uninterrupted disturbance' of the crisis (2013: 48), felt acutely in the university by students and staff alike, allows opposition to neoliberalism to be muted and is used by the 'austerity pushers' (Peck 2014) to drive through the reorganization of higher education.

Critique and resistance

In order to uncover the ideological significance of the use of *enterprise* as used in the official documents of higher education, as I have attempted to show, it is important to interweave questions of political economy and social agency into the analysis. Conceptualizing the social aspects of language must involve an explicit model of the relation between phraseology, speech acts, texts and text-types to social institutions. This means relating things of different scales in time and place and a focus on ideological keywords, as Michael Stubbs acknowledges, can incorporate this dimension. They are words which 'relate to the world' and more broadly and epistemologically, are instances of the relationship of language to society (Stubbs 2010: 21) and have the imprints of social agency. Such words, similar to Volosinov's characterization of verbal-ideological signs, can be 'tips of icebergs: pointers to complex lexical objects which represent the shared beliefs and values of a culture' (Stubbs 2010: 21–22). They are 'binding' words which are 'significant and indicative for certain forms of thought' (Williams 1985: 15; see also Holborow 2012a).

This approach departs from discourse-centered analyses to language and power as articulated within applied and socio-linguistics. Because these have highlighted issues of social power and ideology, it is worth singling out two strands in this thought to assess their capacity to provide a social view of language and their potential concerning paths to critique and resistance.

The first strand falls loosely under the category of Critical Discourse Analysis (CDA) and has included studies of corporate, business and neoliberal language in the university. Following Norman Fairclough's work on the subject (Fairclough 1992, 2007, 2010), Gerlinde Mautner (2005, 2010) and Andrea Mayr (2008) have addressed the spread of corporate discourse in the university although they make only passing reference to wider economic or ideological forces. Mautner notes 'neoliberal agenda of deregulation' (Mautner 2010: 220) but theorizes the marketization of language in terms of an 'interdiscursive alignment' in which business is the 'dominant subsystem' that exerts pressure on other 'subsystems', such as education and health. Management- or business-speak is assumed to

Austerity and the entrepreneurial university   117

form part of a vaguely defined 'creeping enterprise culture' (Mayr 2008: 26–29), but the reasons behind the development of this culture are not discussed. Yet the marketization of language explained in terms of the formal pressures of 'discourse alignment' or of conformity to a trend underestimates the social forces at play. The sheer global uniformity of the adoption of business language, on websites and documents of universities across the English-speaking world, points to orchestrated strategies of legitimization rather than a random wave of changing mind-sets.

Discourse analyses of the marketization of language have been much influenced by the work of Norman Fairclough, who remains an important point of reference in discussion of language and power and ideology (Talbot et al. 2003; Simpson and Mayr 2010). While there is reference to the socio-political context in this work, the marketization of language is seen as part of a wider social development, the more prominent role of discourse in contemporary capitalism. Thus the analysis centres on discourse as a social force. Fairclough's earlier work was important because it drew attention to the language of New Labour which he rightly identified as marking a political departure from traditional social democracy in its use of 'a new political discourse which combine[d] elements from Thatcherite Conservative discourse with elements of communitarian and social democratic discourses' (Fairclough 2010: 171). But New Labour's turn he saw as part of a new social configuration in which 'the complex realities of power relations were condensed in discourse' (2010: 4). The power of discourse he saw as arising from the 'information' and 'knowledge-based society', which conferred discourse with special power, with discourse 'materially grounded and materially promoted' (2010: 506) assuming a formative role in this new form of capitalism. While Fairclough's claim was that discourse and society are 'dialectically relational', in practice the principal actors were 'discursive relations' and 'orders of discourse', and social relations and the social order mere background noise, never concretely analysed nor its specific social agents identified.

For example, Fairclough (2007) described the discursive and semiotic effects of the marketization of higher education in terms of its 're-spacialization' and 're-scaling' which involved taking the neoliberal social landscape as given. He makes uncritical use of neoliberal descriptions of the globalized, 'knowledge-based economy' (2007: 135). For example, quoting approvingly Anthony Giddens (perhaps one of the most influential supporters of social liberalism in the late 1990s)[16] in connection with his identification of 'negotiation through dialogue', 'self-reflexivity' and 'promotional language' as the determining characteristics of our 'post-traditional age' (Fairclough 2010: 97–100). His study of the marketization of language in the university – consisting of the 'informalisation' of society, the 'conversationalisation' of discursive practices, the 'increased reflexivity' of contemporary life (2010: 118) – is seen as confirmation that there has been 'a reconstitution of hegemony', along the lines outlined by Giddens. Fairclough does raise caveats around 'the imaginary for and the partial reality of a knowledge based economy' and 'a global economy', but in conceding that there is a 'heightened significance for discourse', even that 'much is discourse driven' today (2010: 13),

118 *Austerity and the entrepreneurial university*

Fairclough appears to endorse the dominant neoliberal view that communication and information technology drive societies independently of the specific configurations of social relations. While making the call for the need to resist neoliberal discourse, the theoretical tools he deploys do not allow the dynamic of social relations to come into view. What Fairclough describes as the 'ideological legitimisation engineered by market discourse' (2007: 137), makes discourse, rather than social forces, the source of ideological hegemony. Wider social questions of political economy, of class, or of the role of higher education in capitalism, while sometimes formally noted, do not form a central component of the analysis with the result that 'a restructured hegemony' in 'the order of discourse' in the university (2010: 118) comes to occupy all available social space.

A later study, by Norman Fairclough and Ruth Wodak (2010), which specifically deals with discourse in higher education, is illustrative of how an overpowering presence of discourse practices can crowd out social developments. Their study aims to evaluate the implementation of the Bologna process through 'a detailed discourse-analytic study of the "recontextualisation processes of policy documents"' (2010: 19) in Austria and Romania. 'Recontextualisation' and 'operationalised' are core analytical terms in their analysis, although it is not always clear whether these processes are discursive or social. Discourse practices appear to have supplanted social events. In some instances, it is 'election pressures' in local situations which is seen as an example of the 'relations of recontextualisation' for the Bologna process (2010: 22). In others, 'recontextualisation' refers purely to inter-textual 'relations', as when describing the different emphases of the Austrian University Act and the National Report (2010: 30). When the 'discourses have not been operationalised', as noted in the implementation of the Bologna Process in Romania, it is suggested that Romanian society and its resistance to quality assurance modes will simply have to catch up, 'because it is difficult to see how universities can survive otherwise in a higher education *market* which they are thrown into willy-nilly' (2010: 36), a formulation which could be interpreted as an endorsement of neoliberal policies. These contradictions flow from the blurring of the distinction between 'discourse operationalisation' and actual policy implementation, and misconstruing textual representation as social change.

Locating ideology in language need not be taken to mean language is equivalent to social power, or that discourse is at the centre of social relations. But this assumption is often made, with discourse relations – often without distinct social subjects – seen as enacting social power (Fairclough 1992; O'Halloran 2011). This ambiguous formulation tended to lead to the interpretation – although not Fairclough's – that discourse had incorporated, or even replaced, ideology.[17] Such views, extrapolated from Fairclough's more complex characterization of discourse 'inculcation' (Fairclough 2007), maintained that 'hegemonic discourses' were tantamount to individuals fully 'internalising neoliberal or other narratives' (for example, Mesthrie et al. 2009: 316). One account of hegemony through language describes it as 'representations which inculcate identities, beliefs and behaviours confirming the practices and discourses of the ruling group' (quoted in Simpson and Mayr 2010: 3). The discourse/social fusion, expressed as both

Austerity and the entrepreneurial university   119

having 'relations' and 'practices', seemed to invite parallels with Marxist categories of political economy but, as I have argued elsewhere (Holborow 2012c), these formulations were rather short on theoretical elaboration of the implications of discourse domination on the exercise of power in capitalist society.

A discourse-centered view of society presents difficulties when it comes to resistance. Ben Rampton (1995: 243) argues that the main weakness of Fairclough's notion of discourse relations constituting the central hub of social power, that 'all power is expressed in texts' is one of political irrelevance. Pressing discursive practices on to the same plane as non-discursive practices elides the distinction between thought and reality. It projects, as Terry Eagleton has noted, a way of understanding an object onto the object itself and thereby succumbs to an idealism (and 'academicism') in which 'discourse is inflated to the point where it imperialises the whole world' (Eagleton 2007: 19). The more recent claim by Fairclough that the 2008 economic crisis was 'a crisis of discourse', requiring as part of a political strategy a 'Manifesto for Critical Discourse Analysis for a time of crisis' (Fairclough 2010: 13–21), would seem to fall into this trap.[18] Discourse is only part of the present crisis in the sense that it overlaps with descriptions and interpretations of the crisis; it can articulate both dominant neoliberal themes and opposition to them. For discourse analysis to be socially engaged, I believe it needs to make explicit questions of social theory of political economy. Rather than collapsing power into discourse or constructing political progammes around 'discourse relations', it needs to theorize the connections of language to ideology and the social world and how language is interwoven, in an unstable relationship, with actual social forces in the real world.

The second strand within applied linguistic and education theory which has dealt with neoliberalism and language might be categorized as Foucault-inspired versions. These prioritize the notion of subjectivity in the discourses of neoliberalism. The presence of entrepreneurialism in the university, in these accounts, is seen in subjective terms, as the expression not of social forces than of individual subjectivities. Stephen Ball, for example, following Peck's early description (2003) of neoliberalism that is '"in" our heads as well as "in" the economy', takes neoliberalism to be 'the reciprocal relations that exist between state and subjectivity' (Ball 2013: 128). The focus is on the individual, seen here to be the distillation and the embodiment of social relations, a 'molecular' fraction of capital (2013: 132). In an article on the neoliberal university Ball argues that neoliberalism gets into 'our minds and our souls, into the ways in which we think about what we do' and that it 'is "in here" as well as "out there"' (Ball 2012: 20). Interestingly Ball's account deals very fully with the effects of infrastructural economic developments such as the off-shore university and the privatization practices by British universities. However, his stated emphasis is on individual self as the site for neoliberal 'performativity' and 'commitment' (Ball 2013). The Foucauldian view that neoliberalism represented the reorganization of social relations around individual self-control – a set of practices through which we establish a relationship to ourselves, and create ourselves as subjects, 'a technology of living' and the 'care of the self' (Foucault 2008). Ball uses language as an example of how neoliberalism works through individuals. Neoliberalism 'is realised through very mundane ways in our institutions of everyday life and thus it "does us" – speaks and acts through our language, purposes and social relations' (2013: 131). Looking at neoliberalism as it appears in language highlights the limits of seeing social power through the prism of the individual; paradoxically such a view sees the individual as the source of social power and the victim of it. This conceptualization of society throws into question conceptions about how societies are run and also about the possibility of resistance.

Yet the question of social, rather than individual, agency cannot be ignored in understanding the presence of neoliberal ideology including linguistic neoliberalism, in the universities. Discourse-centred analyses tend to cede transformative powers to discursive acts. Discourses are treated as literal forms of social power when in fact discourses, even when articulated from powerful positions in society, are seldom swallowed whole. A distinction needs to be made between public discourses circulating through powerful official channels and the ways in which this speech is received, perceived or identified, and the possibility that interpretations of the discourse may go against, however inchoately, the grain of dominant ideologies. Carl John Way Ng's study of 'corporate brand enactment' in Singaporean universities (2013) provides an interesting commentary on how multimodal representations of students are moulded into the model of the neoliberal hyperactive individual agent, but he assumes that ideology, thus 'semioticised', is the same as its full acceptance. It is claimed that the corporate ethos fully fashions the 'individual "subjectivities" and "co-opts brand recipients"' (2013: 2). Any interpretation of the message that is not in full accordance with the corporate image promoted by the university is discounted. The 'effective transmission' of the message is taken to mean that overall 'corporate brand enactment is achieved', although no actual evidence of student or staff commitment to the neoliberal message is provided. From this, we are pulled towards the conclusion that 'brand recipients' have made themselves 'amenable to the workings of capital', which in turn 'helps to sustain the prevailing neoliberal order' (2013: 1) – which is quite a leap. Ng describes official government policy which accords universities the role of drivers of economic development and the disciplinary modernization of an oppressive paternalist state (2013: 2), but these factors do not appear to influence in any way the 'semantic enactment' of the same values in the study, for it is the individual brand recipients themselves, not broader social issues or tensions, that sustain the existing state of affairs.[19] This interpretation locates power in a putative micro-mental interiority rather than in any larger social forces, thereby, ironically, rendering social critique, the starting point of the study, redundant.

The trend towards discourse centeredness, as this last example indicates, explains perhaps why applied and socio-linguists have been ill-equipped to take a leading role in opposing neoliberal language in the university. Guy Cook (2012), whose study has already been referred to, noted the surprising fact that linguists appeared to have little to say about business language in the university.

The use of what he terms 'PR' language has taken place, he claims, at the behest of communication 'experts', charged with presenting universities in a market-friendly way. We might have expected applied linguistics to have been well positioned to address specifically these language-political issues, owing to its avowed engagement with interdisciplinarity and concern with 'real world problems' (Cook 2012: 31). But this has patently not been the case. Indeed, Cook states that

> we – applied linguists – do as we are told. We have in effect developed two ways of speaking, one which adheres to the rigour and thoughtfulness which characterises our discipline and one which meekly accepts the other way of speaking.
>
> (Cook 2012: 37)

He calls for 'independent analysis and critique', 'a rational counter-current and dissent from academics who should stop "meekly falling into step behind a government directive"' (2012: 41). Cook's call to action opens the way to a different approach to that of CDA or micro-subjectivity models. While 'rationality' and 'informed dissent' may not provide the necessary analytical tools to take on neoliberal ideology (which claims to have these attributes as well)[20] nor uncover the socio-political elements supporting the transformation occurring in higher education, the case for active resistance needs to be made.

Resistance has to start from the standpoint that discourse practices cannot be made blandly equivalent to, or somehow stand in for, social practice. Language, words, and discourse genres must be seen as social activities woven into and inseparable from social existence and conditions. Power relations in language are of a different nature than those in society because linguistic expression is dynamic, contradictory, unpredictable and with no guarantees. Social relations condition and determine discourses in various ways and those with power can use their social leverage, via their own socially dominant channels of communication, to drive forward the articulation of their world view but they cannot be sure that their message will be received as conceived. In order to unpick the ideological content of any language emanating from the ruling class of a society, it is necessary to identify the link between that language and the specific social world that it seeks to represent, including its distortions of reality which have the potential to undermine its hegemony. To grasp how ideology is condensed in certain expressions, it is necessary to see language not as a discursive practice within its own constraints – an 'order of discourse' – but as an utterance which responds to a social order and is fragilely suspended in a social conjuncture. Even written discourses are not finished entities as they depend on an audience for their meaning to be complete. Its complete immersion in social relations allows the word, as Vološinov (1973: 19) noted, 'to register all the transitory, delicate, momentary phases of social change'. In order to uncover the specific ideological elements, instead of turning inwards to the discursive

122   *Austerity and the entrepreneurial university*

mechanisms themselves, we need 'to trace the social life of the sign' (1973: 19), to follow the threads that tie that utterance, with all its ambiguities, to its social world.

Conclusion

In this chapter I have traced the source of the neoliberal keyword *enterprise* to influential think tanks and to Irish state bodies. My argument has been that the presence of neoliberal keywords in the public channels of higher education can be inserted into a wider political project whose aim is to represent the workings of society as an agglomeration of market competitive individuals and, in the aftermath of the crisis, to bolster the entrepreneurial individual as a means of deflecting the social and systemic causes of the crisis. The themes which I have argued may be summarized thus.

Social agency

Social agency – in the form of the OECD, the state and the university – is decisive in the promotion of neoliberal keywords. The uniformity and spread of the language used is evidence of a concerted discourse strategy devised on the part of powerful social actors and which seeks to convey a certain ideology in language interactions in the university. It is a top-down process which, to reorder Peck's (2003) phrase, emanates from the 'out there' rather more than the 'in here'. It is the official language of the university, used in documents and in formal meetings and constitutes a *management-speak* used most by senior academics and administrators.

However, while there may be certain pressures towards conformity to this discourse, these may be less strong in some settings and also undermined by conflicting attitudes to the discourse. 'Seeking partnerships with enterprise' may be said in a faculty meeting by department heads or senior academics but possibly not when conversing among themselves or, if they do, may well find ways of distancing themselves from it (for example, gesturing 'scare' quotes). Furthermore, the use of these neoliberal keywords may be somewhat cynically viewed as the speaker seeking an opportunity to identify with university management, or with other career concerns, but not necessarily as indicative of a strong commitment to the message.

A growing amount of literature would indicate that the present neoliberal hegemony within the university and the discourse with which it is expressed is met with unease, if not outright hostility (Bailey and Freeman 2011; Calhoun 2006; Collini 2012; Deem et al. 2007; Gallagher 2013; Harvie 2004; Head 2010; Walsh 2012; Vincent 2011). Neoliberalism, if these accounts are anything to go by, falls well short of neoliberalism 'speaking and acting through our language'. When the language is objected to as part of a general critique of the privatization of universities, it is met with a sympathetic response (Holborow 2013) and critiques of neoliberal language are often an integral part of campaigns to defend the public university (Bailey and Freeman 2011; Holmwood 2014; Gallagher 2013; Walsh 2012; see also http://defendtheuniversity.ie).

The university itself is instrumental in the diffusion of neoliberal language. Sotiris argues that that the entrepreneurial university should be seen as 'the condensation of class strategies related to the imperatives of hegemony in a period of capitalist restructuring' (Sotiris 2012: 121). The university is both a legitimizer of ruling ideas and also a site of challenge to them. Neoliberals as our account shows, aware of the value of ideological hegemony in the university, strive to make neoliberal keywords common currency. If it is believed that the presence of neoliberal language constitutes our 'subjectivities', if social agency is deflected on to the individual, then challenge to ideological hegemony is also deflected and weakened. A challenge to the neoliberal university must be a collective project: organized campaigns but also directly taking issue with the ideological themes of neoliberalism, including the normalization of neoliberal keywords.

Ideology and political project

There is no denying that the use of neoliberal keywords is widespread and widely used – something which is a given starting point of this study – but to recognize that neoliberalism is hegemonic is not to say that we have all imbibed it or that we are fully committed to its principles. As noted by Mirowski (2013: 92), treating 'the neoliberal self as a monolithic cultural iron cage' ignores the fact that 'many people are sufficiently reflexive that they can and do catch glimpses of worlds outside the neoliberal ambit'.

Keywords such as *enterprise* as discussed here provide can provide an opening into the discussion of ideological hegemony and resistance. *Enterprise*, as I have shown, is an ideological sign that is a repository of ideology, but whose meaning is not settled nor fixed. Ideology is transitorily embedded in keywords, because the force of their meaning depends on their social context. They can both represent ideological hegemony and also, depending on contextual and social factors, ideological vulnerability. Hegemony represents a complex social, political and ideological process, not a stable state of fact and similarly ideological hegemony, as will be explained in more detail in the next chapter, contains contradictory elements which make it dependent on events and developments in the social world and thus potentially open to challenge.

The meanings of a neoliberal keyword such as *enterprise* are, as I have shown, neither fixed nor static. It expresses the tensions of its social content and of what I have termed here its social voice. It has become ideologically laden in that it promotes radical individualism of neoliberal thinking but it is also part of a political project which aims to protect the interests of capital through the social and economic crisis. As used in higher education, *enterprise* points strategically towards targeting private income streams to replace public funding while *entrepreneurial* captures a human capital view of education which treats students mainly as individual competitors on the job market. The endurance of these keywords depends ultimately on the degree to which they measure up to their

124 *Austerity and the entrepreneurial university*

promises. They represent specific ideological inventions whose currency and value depend on a credible relationship with the social world they inhabit.

Keywords as ideological-verbal signs

Volosinov's description of the word as an ideological sign, 'the most sensitive index of social change' and potentially 'a fully-fledged ideological product' captures some the dynamic of neoliberal keywords. Keywords as ideologically contentious signs, or 'nodal points' in discourse (Žižek 1989: 87), can provide a pathway into ideological analysis and critique. When neoliberal keywords such as *enterprise* are understood as having an existential relationship to specific socio-economic contexts and articulating the view of specific social classes, then the theoretical grounds of critique are provided. As Kenneth McGill states, these keywords can be considered as 'specific ideological terms which help to justify and secure dominant interests and whose presence simultaneously presupposes not only a particular referential content, but also the community which stereotypically interprets this content' (McGill 2013). Identification of the ideological content of these keywords, their role in a particular social moment and how their ideological aspirations measure up to actual social relations, events and developments can unravel the accepted common sense of their meanings and open avenues to alternatives views.

Reference has been made in this chapter to the fact that applied linguistics has a special role to play in not only describing and critiquing the language of neoliberalism, but also challenging it. The theoretical underpinning of such an approach lies in a rounded social view of language which attempts to incorporate social agency into an understanding of the use of keywords in official discourse. Neoliberal keywords that appeared to have gained consensus can be contested by participants in the language event. This arises, not as a result of the specialist insights of critical discourse analysts, but from the social nature of language itself. This inherently social and creative quality of language was summarized by Bakhtin:

> The speech act is by its nature social. The word is not a tangible object but an always shifting, always changing means of social communication. It never rests with one consciousness, one voice. Its dynamism consists in a movement from speaker to speaker, from one context to another, from one generation to another. Through it all, the word does not forget its path of transfer and cannot completely free itself from the power of those concrete contexts into which it has entered. … the word enters our context from another context, permeated with the intentions of other speakers.
>
> (Quoted in Titunik 1973: 199)

The challenge for applied linguistics today is to engage critically with the use of neoliberal language in the university and to refocus on the dynamic, social nature of language which, it is argued here, requires the inclusion of political economy analysis and a re-theorization of ideology in relation to language.

Notes

1 Bait-and-switch is a term used in retailing to describe the fraud of sellers getting customers to buy what they wouldn't normally consider buying. Shoppers are 'baited' into supermarkets by advertisements for very low-priced products but, once in the store, they discover that the advertised goods are not on the shelves and they are persuaded, by in-store promotions, to buy (switch to) similar but higher-priced goods.

2 The smaller top 0.5 per cent increased from 3.5 per cent to 7.5 per cent. Michael Taft notes that when the crash hit, due to the property and market crash, the income shares of the top 1 per cent and 0.5 per cent fell slightly but by 2009 this had stabilized and, in the case of the top 10 per cent, started to increase. The Irish wealthy make less than those in the UK but more than the top 1 per cent in other countries (Taft 2011).

3 The two governments were the government led by Fianna Fáil in coalition with the Green Party, who with the support of Sinn Fein, agreed to the bank guarantee, and the following one, led by Fine Gael in coalition with Labour, whose policies were based on accepting its terms.

4 In the National Recovery Plan 2011–14 the word enterprise is used 63 times (http:// www.budget.gov.ie/The%20National%20Recovery%20Plan%202011–14.pdf, accessed 15th December 2014).

5 John Hennessy was the first non-civil servant to hold this post and continues to hold the chairmanship of a holdings company of Ericsson. See http://www.hea.ie/content/ hea-board-members (accessed 15th December 2014).

6 See http://www.ryanacademy.ie/about (accessed 15th December 2014). Tony Ryan was one of the founders of Ryanair.

7 'Business angels' means informal private investors who invest capital in companies during their early stage of development but who also, unlike their name would suggest, are guaranteed a share in any profits made in the company in which they invest.

8 See Chapter 5 for an account of the high profile of enterprise in Ireland and the associations it has.

9 The 'new spirit of capitalism' is used by Boltanski and Chiapello (2005) to describe the dominant ideology which attempts to channel individual experience through a multifaceted consumerist matrix. They see the spirit of capitalism as both legitimizing the system and constraining it, a subject which is discussed further in the concluding chapter.

10 Guy Cook's study of PR language in the British university notes a similar trend. It amounts to a 'government-enabled business stranglehold' on British universities (Cook 2012: 39) and represents the present-day equivalent of the 'propaganda of totalitarian regimes' for whom 'all news is good news, every harvest a bumper harvest, and all workers are happy' (2012: 36).

11 Stefan Collini describes well the predictable glibness of this language: 'I work in the knowledge and human resources industry. My company specialises in two kinds of product: we manufacture high-quality, multi-skilled units of human capacity; and we produce commercially relevant, cutting-edge new knowledge in user-friendly packages of printed material ... We compete in the global market place and our brand-recognition scores are high. The company's name is HiEdBiz plc. and its motto is "World-class products at rock-bottom prices"' (Collini 2012: 132).

12 This strident uniformity rules out any local linguistic variation. For example, in Irish reports the term traditionally used to describe higher education in Ireland – 'third level education' – is simply ignored and 'higher education' used throughout these reports.

13 This amount was deducted directly from the pay of those working in the public service, over a series of budgets after 2009. It does not include salary reductions in terms of spending power over the period.

126 *Austerity and the entrepreneurial university*

14 In the overall drive to 'resource maximization' and 'value for money', university administrations have increasingly adopted corporate management methods of management and with conditions of work for all staff in the university becoming increasingly restructured according to performance outcomes, productivity income generation and top-down surveillance (Lynch et al. 2012).

15 See Chapter 5.

16 For an account of Giddens's agreement with New Labour's adoption of neoliberalism see Callinicos (1999).

17 For example, Canagarajah and Ben Said (2011).

18 The over-discursive focus that Fairclough provides on the proposed manifesto does not help his case. He suggests that it should include identifying 'the emergence of discourses', 'the contestation and dominance between discourses, the recontextualisation of discourses and the operationalization of discourses' (Fairclough 2010: 19–20).

19 The uncritical use of market language – such as 'brand recipients', 'brand enactment' – further adds to the impression of adaptation. Furthermore, other social tensions that threaten to unravel the supposed market harmony are ignored. For example, the Singaporean Management University (SMU) promotes an image of dynamism to potential students through an image in its brochure which shows the smiling SMU President riding a bike alongside a smiling young male student. The graphic is described as acting as an effective metaphor of relaxed, modern, informality coupled with the notion of moving forward (Ng 2013: 10). No mention is made of the fact that the president is white and the student Asian, a strange omission given its potent to disrupt the bland neoliberal narrative.

20 See Mirowski (2013: 116–20) for an account of how neoliberals lay claim to rationalism, and even anti-authoritarianism, to drive their project forward.

7 Conclusion

Implications for understanding ideology in language

This book has demonstrated, from different perspectives, how ideology and language overlap. Analysing the presence of neoliberal ideology in language has shed light on the dynamic nature of this interdependence but also on the contradictions of the ideology itself.

It has shown that language repackaged discursively as a commodity, as described in the first chapter, articulates a neoliberal view, which converts linguistic skills into a *commodity* available to employers for exploitation in service and other industries. This specific angle of the ideology is also aimed at those who potentially possess the necessary language skills, renamed as *human capital*, which, they are told, will bring them the reward of a higher income. This is presented as a return on the 'investment' in education that they have made although, as explored further in Chapter 4, this promise is seldom fulfilled.

I have also shown how the metaphorical personalization of the market bestows greater powers on markets, and this reinforces the neoliberal notion that markets are to be obeyed. Financial markets, in these metaphorical representations, are frozen into essential things and appear as beyond the reach of human intervention. *Entrepreneur, entrepreneurial* and *entrepreneurship* used across different social settings, as analysed in the two preceding chapters, together constitute an ideological keyword cluster in the narrative of neoliberalism which reconfigures capitalist society as a collection of competing individuals and which naturalizes the *entrepreneurial* view of society. Promotion of *entrepreneurialism* in the socially influential arena of higher education, I have argued, constitutes a two-pronged ideological strategy: to deflect attention away from the causes of the market crash of 2008–9 and as a way of managing, as part of the 'austerity' agenda, a significant reduction in public funding for universities.

These examples have illustrated how neoliberal ideology is articulated in language in different settings. They illustrate the fact that language and ideology are coextensive; both develop in concrete social situations, both involve social dialogue, and both affect social consciousness. The focus on specific neoliberal keywords allows the mechanisms whereby language and ideology merge to become visible and amply confirm Vološinov's observation that 'the word is the ideological phenomenon *par excellence*' (1973: 13).

128 *Understanding ideology in language*

But this study, while showing how ideology in various ways functions through language, has also maintained that ideology is not identical, nor reducible to language. This is obvious in the sense that different ideological positions may be expressed within the same language and by different speakers or groups of speakers of that language. There is a dynamic to the presence of ideology in language which is subject to constant change. *Entrepreneur*, I have shown, has not always had the same ideological meaning or social significance that it has in the neoliberal world of today. Ideology constitutes an aspect of the social nature of language and, like all meaning in language, is not contained within linguistic form, but is creatively generative and unpredictable. Words reflect and refract social existence, and the exact nature of the interpretation of that social existence depends on the social situation of the speakers and the larger contending social forces of which they are part. Words, Terry Eagleton aptly explains, are 'pulled this way and that by competing social interests, inscribed from within with a multiplicity of ideological accents' (Eagleton 2007: 19). Words, as this study has attempted to show, are an arena of social conflict and have their own social life. Göran Therborn's conception of ideology includes the '"consciousness" of social actors and the institutionalised thought-systems and discourses of a given society' but, he insists, 'to study these as ideology means to look at them from a particular perspective: not as bodies of thought or structures of discourse *per se* but as manifestations of a particular being-in-the-world of conscious actors, of human subjects' (Therborn 1980: 2). The dimension which Therborn seeks to highlight is that which also underpins this study: that ideology is the medium through which people and social classes directly intervene in history to fashion the world 'as conscious actors' (1980: 3). The ideological force of *markets trying to persuade governments how to act*, students presented as *human capital* or universities as *enterprises* derives from powerful social players who are attempting to steer society further in the direction of their neoliberal vision. In this capacity, they '[strive] to fix a supraclass, eternal character to the ideological sign' (Vološinov 1973: 23). But also from the perspective of those engaged in the social dialogue in which these words appear, the response to these ideological keywords is not given or static, but involves the speech participants fashioning meaning as conscious social actors. There are continual clashes over the meanings of words and in this respect, to paraphrase Marx's well-known formulation (Marx 1969: 504), one might say that language is one of 'the ideological forms' in which people 'become conscious of this conflict [of the forces and relation of production] and fight it out'.

Second, while ideology and language overlap, social consciousness exists to different degrees across the different social situations of language. Not all language, rather obviously, is ideological and ideology tends to find its clearest expression in the more complex forms of language. Mikhail Bakhtin (1986) makes the distinction between 'primary genres' and 'secondary genres': a primary genre, is embedded in immediate experience and represents an unmediated form of communication. 'Could you pass the water?' or 'it's half past three' could hardly be regarded, in normal circumstances, to have an ideological dimension.

Within what Bakhtin terms 'secondary genres' exists the 'more complex and comparatively highly developed and organised cultural communication' consisting of 'primarily written genres' and which are more susceptible to expressing general world views. The 'historical formation' of secondary genres, he writes, 'sheds light on the nature of the utterance and above all on the complex problem of the interrelations among language, ideology and world view' (Bakhtin 1986: 62). In other words, the language–ideology interplay exists with different degrees of intensity in language.[1] Vološinov, likewise, saw how social consciousness is expressed in varying measures within language. He identified *meaning* as pertaining to the constituent parts of the whole, or *theme*, and the meaning may have a formal technical denotation that alters when expressed as part of a theme (Vološinov 1973: 101). He also drew attention to the two extreme poles of language, between what he called the 'I-experience' as immediate consciousness, with the 'We-experience' pole containing greater ideological differentiation (1973: 87). As I have shown here, the relationship between complexity of form and expression of ideology is of direct relevance to the appearance of neoliberal keywords in official discourse. The examples of language expressing neoliberal ideology given in this book are taken from written texts to be found mainly in public discourse, such as the print media or on public websites – in other words, in 'secondary genres', in Bakhtin's terms. Ideology is not present with the same intensity across all forms of language, something which over-extensive understandings of language/discourse as ideology cannot satisfactorily explain.

Third, I have shown that neoliberal ideology can be traced to specific social actors and that its force depends on the institutionalization of class power and the material means of production that its promoters have at their disposal. The degree of uniformity of neoliberal keywords in the university, as I have shown, is achieved in written texts through powerful channels of distribution – such as the OECD, EU institutions and state agencies – which are managed, although not always controlled, by the ruling classes in society.[2] The strong presence of neoliberal language in the university is an example of top-down language emitted from powerful social voices along effective and politically influential transmission chains.

This raises the role of social agency in the presence of neoliberal ideology in language, which has been a dominant theme of this book. Neoliberal practices of market rule have come to be understood as originating less from state-imposed policies than from the individual's adoption of certain practices, captured by Michel Foucault's term 'biopower', or a form of power which is regulated through individual behaviour (Foucault 2008). Accounts in this mould, I have shown, have turned the spotlight away from the actions of governments to the conduct of the governed themselves (Barnett 2010; Ball 2013; Marttila 2013). In this trope, neoliberal ideology comes to be understood as a 'neoliberal rationality floating across the political environment' rendering neoliberalism a 'technique of administration' whose prized metaphor is knowledge – enlightening, intangible and highly mobile – and whose goal was the fostering of 'self-actualization and self-entrepreneurship' (Ong 2007: 4). Neoliberalism becomes a normalizing logic

130 *Understanding ideology in language*

which constructs political subjects through various techniques across different 'sites of self-production' from urban spaces, work, consumption and the body (Larner 2000; Hilgers 2010; Peck and Theodore 2012). Power interpreted as 'government of the self', for reasons that given in Chapter 5, remains notably silent on the role of social class in the neoliberal project and, in an echo of neoliberal ideology itself, views neoliberal rule mainly through the prism of the individual. This understanding of power, I argue, limits the options for opposition to neoliberalism. Stephen Ball expresses this limitation when he writes, paraphrasing Nietzsche, 'while we need to understand how these elements and their relations enter into us and encourage us to work on ourselves in a variety of ways we also need to hold firmly onto a sense that we are none of the things we now do, think or desire' (Ball 2012: 26). While the sentiment is one we can relate to, it offers no general pathway towards resisting neoliberalism, save that of individual values or inclination.

Ideology as a social construction and an analytical tool opens broader avenues of critique and resistance. In an earlier work, I summarized ideology in relation to neoliberalism and language in the following way: it is a one-sided representation, articulated from a particular social class but constructed as a world view, part-believed and part rejected, influenced by real-world events and coextensive with language, but distinct from it (Holborow 2012c). This study has built on this approach and explored, in more detail, the contradictory nature of the ideology of neoliberalism as it appears in language. My intent has been to reveal the ideological nature of language by showing how the use of certain neoliberal keywords in official discourse articulates the interests of capital and, in identifying this social bias, to thereby expose the misleading nature of the reasoning. This approach depends on a distinction between the ideological representation of the world and the lived social world, between how society is presented in neoliberal ideology and the real experience of class conflict in the social world. This principle informs my critical method. Mirowski (2013) also characterizes the hallmark of neoliberal thinking as its 'double truths', an ideological trait which he describes in compelling detail. Neoliberal ideology may proclaim the miraculous powers of *entrepreneurship* or the infallibility of the market, but in practice and in complete contradiction to its supposed shibboleths, neoliberal states seek to closely direct the workings of the market. These inconsistencies make the ideology vulnerable. Furthermore, neoliberal ideology will conflict with the immediate experiences of the majority of the population making its 'common sense' seem less plausible.

Finally, the understanding of ideology in language outlined here flows from the predication that meaning in language is interactional and social and that the tensions of meanings within words derive from their social rootedness. Vološinov expressed the dynamic of language when he wrote 'each living ideological sign has two faces, like Janus. Any current curse word can become a word of praise; any current truth must inevitably sound to many other people as the greatest lie' (Vološinov 1973: 23). Meaning is reflected and refracted by an intersection of social interests, which implies that words, while conveying ideological content in a one-sided (or uni-accentual) manner, always have the potential to have their meaning to be overturned. With this in mind, it can be claimed that identifying the presence of neoliberal ideology in language can be understood, alongside practical political movements of resistance, as another dimension to the much needed challenge to neoliberalism.

Notes

1 See Harman (2007) for greater discussion of the different dimensions of language as social consciousness.
2 Which is why Althusser's label of Ideological State Apparatuses appears too rigid and confining. See Eagleton (2007) for a critique of Althusser's position.

References

Abercrombie, N. A. and Turner, B. (1978). The Dominant Ideology Thesis. *British Journal of Sociology, 29* (2), 149–70.

Agha, A. (2011). Commodity Registers. *Journal of Linguistic Anthropology, 21* (1), 22–53.

——(2005). Voice, Footing, Enregisterment. *Journal of Linguistic Anthropology, 15* (1), 38–59.

Albritton, R. (2012). Commodification and Commodity Fetishism. In A. Saad-Fihlo and B. Fine (Eds.), *The Elgar Companion to Marxist Economics* (pp. 66–72). Cheltenham, UK: Edward Elgar Publishing Inc.

——(2003). Superseding Lukács: A Contribution to the Theory of Subjectivity. In R. Albritton and J. Simoulidis (Eds.), *New Dialectics and Political Economy* (pp. 60–78). Basingstoke: Palgrave.

Allen, K. (2009). *Ireland's Economic Crash: A Radical Agenda for Change.* Dublin: The Liffey Press.

——(2007). *The Corporate Takeover of Ireland.* Dublin: Irish Academic Press.

Allen, K. and O'Boyle, B. (2013). *Austerity Ireland.* London: Pluto.

Althusser, L. (2008). *On Ideology* (Trans. B. Brewster). London: Verso.

Arthur, C. J. (1974). Editor's Introduction. In *The German Ideology: Marx and Engels* (pp. 4–34). London: Lawrence and Wishart.

Ashoka. (2014). *Ashoka: Innovators for the Public.* Retrieved 5th April 2014, from Ashoka: https://www.ashoka.org/social_entrepreneur.

Bailey, M. and Freeman, D. (Eds.). (2011). *The Asssault on Universities: A Manifesto for Resistance.* London: Pluto Press.

Bakhtin, M. (1986). *Speech Genres and Other Late Essays* (Trans. V. W. Magee, Ed. T. B. McGee). Austin, TX: University of Texas Press.

——(1981). *The Dialogic Imagination: Four Essays* (Trans. and Ed. C. Emerson and M. Holquist). Austin, TX: University of Texas Press.

Ball, S. J. (2013). *Foucault, Power and Education.* London: Routledge.

——(2012). Performativity, Commodification and Commitment: An I-Spy Guide to the Neoliberal University. *British Journal of Educational Studies, 60* (1), 17–28.

Barnett, C. (2010). Publics and Markets: What's Wrong with Neoliberalism? In S. Smith, S. Marston, R. Pain and J. P. Jones (Eds.), *The Handbook of Social Geographies* (pp. 269–97). London and New York: Sage.

Barthes, R. (1973). *Mythologies* (Trans. Annette Lavers). London: Paladin Books.

References   133

Beaken, M. (2011). *The Making of Language*. Edinburgh: Dunedin.

Beasley-Murray, J. (2000). Value and Capital in Bourdieu and Marx. In N. Brown and I. Szeman (Eds.), *Pierre Bourdieu: Fieldwork in Culture* (pp. 100–119). New York: Rowman & Littlefield Publishers Inc.

Becker, G. (2010). *Lecture 1: Human Capital and Intergenerational Mobility: An Introduction*. Retrieved 14th February 2014 from University of Chicago: http://www.youtube.com/watch?v=QajILZ3S2RE.

——(2002). The Age of Human Capital. In E. P. Lazear (Ed.), *Education in the Twenty-First Century* (pp. 3–8). Palo Alto: Hoover Institution Press. Retrieved 19th December 2014 from: http://media.hoover.org/sites/default/files/documents/0817928928_3.pdf.

——(1992, 9th December). *The Economic Way of Looking at Life (Nobel Lecture)*. Retrieved 16th February 2014 from University of Chicago: http://home.uchicago.edu/gbecker/Nobel/nobellecture.pdf.

——(1962). Investment in Human Capital: A Theoretical Analysis. Part 2: Investment in Human Beings. *Journal of Political Economy, 70* (5), 9–49.

Beckwith, L. (2006). *The Dictionary of Corporate Bullshit: An A to Z Lexicon of Empty, Enraging and Just Plain Stupid Office Talk*. New York: Broadway Books.

Birch, K. and Mykhnenko, V. (2010). *The Rise and Fall of Neo-Liberalism: The Economic Decline of an Economic Order*. London: Zed Books.

Blackledge, A. and Creese, A. (2012). Pride, Profit and Dsictinction: Negotiations across Time and Space. In A. Duchêne and M. Heller (Eds.), *Language in Late Capitalism: Pride and Profit* (pp. 116–42). London: Routledge.

Blackledge, P. (2013). Thinking about (New) Social Movements: Some Insights from the British Marxist Historians. In C. Barker, L. Cox, J. Krinsky and G. Nilsen (Eds.), *Marxism and Social Movements* (pp. 262–76). Amsterdam: Brill.

Block, D. (2014). *Social Class in Applied Linguistics*. London: Routledge.

Block, D. and Cameron, D. (2002). *Globalization and Language Teaching*. London: Routledge.

Block, D., Gray, J. and Holborow, M. (2012). *Neoliberalism and Applied Linguistics*. London: Routledge.

Blommaert, J. (2012). Chronicles of Complexity: Ethnography, Supediversity and Linguistic Landscapes. *Tilburg Papers in Culture Studies, 29*, 1–149.

——(2005). *Discourse*. Cambridge: Cambridge University Press.

Blommaert, J. and Rampton, B. (2011). Language and Superdiversity. *Diversities, 13* (2), 1–21.

Blyth, M. (2013). *Austerity: The History of a Dangerous Idea*. Oxford: Oxford University Press.

Boltanski, L. and Chiapello, E. (2005). *The New Spirit of Capitalism*. London: Verso.

Bottomore, T. L. with Harris, L., Kiernan, V.G. and Miliband, R. (Eds.) (1983). *A Dictionary of Marxist Thought*. Oxford: Basil Blackwell.

Bourdieu, P. (2005). *The Social Structures of the Economy*. Cambridge: Polity.

——(2003). *Firing Back; Against the Tyranny of the Market 2* (Trans. R. Nice, Ed. T. L. Wacquant). New York: The New Press.

——(2000). *Pascalian Mediations* (Trans. R. Nice). Cambridge: Polity Press.

——(1999). *The Weight of the World: Social Suffering in the Contemporary World* (Trans. P. P. Furguson et al.). Cambridge: Polity.

——(1998, December). Utopia of Endless Exploitation: The Essence of Neoliberalism. *Le Monde Diplomatique*. Retrieved 16th August 2014 from: http://mondediplo.com/1998/12/08bourdieu.

134 *References*

——(1991). *Language and Symbolic Power* (Trans. G. Raymond, Ed. J. B. Thompson). Cambridge: Polity.

——(1990). *In Other Words: Essays Towards a Reflexive Sociology* (Ed. T. M. Adamson). Stanford, CA: Stanford University Press.

——(1987). What Makes Social Class? On the Theoretical and Pracatical Existence of Groups. *Berkeley Journal of Sociology, 32*, 1–18.

——(1986). The Forms of Capital. In J. G. Richardson (Ed.), *Handbook of Theory and Research of Education* (pp. 241–58). New York: Greenwood.

——(1979). *Distinction: A Social Critique of the Judgement of Taste* (Trans. R. Nice). Cambridge, MA: Harvard University Press.

Bourdieu, P. and Boltanski, L. (1975). Le fétichisme de la langue. *Actes de la Recherce en Sciences Sociales, 1* (4), 2–32.

Bourdieu, P. and Eagleton, T. (1992, January–February). Doxa and Common Life. *New Left Review, 191*, 111–21.

Boutet, J. (2012). Language Workers: Emblematic Figures of Late Capitalism. In A. Duchêne and M. Heller (Eds.), *Language in Late Capitalism: Pride and Profit* (pp. 207–29). New York: Routledge.

——(2001). La part langagière du travail: bilan et évolution. *Langage et Société., 4*, 17–42.

Braverman, H. (1974). *Labour and Monopoly Capital*. New York: Monthly Review Press.

Brenner, N. J., Peck, J. and Theodore, N. (2010). Variagated Neoliberalization: Geographies, Modalities, Pathways. *Global Nextworks, 10*, 182–222.

British Council (2013). *Corporate Plan 2013–15*. British Council, London. Retrieved 15th August 2014 from: http://www.britishcouncil.org/sites/britishcouncil.uk2/files/corporate-plan-2013–15.pdf.

Brône, G. and Feyaerts, K. (2006). Headlines and Cartoons in the Economic Press: Double Grounding as Discourse Supporting Strategy. In Guido Erreygers and Geert Jacobs (Eds.), *Language Communication and the Economy* (pp. 73–99). Amsterdam and Philadelphia: John Benjamins.

Brown, P. and Lauder, H. (2012). The Great Transformation in the Global Labour Market. *Soundings, 5*, 41–42.

——(2006). Globalisation, Knowledge and the Myth of the Magnet Economy. *Globalisation, Societies and Education, 1* (4), 25–57.

Brown, P., Lauder, H. and Ashton, D. (2011). *The Global Auction: The Broken Promises of Education, Jobs and Incomes*. Oxford: Oxford University Press.

——(2008). *Education, Globalisation and the Knowledge Economy*. London: Teaching and Learning Research Programme. Retrieved 15th December 2014 from: http://www.tlrp.org/pub/documents/globalisationcomm.pdf.

Browne, H. (2013). *The Frontman: Bono (In the Name of Power)*. London: Verso (Counterblasts).

Bunting, M. (2004). *Willing Slaves: How the Overwork Culture is Ruling our Lives*. London: HarperCollins.

Burawoy, M. (2011, 1st February). Learning from the Global Phenomenon of 'Universities in Crises'. *Irish Times*, Opinion Section.

——(2010). Public Institutions and the Public Good, Universities and the Public Sphere. SSRC. Retrieved 12th June 2014 from: http://publicsphere.ssrc.org/burawoy-redefining-the-public-university.

——(1982). *Manufacturing Consent: Changes in the Labour Process under Monopoly Capitalism*. Chicago: University of Chicago.

References 135

Burke, N. (2008, 5th August). Confessions of a Call-Centre Drone. *Irish Independent.* Retrieved 15th December 2014 from: http://www.independent.ie/lifestyle/confessions-of-a-callcentre-drone-26467224.html.

Burke-Kennedy, E. (2011, 31st March). Irish Banks Require an Extra €24 billion Recapitalisation. *The Irish Times.*

Cahill, A. (2013). Austerity Filling the Pockets of Ireland's Richest. *Irish Examiner,* 12th September. Retrieved 15th December 2014 from: http://www.irishexaminer.com/ireland/austerity-filling-the-pockets-of-irelands-richest-242779.html.

Calhoun, C. (2006, May/June). Is the University in Crisis? *Society,* pp. 8–18.

——(2002). *Pierre Bourdieu in Context.* Retrieved 13th January 2014 from: www.nyu.edu/classes/bkg/objects/calhoun.doc.

Callinicos, A. (2012). Contradictions of Austerity. *Cambridge Journal of Economics,* 36 (1), 65–77.

——(2010). *Bonfire of Illusions: The Twin Crises of the Liberal World.* Cambridge: Polity.

——(2006). *The Resources of Critique.* Cambridge: Polity.

——(2003). *An Anti-Capitalist Manifesto.* London: Wiley.

——(1999). Social Theory Put to the Test of Politics: Pierre Bourdieu and Anthony Giddens. *New Left Review, 1* (236), 76–102.

——(1983). *Marxism and Philosophy.* London: Clarendon Press.

Cameron, D. (2005). Communication and Commodification: Global Economic Change in Sociolinguistic Perspective. In G. Erreygers and G. Jacobs (Eds.), *Language, Communication and the Economy* (pp. 9–23). Amsterdam: John Benjamins.

——(2001, 5th November). The Tyranny of Nicespeak. *New Statesman,* pp. 25–27. Retrieved 15th December 2014 from: http://www.newstatesman.com/node/141564.

——(2000). *It's Good to Talk: Living and Working in a Communication Culture.* London: Sage.

Campus Entrepreneurship Enterprise Network. (2014). *Campus Entrepreneurship Enterprise Network (CCEN).* Retrieved 21st July 2014 from Campus Entrepreneurship Enterprise Network: http://www.ceen.ie/library-educators.

Canagarajah, S. and Ben Said, S. (2011). Lingusitic Imperialism. In J. Simpson (Ed.), *The Routledge Handbook of Applied Linguistics* (pp. 388–401). London: Routledge.

Cardillo, D. (2014). *Nursing and Entrepreneurship: Perfect Together.* Retrieved 16th March 2014 from: http://donnacardillo.com/articles/perfect-together.

Castells, M. (2009). *Communication Power.* Oxford: Oxford University Press.

Chandler, D. (2007). *Semiotics: The Basics.* Abingdon: Routledge.

Chiapello, E. and Fairclough, N. (2002). Understanding the New Management Ideology: A Transdisciplinary Contribution from Critical Discourse Analysis and New Sociology of Capitalism. *Discourse and Society, 13* (2), 185–208.

Chilton, P. (2004). *Analysing Political Discourse: Theory and Practice.* London: Routledge.

Chomsky, N. (2012, 30th April) What Next for Occupy? (Naom Chomsky interviewed by Mikal Mamil and Ian Escuela). *The Guardian.* Retrieved 15th December 2014 from: http://www.chomsky.info/interviews/20120530.htm.

Chun, C. W. (2014). Reflexivity and Critical Language Education in Occupy L.A. In J. B. Clark and F. Dervin (Eds.), *Reflexivity in Language and Education: Rethinking Multilingualism and Interculturality* (pp. 172–92). London: Routledge.

——(2009). Contesting Neoliberal Discourse in EAP: Critical Praxis in an IEP Classroom. *Journal of English for Academic Purposes, 8,* 111–20.

136 References

Clancy, P. (2007). Education. In S. O'Sullivan (Ed.), *Contemporary Ireland: A Sociological Map* (pp. 101–20). Dublin: University College Dublin Press.

Clancy, P., O'Connor, N. and Dillon, K. (2010). *Mapping the Golden Circle*. Dublin: TASC.

Clark, J. (2013). *The True Cost of Austerity and Equality: Ireland a Case Study*. Crowley: Oxfam International. Retrieved 17th August 2014 from: https://www.oxfam ireland. org/sites/default/files/upload/pdfs/austerity-ireland-case-study.pdf.

Collini, S. (2012). *What are Universities For?* London: Penguin Books.

Cook, B., Dodds, C. and Mitchell, W. (2003). Social Entrepreneurship – False Premises and Dangerous Forebodings. *Australian Journal of Social Issues, 38* (1), 57–72.

Cook, G. (2012). British Applied Linguistics: Impacts of and Impacts on. *Applied Linguistics Review, 3* (1), 25–45.

Corcoran, M. P. and Lalor, K. (Eds.). (2012). *Reflections on Crisis: The Role of the Public Intellectual*. Dublin: Royal Irish Academy.

Coulmas, F. (1992). *Language and Economy*. Oxford: Blackwell.

Coulter, C. (n.d.). *Factory Farms for the Mind*. Retrieved 18th August 2012 from Politics.ie: http://politico.ie/index.php?option=com_content&view=article&id=701: factory-farms-for-the-mind.

Coupland, N. (2003). Sociolinguistics and Globalisation. Special Issue. *Journal of Sociolinguistics, 7* (4), 465–72.

Crehan, K. (2011). Gramsci's Concept of Common Sense: A Useful Concept for Anthropologists? *Journal of Modern Italian Studies, 16* (2), 273–87.

Crouch, C. (2011). *The Strange Non-Death of Neoliberalism*. Cambridge: Polity.

Crowley, T. (1996). *Language in History: Theories and Texts*. London: Routledge.

Deem, R. S., Hillyard, S. and Reed, M. (2007). *Knowledge, Higher Education and the New Managerialism: The Changing Management of UK Universities*. Oxford: Oxford University Press.

Dees, G. J. (2012). *What Exactly is Social Entrepreneurship?* Retrieved 8th May 2014 from Forbes: http://www.forbes.com/sites/greggfairbrothers/2012/05/28/what-exactly-is-social-entrepreneurship.

Delaney, A. and Healy, T. (2014). *We Need to Talk about Higher Education*. Dublin: Nevin Economic Research Institute.

Department of Education and Skills. (2011). *National Strategy for Higher Education to 2030 (The Hunt Report)*. Dublin: Department of Education and Skills.

Department of Education, Ireland. (2014, 14th April 14). *Address by the Minister for Education and Skills to the 5th International Exhibition and Conference on Higher Education*. Retrieved 30th April 2014 from: http://www.education.ie/: http://www. education.ie/en/Press-Events/Speeches/2014-Speeches/SP14-04-15.html.

Department of Finance. (2011). *National Recovery Plan 2011–2014*. Dublin: Department of Finance/An Roinn Airgeadas. Retrieved 8th August 2014 from: http://www.budget. gov.ie/The%20National%20Recovery%20Plan%202011–14.pdf.

Department of Jobs, Enterprise and Innovation. (2014). *Action for Jobs 2014 Department of Jobs Enterprise and Innovation Ireland*. Retrieved 17th March 2014 from Department of Jobs Enterprise and Innovation: http://www.djei.ie/enterprise/ apj.htm.

Donnelly, K. (2014, 14th April). Third Level Staff Cuts Equal to Entire UCD Workforce. *Irish Independent*. Retrieved 15th December 2014 from: http://www.independent.ie/ irish-news/thirdlevel-staff-cuts-equal-to-entire-ucd-workforce-30182775.html.

Doogan, K. (2009). *New Capitalism: The Transformation of Work?* Cambridge: Polity.

References   137

Drennan, J. (2013, 5th July). Budget will be Tough, Gilmore Warns Householders. *Irish Indpependent*, pp. 6–7. Retrieved 15th December 2014 from: http://www.independent.ie/irish-news/budget-will-be-tough-gilmore-warns-householders-29453812.html.

Dublin City University. (2012). *Strategic Plan 2012–2017*. Dublin: Dublin City University. Retrieved 15th December 2014 from: http://www.dcu.ie/external-strategic-affairs/strategic-plan.shtml.

Duchêne, A. and Heller, M. (Eds.) (2012). *Language in Late Capitalism: Pride and Profit*. New York: Routledge.

Duménil, G. and Lévy, D. (2011). *The Crisis of Neoliberalism*. Cambridge, MA: Harvard University Press.

——(2004). *Captial Resurgent: Roots of the Neoliberal Revolution*. Cambridge, MA: Harvard University Press.

Eagleton, T. (2010, 17th December).The Death of Universities. *The Guardian*. Retrieved 15th May 2014 from: www.theguardian.com/commentisfree/2010/dec/17/death-universities-malaise-tuition-fees.

——(2007). *Ideology: An Introduction*. London: Verson.

——(2001). Ideology, Discourse and the Problems of Post-Marxism. In S. Malpas (Ed.), *Postmodern Debates* (pp. 79–92). Basingstoke: Palgrave.

——(1989). Base and Superstructure in Raymond Williams. In T. Eagleton (Ed.), *Raymond Williams: Critical Perspectives* (pp. 165–75). Boston, MA: Northeastern University Press.

Ehrenreich, B. (2006). *Bait and Switch: The Futile Pursuit of the Amercan Corporate Dream*. London: Granta Books.

European Commission (2012a). *Effects and Impact of Entrepreneurship Programmes in Higher Education*. Brussels: Entrepreneurship Unit, Directorate General of Enterprise and Industry.

——(2012b). *Ireland's Economic Crisis: How Did It Happen and What is Being Done about It?* Brussels: European Commission. Retrieved on 15th December 2014 from: http://ec.europa.eu/ireland/economy/irelands_economic_crisis/index_en.htm.

European Commisssion Industry and Enterprise (2012). *A Survey of Entrepreneurship in Higher Education in Europe*. Brussels: European Commission. Retrieved 15th December 2014 from: http://ec.europa.eu/enterprise/policies/sme/promoting-entrepreneurship/education-training-entrepreneurship/higher-education/index_en.htm.

Fairclough, N. (2010). *Critical Discourse Analysis*. London: Longman.

——(2007). Global Capitalism and Change in Higher Education: Dialectics of Language and Practice, Technology, Ideology. *Proceedings of the BAAL conference 2007* (pp. 131–41). Retrieved 15th December 2014 from: http://www.baal.org.uk/proc07/36_norman_fairclough.pdf.

——(2006). *Language and Globalisation*. London: Routledge.

——(1992). *Discourse and Social Change*. Cambridge: Polity.

Fairclough, N. and Wodak, R. (2010). Recontextualising European Higher Education Policies: The Cases of Austria and Romania. *Critical Discourse Studes, 7* (1), 19–40.

Fine, B. (2002). It Ain't Social, It Ain't Captal and It Ain't Africa. *Studia Africana, 13*, 18–33.

Fitzsimons, P. and O'Gorman, C. (2010). *Global Enterprise Monitorship (GEM) Report*. Dublin: Enterprise Ireland.

Flores, N. (2013). The Unexamined Relationship between Neoliberalism and Plurilingualism: A Cautionary Tale. *TESOL Quarterly, 47* (3), 500–520.

Forfás (2013). *Social Enterprise in Ireland: Sectoral Opportunities and Policy Issues*. Forfás, Dublin. Retrieved 1st September 2014 from: http://www.forfas.ie/

138 References

media/23072013-Social_Enterprise_in_Ireland-Sectoral_Opportunities_and_Policy_Issues-Publication.pdf.

Foucault, M. (2008). *The Birth of Biopolitics: Lectures at the Collège de France 1979–1979* (Trans. G. Burchill, Ed. M. Senellart). Basingstoke: Palgrave Macmillan.

——(2002). *Power: Essential Works of Foucault 1954–1984: Volume 3* (Trans. Robert Hurley et al.). London: Penguin.

——(1988). 'Practicing Criticism' or 'Is it Really Important to Think?' (Didier Eribon interview, 30th–31st May, 1981). In L. D. Kritzman (Ed.), *Michel Foucault: Politics, Philosophy, Culture. Interviews and other writings 1977–1984* (pp. 152–58). London: Routledge.

Fraser, A., Murphy, E. and Kelly, S. (2013). Deepening Neoliberalism via Austerity and Reform; The Case of Ireland. *Human Geography, 6* (2), 38–53.

Freyne, P. (2014, 15th March). How You Can Help Fix Ireland *The Irish Times*. Retrieved 15th December 2014 from: http://www.irishtimes.com/life-and-style/how-you-can-help-fix-ireland-1.1725648?page=3.

Fridell, G. and Konings, M. (2013). Introduction: Neoliberal Capitalism as the Age of Icons. In G. Fridell and M. Konings (Eds.), *Age of Icons: Exploring Philantrhocapitalism in the Contemporary World* (pp. 3–26). Toronto: University of Toronto Press.

Fuentes-Nieva, R. and Galasso, N. (2014, Jan. 20). *Working for the Few: Political Capture and Economic Inequality*. Retrieved 10th May 2014 from Oxfam: http://www.oxfam.org/en/policy/working-for-the-few-economic-inequality.

Gal, S. (1989). Language and Political Economy. *Annual Review of Anthropology, 18*, 345–67.

Gallagher, M. (2013). *Academic Armageddon: An Irish Requiem for Higher Education*. Dublin: The Liffey Press.

Gartland, F. (2014, 7th February). Derivatives like Backing Horses, Economist Tells Trial. *Irish Times*. Retrieved 15th June 2014 from: http://www.irishtimes.com/news/crime-and-law/courts/derivatives-like-backing-horses-economist-tells-trial-1.1682593.

Garvin, T. (2012, 1st May The Bleak Future of the Irish University. *Irish Times*. Retrieved 1st May 2014 from: http://www.irishtimes.com/newspaper/education/2012/0501/1224315400547.html.

Geras, N. (1990). Essence and Appearance: Aspects of fetishism in Marx's Capital. *New Left Review, 1* (65), 69–85.

Giddens, A. (1998). *The Third Way: The Renewal of Social Democracy*. Cambridge: Polity.

Gill, R. (2009). Breaking the Silence: The Hidden Injuries of Neo-liberal Academia. In R. Gill and R. Ryan-Flood (Eds.), *Secrecy and Silence in the Research Process: Feminist Reflections* (pp. 228–45). London: Routledge.

Glynn, I., Kelly, T. and Mac Éinrí, P. (2013). *Emigration in an Age of Austerity*. Cork: Department of Geography/Insititute for the Social Sciences, University of Cork. Retrieved 1st September 2014 from: http://research.ie/intro_slide/research-funded-irish-research-council-irish-emigration-age-austerity.

Goatly, A. (2007). *Washing the Brain: Metaphor and Hidden Ideology*. Amsterdam: John Benjamins.

——(2006). Ideology and Metaphor. *English Today, 22* (13), 25–29.

Graeber, D. (2001). *Towards an Anthropological Theory of Value: The False Coin of Our Own Dreams*. New York: Palgrave.

Gramsci, A. (2011). *Prison Notebooks Volume 3* (Trans. and Ed. J. A. Buttigieg). New York: Columbia University Press.

References 139

——(1971). *Selections from Prison Notebooks* (Trans. and Ed. Q. Hoare and N. Smith). London: Lawrence and Wishart.

Gray, J. (2012). English the Industry. In Ann Hewings and Caroline Tagg (Eds.), *The Politics of English: Conflict, Competition, Co-existence* (pp. 137–62). Milton Keynes, UK: Open University/Routledge.

——(2010). *The Construction of English: Cuture, Consumerism and Promotion in the Global ELT Coursebook.* Basingstoke: Palgrave Macmillan.

Grenfell, M. (Ed.). (2011). *Bourdieu, Language and Linguistics.* London: Continuum.

Gu, Q. and Schweisfurth, M. (2011). Rethinking University Internationalisation: Towards Transformative Change. *Teachers and Teaching: Theory and Practice, 17* (6), 611–17.

Hall, S. (1986). The Problem of Ideology: Marxism without Guarantees. *Journal of Communication Inquiry, 10* (2), 28–44.

Hardt, M. and Negri, A. (2000). *Empire.* Cambridge, MA: Harvard University Press.

Harman, C. (2009). *Zombie Capitalism: Global Crisis and the Relevance of Marx.* London: Bookmarks.

——(2007). Gramsci, The Prison Notebooks and Philosophy. *International Socialism, 114,* 105–23.

——(1986). Base and Superstructure. *International Socialism, 2,* 3–43. Retrieved 13th August 2014 from: http://www.marxists.org/archive/harman/1986/xx/base-super.html.

Hart, C. (2008). Critical Discourse Analysis and Metaphor: Towards a Theoretical Framework. *Critical Discourse Studies, 5* (2), 91–106.

Harvey, D. (2014). *Seventeen Contradictions and the End of Capitalism.* London: Profile Books.

——(2012). *Rebel Cities: From the Right to the City to Urban Revolution.* London: Verso.

——(2010a). *Companion to Marx's Capital.* London: Verso.

——(2010b). *Organising for the Anti-capitalist Transition: Talk Given at the World Social Forum 2010 (Porto Alegre).* Retrieved 28th January 2014 from: http://davidharvey. org/2009/12/organizing-for-the-anti-capitalist-transition.

——(2005). *A Brief History of Neoliberalism.* Oxford: Oxford University Press.

Harvie, D. (2004). Commons and Communities in the University: Some Notes and Comments. *The Commoner, 8* (Autumn/Winter), 1–10. Retrieved 20th May 2014 from: http://www.commoner.org.uk/08harvie.pdf.

Hasan, R. (2003). Globalisation, Literacy and Ideology. *World Englishes, 22* (4), 433–48.

Hazelkorn, E. and Massaro, V. (2010). A Tale of Two Strategies for Higher education and Economic Recovery. *IMHE* (pp. 1–13). Retrieved 1st September 2014 from: http:// arrow.dit.ie/cgi/viewcontent.cgi?article=1007& context = csercon.

Head, S. (2014). *Mindless: Why Smarter Machines are Making Dumber Humans.* New York: Basic Books.

——(2010, 13th January). The Grim Threat to British Universities. *The New York Review of Books.*

Healy, T. (2014, 7th February). *Time for a Debate on Higher Education.* Retrieved 6th June 2014 from NERI (Nevin Economic Research Institute): http://www.nerinstitute. net/blog/2014/02/07/time-for-a-debate-on-higher-education.

Heller, M. (2010a). Language as Resource in the Globalized New Economy. In N. Coupland (Ed.), *The Handbook of Language and Globalization* (pp. 349–65). Malden, MA: Blackwell.

140   References

——(2010b). The Commodification of Language. *Annual Review of Anthopology, 39*, 101–14.

Henry, M., Lingard, B., Rizvi, F. and Taylor, S. (2001). *The OECD, Globalisation and Education Policy*. Bingley: Emerald Group Publishing.

Higher Education Authority (2013). *Towards a Performance Evaluation Framework: Profiling Irish Higher Education*. Higher Education Authority, Dublin. Retrieved 12th August 2014 from: http://www.hea.ie/sites/default/files/performance_evaluation_full_report_a4_format.pdf.

——(2012a). *HEA Strategic Plan*. Retrieved 1st September 2014 from: http://www.hea.ie/files/HEA-STRATEGIC-PLAN.pdf.

——(2012b). *Policy*. Retrieved 18th August 2012 from http://www.hea.ie/en/node/246.

Hilgers, M. (2010). The Three Anthropological Approaches to Neoliberalism. *International Social Science Journal, 61* (202), 351–64.

Hill, C. (1990). *Nation of Change and Novelty: Radical Politics,Religion and Literature in Seventeenth-Century England*. London: Routledge.

Hill, D. (2007). Critical Teacher Education, New Labour and the Global Project of Neoliberal Capital. *Policy Futures in Education, 5* (2), 204–25.

HM Government (2013a). *International Education: Global Growth and Prosperity*. London: Department of Business, Innovation and Skills. Retrieved 15th May 2014 from: https://www.gov.uk/government/uploads/system/uploads/attachment_data/file/229844/bis-13-1081-international-education-global-growth-and-prosperity.pdf.

——(July 2013b). *International Education: Global Growth and Prosperity*. London: Department of Business, Innovation and Skills.

Hodge, R. I. and Kress, G. (1993). *Language as Ideology*. London: Routledge.

Holborow, M. (2013). Applied Linguistics in the Neoliberal University: Ideological Keywords and Social Agency. *Applied Linguistics Review, 4* (2), 227–55.

——(2012a). Neoliberal Keywords and the Contradictions of an Ideology. In D. Block, J. Gray and M. Holborow (Eds.), *Neoliberalism and Applied Linguisitics* (pp. 14–33). Abingdon: Routledge.

——(2012b). Neoliberalism, Human Capital and the Skills Agenda – The Irish Case. In D. Hill and K. Skodoulis (Ed.), *Critical Education: Proceedings of the 1st International Conference 12–16 July 2011* (pp. 143–66). Athens: Nissos Publications.

——(2012c). What is Neoliberalism? Discourse, Ideology and the Real World. In D. Block, J. Gray and M. Holborow (Eds.), *Neoliberalism and Applied Linguistics* (pp. 14–32). London: Routledge.

——(2007). Language Ideology and Neoliberalism. *Journal of Lnaguage and Politics, 6* (1), 51–73.

——(2006a). Ideology and language: Interconnections between Neo-liberalism and English. In J. Edge (Ed.), *(Re)locating TESOL in an Age of Empire* (pp. 84–104). Basingstoke: Palgrave Macmillan.

——(2006b). Putting the Social Back into Language: Marx, Volosinov and Vygotsky Reexamined. *Studies In Language And Capitalism, 1*, 1–28.

——(1999). *The Politics of English: A Marxist View of Language*. London: Sage Publications.

Holmwood, J. (2014). Academic Freedom and the Corporate University. Retrieved 30th July 2014 from: http://publicuniversity.org.uk/2014/07/04/academic-freedom-and-the-corporate-university.

Horner, J. R. (2011). Clogged Systems and Toxic Assets; New metaphors, Neoliberal Ideology and the United States 'Wall Street Bailout' of 2008. *Journal of Language and Politics, 10* (1), 29–49.

Humphreys, D. (2009). Discourse as Ideology: Neoliberalism and the Limits of International Forest Policy. *Forest Policy and Economics, 11*, 319–25.

Humphries, J. (2014, 21st June). How Will You Fill Your 168-Hour Week? *The Irish Times*. Retrieved 26th December 2014 from: http://www.irishtimes.com/news/education/how-will-you-fill-your-168-hour-week-1.1839914?page=3.

Hunt, C. (2011). *National Strategy for Higher Education to 2030*. Dublin: Department of Education and Skills. Retrieved 15th December 2014 from: http://www.hea.ie/sites/default/files/national_strategy_for_higher_education_ 2030.pdf.

Hymes, D. (1996). *Ethnography, Linguistics and Narrative Inequality: Towards an Understanding of Voice*. London: Taylor and Francis.

Irish Congress of Trade Unions (ICTU) (2011). *International Labour Organanisation Aid Partners*. Retrieved 4th May 2014 from: http://www.ictu.ie/globalsolidarity/workers rights/iloirishaidpart.html.

Ives, P. (2004). *Language and Hegemony in Gramsci*. London: Pluto.

Jones, C. (2013). *Can the Market Speak?* Winchester: Zero.

——(2011). What Kind of Subject is the Market? *New Formations, 72*, 131–44.

Jones, P. (2004). Discourse and the Materialist Conception of History: Critical Comments on Critical Discourse Analysis. *Historical Materialism, 12* (1), 97–125.

Jørgensen, J. N., Karrebæk, M., Madsen, L. M. and Møller, J. S. (2011). Polylanguaging in superdiversity. *Diversities, 13* (2), 23–38.

Keeling, R. (2006). The Bologna Proces and the Lisbon Research Agenda: The European Commission's Expanding Role in Higher Education Discourse. *European Journal of Education, 41* (2), 203–23.

Kellaway, L. (2007, 4th November). The Battle is Lost, Going Forward. *Financial Times*.

Kelly-Holmes, H. and Mautner, G. (Eds.). (2010). *Language and the Market*. Basingstoke: Palgrave.

Klein, N. (2007). *The Shock Doctrine: The Rise of Disaster Capitalism*. New York: Metropoitan Books/Henry Holt.

Kubota, R. (2011). Questioning Linguistic Instrumentalism: English, Neoliberalism and Language Tests in Japan. *Linguistics and Education, 22*, 248–60.

Labriola, A. (2005). *Essays on the Materialist Conception of History* (Trans. C. H. Kerr). New York: Consimo.

Lakoff, G. (2008). *The Political Mind: Why You Can't Understand 21st Century American Politics with an 18th Century Brain*. New York: Viking Penguin.

Lakoff, G. and Johnson, M. (2003). *The Metaphors We Live By*. Chicago: Chicago University Press.

Lam, A. S. L. and Wang, W. (2008). Negotiating Language Value in Multilingual China. In Peter K. W. Tan and Rani Rubdy (Ed.), *Language as Commodity* (pp. 147–70). London: Continuum.

Lane, J. F. (2000). *Pierre Bourdieu: A Critical Introduction*. London: Pluto.

Larner, W. (2000). Neo-liberalism, Policy Ideology, Governmentality. *Studies in Political Economy, 63*, 5–25.

Larrain, J. (1979). *The Concept of Ideology*. London: Hutchinson.

Lauder, H. M., Young, M., Daniels, H., Balarin, M. and Lowe, J. (2012). *Educating for the Knowledge Economy? Critical Perspectives*. Abingdon: Routledge.

Lemke, T. (2001). The Birth of Biopolitics: Michel Foucault's Lecture at the College de France on Neo-liberal Governmentality. *Economy and Society 30* (2), 190–207.

Lévy, D. and Duménil, G. (2012). Neoliberalism. In B. Fine and A. Saad-Fihlo (Eds.), *The Elgar Companion to Marxist Economics* (pp. 240–45). Cheltenham: Edward Elgar.

142 *References*

Lo Bianco, J. (2008). Foreword. In P. K. Tan (Ed.), *Language as Commodity: Global Strucutres, Local Marketplaces* (p. xii). London: Continuum.

——(1999). *Globalisation: Frame Word for Education, Training, Human Capital and Human Development/Rights.* Melbourne: Language Australia, National Languages and Literacy Institute of Australia.

Lukács, G. (1971). *History and Class Consciousness: Studies in Marxist Dialectics* (Trans. R. Livingstone). London: Merlin Press.

Lynch, K., Grummell, B. and Devine, D. (2012). *New Managerialism in Education: Gender,Commercialisation and Carelessness.* Basingstoke: Palgrave Macmillan.

Lynch, S. (2013, 14th November. Ireland's Bailout Exit of Huge Significance for Europe. *Irish Times.* Retrieved 15th December 2014 from: http://www.irishtimes.com/news/politics/ireland-s-bailout-exit-of-huge-significance-for-europe-1.1594773?mode=print&ot=example.AjaxPageLayout.ot.

Marttila, T. (2013). *The Culture of Enterprise in Neoliberalism.* New York: Routledge.

Marx, K. (1999). *Wage, Labour and Capital.* Retrieved 15th December 2014 from: http://www.marxists.org/archive/marx/works/1847/wage-labour/ch02.htm.

——(1991). *Capital: A Critique of Political Economy Volume Three* (Trans. D. Fernbach). London: Penguin.

——(1981). *Capital: A Critique of Critical Economy Vol 3* (Trans. D. Fernbach). London: Penguin Books in association with New Left Review.

——(1974). *Capital: A Critique of Political Economy, Volume 1* (Trans. B. Fowkes). Harmondsworth: Penguin Classics.

——(1973). *Gundrisse: Foundations of the Critique of Political Economy (Rough Draft)* (Trans. M. Nicolaus. London: Penguin Books in association with New Left Review.

——(1969). Preface to A Contribution to the Critique of Political Economy. In *K. Marx and F. Engels: Seclected Works: Vol 1.* Moscow: Progress Publishers. Retrieved 2nd September 2014 from: http://www.marxists.org/archive/marx/works/1859/critique-pol-economy/preface.htm.

——(1964). *Karl Marx: Early Writings* (Trans. and Ed. T. Bottomore). New York: McGraw-Hill.

Marx, K. and Engels, F. (1974). *The German Ideology* (Ed. C. J. Arthur). London: Lawrence and Wishart.

Massey, D. (2013, 11th June). *Vocabularies of the Economy.* Retrieved 30th July 2014 from: http://www.open.ac.uk/researchcentres/osrc/news/vocabularies-of-the-economy.

Mautner, G. (2010). The Spread of Corporate Discourses to Other Domains. In H. Kelly-Holmes and G. Mautner Eds.), *Langauge and the Market* (pp. 215–25). Basingstoke: Palgrave Macmillan.

——(2005). The Entrepreneurial University: A Discursive Profile of Higher Education. *Critical Discourse Studies 2,* 95–120.

Mayr, A. (2008). *Language and Power: An Introduction to Institutional Discourse.* London: Continuum.

McCrum, R. (2010). *Globish: How the English Language Became the World's Language.* London: Viking.

——(2006, 3rd December). So What is this Globish Revolution? *The Observer.* Retrieved 3rd September 2014 from: http://www.theguardian.com/theobserver/2006/dec/03/features.review37.

McGill, K. (2013). Political Economy and Language: A Review of Some Recent Literature. *Journal of Linguistic Anthropology, 23* (2), E84–E101.

McGuigan, J. (2005). Neo-liberalism, Culture and Policy. *International Journal of Cultural Policy, 11* (3), 229–41.

McNally, D. (2001). *Bodies of Meaning: Studies on Language, Labor and Liberation.* Albany, NY: State University of New York.

McNally, F. (2010, 3rd September). An Irishman's Diary. *The Irish Times.*

Mesthrie, R. J., Swann, J., Deumert, A. and Leap, W. (2009). *Introducing Sociolinguistics.* Edinburgh: Edinburgh University Press.

Mirowksi, P. (2013). *Never Let a Serious Crisis Go to Waste: How Neoliberalism Survived the Financial Crisis.* New York: Verso.

——(2009). Postface: Defining Neoliberalism. In P. Mirowski and D. Plehwe (Eds.), *The Road from Mont Pelerin: The Making of the Neoliberal Thought Collective* (pp. 417–50). Cambridge, MA: Harvard University Press.

Mirowski, P. and Plehwe, D. (Eds.). (2009). *The Road from Mont Pelerin: The Making of the Neoliberal Thought Collective.* Cambridge, MA: Harvard University Press.

Munck, R. (2014, 30th May). *'Defend the Irish University' Reviews Grant Thornton's 'Review of the Financial Health of the Irish Higher Education Sector.* Retrieved 6th June 2014 from: http://defendtheuniversity.ie/?page_id=378.

Newsinger, J. (2012). *Fighting Back: The American Working Class in the 1930s.* London: Bookmarks Publications.

Ng, C. W. (2013). Semioticizing Capitalism in Corporate Brand Enactment: The Case of Singapore's Corporatized Universities. *Critical Discourse Studies.* Retrieved 18th December 2014 from: htttp://dx.doi.org/10.1080/17405904.2013.836116.

NUIG, Marketing and Communications Office (2014, 1st July). *Irish Higher Education Institutes Partnership Leading a National Education Revolution.* Retrieved 4th July 2014 from NUI Galway: http://www.nuigalway.ie/about-us/news-and-events/latest-news/irish-higher-education-institutes-partnership-leading-a-national-education-revolution.html.

O'Connor, D. and Millar, R. (2013). *The Role of Philanthropy in Funding Irish Universities.* Dublin: Two into Three.

O'Connor, F. (2011, 21st November). Look back: Ireland's Bail-out. *The Sunday Business Post.* Retrieved 1st September from: http://www.businesspost.ie/#!story/Home/News/Look+back%3A+Ireland%E2%80%99s+bail-out/id/19410615-5218-4eca-194e-e8b508863012.

O'Halloran, K. (2011). Critical Discourse Analysis. In J. Simpson (Ed.), *The Routledge Handbook of Apllied Lingusitics* (pp. 445–60). Abingdon: Routledge.

OECD (2013). *Education at a Glance: Ireland.* Paris: Organisation for Economic Co-operation and Development. Retrieved 20th June 2014 from: http://www.oecd.org/ireland/educationataglance2013-countrynotesandkeyfacttables.htm.

——(2011). *Education at a Glance 2011 OECD Indicators.* Paris: Organisation for Economic Co-operation and Development. Retrieved 2nd September 2014 from: http://www.oecd.org/education/skills-beyond-school/48631582.pdf.

——(2009). *Evaluation of Programmes Concerning Education for Entrepreneurship.* Paris: Organisation for Economic Co-operation and Development. Retrieved 12th June 2014 from: http://www.oecd.org/industry/smes/42890085.pdf.

——(2008). *Tertiary Education for the Knowledge Society: Volume 1: Special features: Governance, Funding, Quality – Volume 2: Special features: Equity, Innovation, Labour Market, Internationalisation.* Paris: Organisation for Economic Co-operation and Devolpment. Retrieved 1st September 2014 from: http://www.oecd.org/edu/skills-beyond-school/tertiaryeducationfortheknowledgesocietyvolume1specialfeaturesgovernancefundingquality-volume2specialfeaturesequity innovationlabourmarketinternationalisation.htm.

144 References

——(2004). *Review of National Policies for Education: Review of Higher Education in Ireland. Examiners Report*. Organisation for Economic Co-operation and Development. Retrieved 1st September 2014 from: http://www.oecd.org/ireland/reviewsofnational policiesforeducation-highereducationinireland.htm.

O'Halloran, K. (2011). Critical Discourse Analysis. In J. Simpson (Ed.), *The Routledge Book of Applied Linguistics* (pp. 445–60). London: Routledge.

Oliver, E. (2012, 30th November). Bank Rescue is the Third Most Expensive in History. *Irish Independent*. Retrieved 3rd September 2014 from: http://www.independent.ie/business/irish/bank-rescue-is-the-third-most-expensive-in-history-26647585.html.

Ollman, B. (1971). *Alienation: Marx's Concept of Man in Capitalist Society*. New York: Cambridge University Press.

Ong, A. (2007). Neoliberalism as a Mobile Technology. *Transactions of the Insititute of British Geographers, 32*, 3–8.

O'Regan, J. P. (2014). English as a Lingua Franca: An Immanent Critique. *Applied Linguistics, 35* (2), 1–21.

Orwell, G. (1981 [1946]). The Politics of the English Language. In *A Collection of Essays* (pp. 157–71). New York: Harvest, Harcourt Inc.

Osman, H. (2008). Re-branding Academic Institutions with Corporate Advertising: A Genre Perspective. *Discourse and Communication, 2* (1), 57–77.

Osuji, E. and Pennycook, A. (2011). Metrolingualism: Fixity, Fluidity and Language in Flux. *International Journal of Multilingualism 7* (3), 240–54.

O'Toole, F. (1998, 16th October). Turning the Famine into a Corporate Celebration. *The Irish Times*. Retrieved 12th September 2014 from: http://www.irishtimes.com/debate/oct-16th-1998-turning-the-famine-into-a-corporate-celebration-1.1600212.

Park, J. S.-Y. (2013). Metadiscursive Regimes of Diversity in a Multinational Corporation. *Language in Society, 42*, 557–77.

——(2011). The Promise of English: Linguistc Capital and the Neoliberal Worker in the South Korean Job Market. *International Journal of Bilingual Education and Bilingualism, 14* (4), 443–55.

Park, J. S.-Y. and Lo, A. (2012). Transnational South Korea as a Site for a Sociolinguistics of Globalization: Markets, Timescales, Neoliberalism. *Journal of Sociolinguistics, 16* (2), 147–64.

Park, J. S.-Y. and Wee, L. (2012). *Markets of English: Linguistc Capital and Language Policy in a Globalising World*. New York: Routledge.

Peck, J. (2014). Pushing Austerity: State Failure, Municipal Bankrupcy and the Crisis of Fiscal Federalism in the USA. *Cambridge Journal of Regions, Economy and Society, 7*, 17–44.

——(2010). *Constructions of Neoliberal Reason*. Oxford: Oxford University Press.

——(2003). Geography and Public Policy: Mapping the Penal State. *Progress in Human Geography, 27* (2), 222–32.

Peck, J. and Theodore, N. (2012). Reanimating Neoliberalism: Process Geographies of Neoliberalisation. *Social Anthropologies 20* (2), 177–85.

Peck, J. and Tickell, A. (2002). Neoliberalising Space. *Antipode, 34* (3), 380–404.

Pennycook, A. (2010). Critical and Alternative Directions in Applied Linguistics. *Australian Review of Applied Linguistics, 33* (2), 1–18.

——(2007). *Global Englishes and Transcultural Flows*. London: Routledge.

——(2001). *Critical Applied Linguistics: A Critical Introduction*. London: Critical Applied Linguistics.

Perry, F. L. (2011). *Research in Applied Linguistics: Becoming a Discerning Consumer*. New York: Routledge.

References   145

Phillips, S. U. (1998). Language Ideologies in Institutions of Power: A Commentary. In B. B. Schieflin, K. A. Woolard and P. V. Kroskrity (Eds.), *Language Ideologies* (pp. 211–25). New York: Oxford University Press.

Phillipson, R. (2003). *Engish-Only Europe: Challenging Language Policy*. London: Routledge.

——(2008). The Linguistic Imperialism of Neoliberal Empire. *Critical Enquiry in Language Studies*, 5 (1), 1–43.

Piketty, T. (2014). *Capital in the Twenty-First Century* (Trans. A. Goldhammer). Cambridge, MA: Harvard Unverisity Press.

Piller, I. (2013). Neoliberalism as Language Policy. *Language in Society*, 42 (1), 23–44.

Pinker, S. (2007). *The Stuff of Thought: Language as a Window into Human Nature*. New York: Viking.

——(2002).*The Blank Slate: The Modern Denial of Human Nature*. New York: Viking.

Plehwe, D. and Walpen, B. (2006). Between Network and Complex Organisation: The Making of Neoliberal Knowledge and Hegemony. In D. Plehwe, B. Wlapen and G. Neunhoffer (Eds.), *Neoliberal Hegemony: A Global Critique* (pp. 27–51). Abingdon: Routledge.

Rampton, B. (2006). *Language in Late Modernity: Interaction in an Urban School*. Cambridge: Cambridge University Press.

——(1995). Politics and Change in Research in Applied Linguistics. *Applied Linguistics*, 16 (2), 233–54.

Reagan, R. (1983, May 14). *Radio Adress to the Nation on Small Business*. Retrieved 13th June 2014 from The American Presidency Project: Online by Gerhard Peters and John T. Woolley, The American Presidency Project: http://www.presidency.ucsb.edu/ws/?pid=41324

Reilly, G. (2013, 22nd May). *The World's Wealthy 'Could be Hiding €707 Billion in Ireland'*. Retrieved 12th May 2014 from: http://www.thejournal.ie/oxfam-hidden-wealth-ireland-e707-billion-921414-May2013.

Rhoades, G. and Slaughter, S. (2009). *Academic Capitalism and the New Economy*. Baltimore, MD: Johns Hopkins University Press.

Rose, H. (1999). Changing Constructions of Consciousness. *Journal of Consicousness Studies*, 6 (11/12), 251–58.

Rose, N. (1996). Death of the Social. *Economy and Society*, 25 (3), 327–56.

Rose, N. and Miller, P. (1992). Political Power beyond the State: Problematics of Government. *British Journal of Sociology*, 43 (2), 173–205.

Rose, S. (2006). *The Twentieth Century Brain: Explaining Mending, and Manipulating the Mind*. London: Vintage.

Russell Hochschild, A. (2012). *The Outsourced Self: Intimate Life in Market Times*. New York: Metropolitan Press.

——(2003). *The Commercialisation of Intimate Life*. San Francisco, CA: University of California Press.

Saad-Fihlo, A. and Johnston, D. (2005). *Neoliberalism: A Critical Reader*. London: Pluto.

Sandel, M. (2012, April). What Isn't For Sale? *Atlantic*.

Saussure, F. D. (1971). *Cours de Linguistique Générale* (C. Bally and A. Sechehaye, Eds.). Paris: Payot.

Scacco, J. (2009). Shaping Economic Reality: A Critical Metaphor Analylsis of President Obama's Economic Language During His First 100 Days. *Gnovis Journal*, 10 (1), 1–8. Retrieved 15th May 2014 from: http://gnovisjournal.org/2009/12/22/

146 References

shaping-economic-reality-critical-metaphor-analysis-president-barack-obama-s-econom ic-langua.

Schieflin, B. B., Woolard, K. A. and Kroskrity, P. V. (1998). *Language Ideologies: Practice and Theory*. New York: Oxford University Press.

Seacombe, M. (2011, 30th August). Going Forward: Let's Consign this Inane Phrase to History. *The Guardian*.

Seargeant, P. (2012). Disciplinarity and the Study of World Englishes. *World Englishes, 31* (1), 113–29.

Showstack-Sassoon, A. (2010). Gramsci's Subversion of the Language of Politics. In P. Ives and R. Lacorte (Eds.), *Gramsci, Language and Translation* (pp. 243–55). Lanham, MD: Lexington Books.

Silverstein, M. (1998). The Uses and Utility of Ideology: A Commentary. In B. B. Shieffelin, K. A. Woolard and P. V. Kroskrity (Eds.), *Language Ideologies* (pp. 123–45). New York: Oxford University Press.

Simpson, J. (2011). *The Routledge Handbook of Applied Linguistics*. London: Routledge.

Simpson, P. and Mayr, A. (2010). *Language and Power: A Resource Book for Students*. London: Routledge.

Social Entrepreneurs Ireland (2014). *Think Big Act Big*. Retrieved 20th August 2014 from Social Entrepreneurs Ireland: http://socialentrepreneurs.ie/about/our-story.

Sotiris, P. (2012). Theorising the Entrepreneurial University. In K. S. Hill (Ed.), *Critical Education: Proceedings of the 1st International Conference 12–16 July 2011* (pp. 403–19). Athens: Nissos Publications.

Spring, J. (2008). Research on Globalisation and Education. *Review of Educational Research 78* (2), 330–63.

Steen, M. (2013, 24th September). Consultants who Praised Defunct Bank to Advise on New ECB Review. *Financial Times*. Retrieved 13th September 2014 from: http://www. ft.com/intl/cms/s/0/9639e43e-2530-11e3-b349–00144feab7de.html#axzz2xiFcZAg1.

Steinberg, M. (1999). *Fighting Words: Working Class Formative Collective Action and Discourse in Early Nineteenth Century England*. New York: Cornell University Press.

Stubbs, M. (2010). Three Concepts of Keywords. In M. Bondi (Ed.), *Keyness in Texts* (pp. 21–43). Amsterdam, The Netherlands: John Benjamins.

Sweeney, P. (2013). An Inquiry into the Declining Labour Share of National Income and the Consequences for Economies and Societies. *Journal of the Statistical and Social Inquiry Society of Ireland*. Retrieved 14th September 2014 from: http://www.tara.tcd. ie/handle/2262/9206/browse?value=Sweeney%2C+Paul&type=author.

Taft, Michael (2014a). *Notes from the Front*. Retrieved 10th May 2014 from: http:// notesonthefront.typepad.com/politicaleconomy.

——(2014b). *UNITE Trade Union*. Retrieved 19th July 2014 from: http://notesonthefront. typepad.com/politicaleconomy/2014/01/with-the-great-and-the-good-meeting-in-davos-it-is-worthwhile-taking-a-look-at-how-the-top-1-percent-is-doing-courtesy-of-a.html.

——(2011). *Unite's Notes from the Front*. Retrieved 15th December 2014 from: http:// notesonthefront.typepad.com/politicaleconomy/2011/11/the-dublin-council-of-trades-unions-march-against-austerity-tomorrow-12-noon-from-the-garden-of-remembrance.

Talbot, M., Atkinson, K. and Atkinson, D. (2003). *Language and Power in the Modern World*. Edinburgh: Edinburgh University Press.

Tan, P. K. W. and Rubdy, R. (2008). *Language as Commodity*. London: Continuum.

Tannen, D. (1993). *Framing in Discourse*. New York: Oxford University Press.

Teasdale, S. (2012). What's in a Name? Making Sense of Social Enterprise Discourses. *Public Policy and Administration, 27*, 99–119.

References   147

Tellmann, U. (2009). Foucault and the Invisible Economy. *Foucault Studies, 6,* 5–24.

Therborn, G. (1980). *The Ideology of Power and the Power of Ideology.* London: Verso.

Thomas, P. D. (2009). *The Gramscian Moment: Philosophy, Hegemony and Marxism.* Leiden, Netherlands: Brill.

Thompson, J. B. (1990). *Ideology in Modern Culture: Critical Social Theory in the Era of Mass Communication.* Stanford, CA: Stanford University Press.

——(1984). *Studies in the Theory of Ideology.* Cambridge: Polity Press.

Titunik, I. (1973). The Formal Method and the Sociological Method (M.M. Baxtin, P.N. Medvedev, V.N. Volosinov) in Russian Theory and Study of Literature. In V. V. N (Ed.), *Marxism and the Philosophy of Language* (pp. 175–200). Cambridge, MA: Harvard University Press.

Torfing, J. (1999). *New Theories of Discourse: Laclau, Mouffe and Žižek.* Oxford: Blackwell.

Trowler, P. (2001). Captured by the Discourse? The Socially Constitutive Power of New Higher Education Discourse in the UK. *Organzation, 8* (2), 183–201.

Urciuoli, B. (2008). Skills and Selves in the New Workplace. *Amercian Ethnologist, 35* (2), 211–28.

Urciuoli, B. and LaDousa, C. (2013). Language Management/Labour. *Annual Review of Anthropology, 42,* 175–90. Retrieved 3rd September 2014 from: http://www.academia.edu/4844662/2013_Urciuoli_and_LaDousa_Language_Management_Labor.

van Dijk, T. A. (2008). *Discourse and Power.* Basingstoke: Palgrave Macmillan.

——(2001). *Discourse Ideology and Content. Folia Linguistica 30* (1–2), 2001, 11–40. Retrieved 23rd July 2013 from: http://www.discourses.org/Old Articles/Discourse,%20ideology%20and%20context.pdf.

Verschueren, J. (2012). *Ideology in Language Use.* Cambridge: Cambridge University Press.

Vincent, A. (2011). Ideology and the University. *The Political Quarterly, 82* (3), 332–40.

Vološinov, V. (1973). *Marxism and the Philosophy of Language* (Trans. L. Matejka and I. R Tututink). Cambridge, MA: Harvard University Press.

Wacquant, L. (2012). Three Steps to a Historical Anthropology of Actually Existing Neoliberalism. *Social Anthropology/Anthropologie Sociale 20* (1), 66–79.

Wales, J. (2008, 22nd June). The Wisdom of Crowds. *The Observer.* Retrieved 1st August 2014 from: http://www.theguardian.com/commentisfree/2008/jun/22/wikipedia.internet/print.

Walsh, B. (2012). *Degrees of Nonsense: The Demise of the University in Ireland.* Dublin: Glasnevin Publishing.

Ward, S. C. (2012). *Neoliberalism and the Global Restructuring of Knowledge and Education.* New York: Routledge.

Washburn, J. (2005). *University, Inc.: The Corporate Corruption of Higher Education.* New York: Basic Books.

Watkins, T. (1993). *The Great Depression: America in the 1930's.* New York: Back Bay Books, Little Brown and Company.

Wayne, M. (2005). Fetishism and Ideology: A Reply to Dimoulis and Milios. *Historical Materialism, 13* (3), 193–218.

Wee, L. (2005). Class Inclusion and Correspondence Models as Discourse Types: A framework for Approaching Metaphorical Discourse. *Language in Society, 34,* 201–38.

Weninger, C. (2009). Urban Pioneers in the Making: Recontextualisation and the Reemergence of the Engaged Rresident in Redeveloping Communities. *Journal of Sociolinguistics, 13* (1), 83–105.

148 References

White, B. (2014, 4th May). The Sunday Interview: Chris Horn: You May Not be Able to Define an Entrepreneur, but You'd Recognise One if You Saw One. *Sunday Business Post*, p. 15.

Whitehead, F. (2011, 1st August). *British Universities Overseas: It's about More than Just a Pieceof Paper*. Retrieved 15th August 2012 from *The Guardian*: http://www.guardian.co.uk/higher-education-network/2011/aug/01/british-universities-overseas-piece-paper.

Williams, R. (1996). Literature. In T. Eagleton and D. Milne (Eds.), *Marxism and Literary Theory: A Reader* (pp. 261–68). Oxford: Blackwell.

——(1985). *Keywords: A Vocabulary of Culture and Society*. New York: Oxford University Press.

——(1977). *Marxism and Literature*. Oxford: Oxford University Press.

——(1973). Base and Superstructure in Marxist Cultural Theory. *New Left Review*, 1 (32), 3–16.

Wolf, M. (2011, 6th September). We Must Listen to What the Bondmarkets Tell Us. *Financial Times*. Retrieved 1st September 2014 from: http://www.ft.com/intl/cms/s/0/9cbe577a-d872–11e0–8f0a-00144feabdc0.html#axzz2xiFcZAg1.

Wood, E. M. (1998). Modernity, Post-modernity and Capitalism. In R. W. McChesney (Ed.), *Capitalism and the Information Age* (pp. 27–50). New York: Monthly Review Press.

Woolard, K. A. (1998). Introduction: Language Ideology as Field of Enquiry. In B. B. Shieffelin, K. A. Woolard and P. V. Krotskrity (Eds.), *Language Ideologies* (pp. 3–47). New York: Oxford University Press.

Wright, S. and Ørberg, J. (2012). The Double Shuffle of University Reform – the OECD/Denmark Policy Interface. In A. Nyhagen and H. Tor (Eds.), *Academic Identities – Academic Challenges? American and European Experience of the Transformationof Higher Education and Research* (pp. 269–93). Newcastle upon Tyne: Cambridge Scholar Press.

Yates, M. D. (2012). *Wisconsin Uprising: Labour Fights Back*. New York: Monthly Review Press.

Zimmerman, D. (2010). Commentary. *American Literary History, 23* (1), 56–68.

——(2006). *Panic! Markets, Crises and Crowds in American Fiction*. Chapel Hill, NC: University of North Carolina Press.

Žižek, S. (2012b). How Did Marx Invent the Symptom? In S. Žižek (Ed.), *Mapping Ideology* (pp. 296–331). London: Verso.

——(2012a). The Spectre of Ideology. In S. Žižek (Ed.), *Mapping Ideology* (pp. 1–33). London: Verso.

——(2009). *First as Tragedy, then as Farce*. London: Verso.

——(1989). *The Sublime Object of Ideology*. London: Verso.

Index

Note: Page numbers in *italic* refer to figures. Page numbers followed by an 'n' refer to notes.

abstract labour power, 18; *see also* Marx, Karl
Agha, Asaf, 24
Albritton, Robert, 88
Allen, Kieran, 38, 115
Althusser, L., 10
Anglo Irish Bank trial, 40
austerity, role in neoliberalism, 97

bailouts, 35, 38
Bait and Switch: The Futile Pursuit of the Corporate Dream (Ehrenreich 2006), 78–79
Bakhtin, Mikhail, 107–8, 124, 128–29
Ball, Stephen, 119, 130
bank bailouts, 35, 38
Barthes, Roland, 90–91
Becker, Gary
  on economic activity, 26
  homo oeconomicus, 86–87
  and human capital, 15–16
'biopower,' Foucault's use of term, 129
'The Birth of Biopolitics' lectures, 85, 88
Block, David, 8, 16, 18–19
Bono, 75, 82
Bourdieu, Pierre, 49, 55–64
Boutet, Josiane, 23–24
Braverman, Henry, 22
'business angels,' 125 n7

Calhoun, Craig, 60
call centres, 22–23; *see also* language, commodification of
Callinicos, Alex, 28, 60

Cameron, Deborah
  on call centres, 24
  and work in capitalism, 20
Cantillon, Richard, 74
capital
  human capital, 15–16
  linguistic capital, 65–69
  re-appropriation of term, 64
capitalism
  commodification in, 14–16
  and language, 20–21
  language as a commodity in, 20–21
Chilton, Paul, 39
Chun, Christian, 6, 8
Coffey, Séamus, 40
Collini, Stefan, 125 n11
commodification of language, 16–17, 20
commodities
  in capitalism, 14–16
  Marx's description of, 18
  nature of, 18
  signs as, 53–54
commodity fetishism, theoretical framework of, 27–31
common sense, Gramsci's concept of, 4
conceptual metaphors
  kinds of, 44
  and neoliberalism, 43–47
consciousness, and reality, 27–31
Cook, Guy, 103, 120–21
Coolidge, Calvin, 93
Coulmas, Florian, 54
Coupland, Nikolas, 19
Critical Discourse Analysis (CDA), 116
Cullen, Bill, 75

150   *Index*

discourse
 ideology in language as, 11
 strand in applied linguistic and
  education theory, 119
Dublin City University, 100–104
Duchêne, Alexandre, 64–69

Eagleton, Terry, 28, 29, 61, 128
economic crisis of 2008, 34, 78–79, 96–97,
 109–11
Ehrenreich, Barbara, 78–79, 82
English as a Lingua Franca (ELF), 30
English competence testing, 68
Enterprise Ireland, 75–76
enterprises, universities as, 98–104,
 108–14
entrepreneur/entrepreneurship
 definitions and use of terms,
  72–74
 ideology as, 89–91
 neoliberal invention of, 92–94
 role in neoliberalism, 77
 and social enterprise, 79–84
 statistics, 92

Fairclough, Norman, 117–18
Farrell, Colman, 82–83
fetishization, of skills, 25
*Firing-back: Against the Tyranny of the
 Market* (Bourdieu 2003), 58
Flores, Nelson, 19
Foucault, Michel
 'biopower,' 129
 'The Birth of Biopolitics' lectures,
  85, 88
 entrepreneurialism as ideology,
  89–91
 on entrepreneurs role in
  neoliberalism, 77
fragmented self, 77–78

Gal, Susan, 13–14
Giddens, Anthony, 65, 117
Globish metaphor, 54
Goatly, Andrew, 44, 54
governmentality, and neoliberalism,
 84–89
graduates, 111–14
Graeber, David, 54
Gramsci, Antonio
 concept of common sense, 4
 concept of hegemony, 5–6
 on the ideological role of metaphors in
  language, 49

on the presence of ideology in
 language, 2
use of the term 'language,' 3–4
Gray, John, 8, 17, 19

habitus
 Bourdieu's use of term, 57
 Park and Wee's analysis of, 67
Hall, Stuart, 90–91
Harding, Warren, 93
Harman, Chris, 9, 11, 15, 21, 32 n3, 69,
 131 n1
Harvey, David, 34, 63, 96
Hayek, Frederick, 42–43
hegemony, Gramsci's concept of, 5–6
Heller, Monica
 and linguistic capital, 64–69
 on linguistic resources, 17
homo oeconomicus, 86–87
'hooray' words, 103
human and social activities, as markets,
 41–43
Human Capital Theory, 15–16, 26,
 111–14
human skills 21–24; *see also* language,
 commodification of
Hunt report, 99–100

ideology
 entrepreneurship as, 89–91
 and language, 2–7
 neoliberalism as, 9–11
 understanding through commodity
  fetishism, 28–29
 and universities, 114–16
income inequality, 93
information economy, 22
inherited wealth, 93
Ireland
 Anglo Irish Bank trial, 40
 economic crisis of 2008, 96–97
 Enterprise Ireland, 75–76
 entrepreneurs in, 74–76
 government of, 38, 75–76
 graduates, 112–13
 Hunt report, 99–100
 income inequality in, 93
 social enterprise in, 79–84
 Social Entrepreneurs Ireland, 80–81
Italy, government of, 34
Ives, Peter, 2, 3, 11 n2, 49

jaebols, English competence testing, 68
Jones, Campbell, 37–38, 42

Index 151

keywords
  as ideological-verbal signs, 124
  and social agency, 104–8
  study of, 71–72
  use of, 123
Klein, Naomi, 84
knowledge, as the marketplace of ideas,
    42–43

labour, commodification of, 15
labour power, 18, 21
Lakoff, G., 44–45, 50–51
language
  and capitalism, 20–21
  commodification of, 16–17, 20
  Gramsci's use of term, 3–4
  and ideology, 2–7
  Marx's view of, 4
  and new technologies, 21–24
  in Occupy Movement, 6
  role of metaphors, 49
'Language and Political Economy' (Gal),
    13–14
language workers, 17
Larrain, Jorge, 26–27
Lemke, Thomas, notion of
    governmentality, 85
linguistic capital, 65–69
linguistic habitus, 57
linguistic market, 55–64
Lo Blanco, Joseph, 19
Lukács, Georg, 40–41
Lynch, Suzanne, 38–39

marketplace of ideas, knowledge as,
    42–43
markets
  human and social activities as,
    41–43
  personification of, 35–41
Marttila, Thomas, 76
Marx, Karl
  abstract labour power, 18
  description of commodities, 18
  theory of commodity fetishism,
    27–31
  view of language, 4
  'vulgar' economics, 27
Massey, Doreen, on language pertaining
    to customers, 1–2
McGill, Kenneth, 20, 65–66
McNally, David, 53
metaphors
  conceptual metaphors, 43–47

Globish metaphor, 54
  ideological role of, 2, 49
  metaphorical mapping, 43–44
  ontological metaphors, 44; *see also*
    conceptual metaphors
  representations of financial markets,
    35–41
  role in language, 49
  social reality of, 47–50
metonymy, 42
Mirowski, Philip, 43, 77–78
Monti, Mario, 34

neoliberalism
  analysis of term, 7–8
  Bourdieu's view of, 58–59
  and conceptual metaphors,
    43–47
  and governmentality, 84–89
  as ideology, 9–11
  resistance to, 19, 58, 63–64, 89, 98,
    116–22
new technologies, and language,
    21–24
Ng, Carl John Way, 120
nonverbal communication, 24

O'Boyle, Brian, 38
Occupy Movement, language in, 6
Ollman, Bertell, 25
Ong, Aihwa, 7, 129
ontological metaphors, 44; *see also*
    conceptual metaphors
O'Regan, John, 30
Organisation of Economic Cooperation
    and Development (OECD),
    105–9, *108*

Park, Joseph Sung-Yul, 32 n4, 61, 66,
    67–68
Peck, Jamie, 97
Phillips, Susan, 29
Piketty, Thomas, 93
Pinker, Stephen, 45–47
political economy, 30

Rampton, Ben, 119
reality, and consciousness, 27–31
reification
  and the anthropomorphizing financial
    markets, 40–41
  of skills, 25
resistance (to neoliberalisim), 19, 58,
    63–64, 89, 98, 116–22

152 Index

Saussure, Ferdinand de, and the market metaphor, 52–55
self-fragmentation, 77–78
signs as commodities, 53–54
Singaporean Management University (SMU), 126 n19
social activities, as markets, 41–43
social agency
and the promotion of neoliberal keywords, 104–8
theme of, 122
social consciousness, and ideology and language, 3–4
social enterprise, 79–84
Social Entrepreneurs Ireland, 80–81
social reality of metaphors, 47–50
Sotiris, Panagiotis, 114–15
structural sociology, Bourdieu's view of, 57
Stubbs, Michael, 116
The Stuff of Thought (Pinker 2007), 45
subjectivity, in the discourses of neoliberalism, 119
surface relations, 25–27

Tannen, Deborah, 47
technologies, and language, 21–24
Tellmann, Ute, 95 n5
Test of English for International Communication (TOEIC), 68
Therborn, Göran, 128

universities
as enterprises, 98–104, 108–14
funding for, 109–11
graduates, 111–14
and ideology, 114–16
Urciuoli, Bonnie, on communication skills, 25–27
US Occupy Movement, language in, 6

Vincent, Andrew, 115
Vološinov, Valentin, 91, 97–98, 129
'vulgar' economics, 27

Wacquant, Loïc, 87
Wales, Jimmy, 42–43
Ward, Steven, 105
wealth, inherited, 93
Wee, Lionel, 66, 67
The Weight of the World (Bourdieu 1999), 60
Wikipedia, 42–43
Williams, Raymond, 29, 71–72
Wodak, Ruth, 118
Wolf, Martin, 36–37
Woolard, Kathryn, 29
work, commodification of, 15

Zimmerman, David, 50–51
Žižek, Slavoj, 28, 63, 72, 87